An Introduction to Antonio Gramsci

An Introduction to Antonio Gramsci

His Life, Thought and Legacy

GEORGE HOARE AND NATHAN SPERBER

Bloomsbury Academic
An imprint of Bloomsbury Publishing Plc

B L O O M S B U R Y
LONDON · OXFORD · NEW YORK · NEW DELHI · SYDNEY

Bloomsbury Academic

An imprint of Bloomsbury Publishing Plc

50 Bedford Square
London
WC1B 3DP
UK

1385 Broadway
New York
NY 10018
USA

www.bloomsbury.com

BLOOMSBURY and the Diana logo are trademarks of Bloomsbury Publishing Plc

First published 2016

British Library Cataloguing-in-Publication Data
A catalogue record for this book is available from the British Library.

ISBN: HB: 978-1-4725-7277-6
PB: 978-1-4725-7276-9
ePDF: 978-1-4725-7278-3
ePub: 978-1-4725-7279-0

Library of Congress Cataloging-in-Publication Data
Hoare, George, 1984-
An introduction to Antonio Gramsci : his life, thought and legacy / George Hoare and Nathan Sperber.
pages cm
Includes bibliographical references and index.
1. Gramsci, Antonio, 1891-1937–Political and social views. 2. Gramsci, Antonio, 1891-1937–Influence. 3. Political science–Philosophy–History–20th century.
I. Sperber, Nathan, 1986- II. Title.
JC265.G68H63 2015
320.53'2092–dc22
2015007546

Typeset by Integra Software Services Pvt. Ltd.
Printed and bound in India

Contents

A Note on the Text

Throughout, references to Gramsci's prison writing follow the international standard: notebook number, according to the 1975 Italian critical edition (edited by Valentino Gerratana), followed by number of note. In this way, notebook (*quaderno*) 12, note 3 becomes Q12§3. We have also given page references to one of the English anthologies of Gramsci's writings, where possible. In referring to Gramsci's writings we have used the following abbreviations:

SPN: *Selections from Prison Notebooks*, edited and translated by Quintin Hoare and Geoffrey Nowell-Smith (London: Lawrence and Wishart, 1971).

SPWI: *Selections from Political Writings (1910–1920)*, edited by Quintin Hoare and translated by John Mathews (London: Lawrence and Wishart, 1977).

SPWII: *Selections from Political Writings (1921–1926)*, edited and translated by Quintin Hoare (London: Lawrence and Wishart, 1978).

LP: *Letters from Prison by Antonio Gramsci*, edited and translated by Lynne Lawner (London: Quartet, 1979).

SCW: *Selections from Cultural Writings*, edited by David Forgacs and Geoffrey Nowell-Smith and translated by William Boelhower (London: Lawrence and Wishart, 1985).

FSPN: *Further Selections from the Prison Notebooks*, edited and translated by Derek Boothman (London: Lawrence and Wishart, 1995).

GR: *The Gramsci Reader: Selected Writings, 1916–1935*, edited by David Forgacs (New York: New York University Press, 2000).

Introduction

Thinking through Gramsci

It may be asked how we can read Gramsci today. Any answer to this question is inevitably complicated by the emergence since his death, and particularly in the English- and Italian-speaking academic communities, of a veritable 'Gramsci industry' with a great many different Gramscis. Thus, we see a Gramsci in International Relations, in Cultural Studies, in Political Theory, in Literary Theory and in Postcolonial Studies. There is a Gramsci used by the Right and one claimed by the Left.

In place of these diverse and split 'Gramscis', we instead argue for a unified and consistent Gramsci, a Gramsci essential for critical thought today. This unified Gramsci is centred on his attempt to develop the tools and resources he needed to understand his own historical situation in a way that would simultaneously renew and extend Marxism. We contend that the challenge Gramsci presents us is not the doctrinaire establishment of the precise meaning of Gramscian concepts, but rather a textual and philological fidelity allied with an understanding of the essential rhythm of his thought. We propose a challenge to the reader of 'thinking through' Gramsci: of using Gramsci's thought to think through – to unpack and to begin to understand – the historical situation in which we find ourselves today.

When reading Gramsci we should begin with the *concrete*: Gramsci's analyses of intellectuals, education, journalism and common sense provide a number of starting points for the analysis of ideology in late capitalism; his understanding of the State and civil society helps us comprehend the constellations of power operating today. Thinking through Gramsci must be dialectical, flexible, open-minded and generative, attempting to open new avenues rather than discover new dead ends. At the same time, thinking through Gramsci involves investigating how concrete forms of thought and practice are linked to politics – Gramsci's conceptual *and political* horizon remains that of hegemony, or the methods of *organizing consent* that involve both material and ideological elements. We have not yet moved beyond this horizon. We must also take lessons from Gramsci in the matters of personal courage and conviction: those who would think critically must attempt to generate an unbending fidelity to the intellectual and practical consequences of their ideas. Finally, the task Gramsci sets us is nothing less than that of forming a new common sense. Gramsci sees in all his analyses that superstructures do all they do for capital – to put it another way, capitalism is glimpsed as a whole form of social life. The alternative to capitalism has to be a whole form of social life, too. Therefore, as much as we need Gramsci's famous 'pessimism of the intellect, optimism of the will', we also need his idea that the goal of thought and practice is to trace the thread of a new conception of the world and to struggle to bring it into being. This is Gramsci's core lesson for our times.

The structure of the book

This book is broken down into four parts. The first gives an overview of Gramsci's biography, intellectual development and some of his pre-prison writing (Chapter 1). Gramsci's life shows him to be one of the most determined, uncompromising and – depending on your reading – tragic and/or inspiring figures in the history of the Left.

The second examines in detail Gramsci's thought as developed in his *Prison Notebooks*. It is composed of four chapters that deal, successively, with Gramsci's thought on culture (Chapter 2), politics (Chapter 3), philosophy (Chapter 4) and hegemony (Chapter 5). We have attempted, albeit in a broad and open way, to begin with the tripartite structure of the most popular collection of Gramsci's writings in English, *Selections from the Prison Notebooks*

(*SPN*).[1] We think it likely that most readers coming to Gramsci will use this collection, and moreover we judge it to be an excellent (if, of course, partial) selection and translation of many of Gramsci's most interesting, difficult and thought-provoking prison notes. Our structure should also be useful to those coming to Gramsci through other avenues. After three substantive chapters that correspond more or less closely to the three parts of *SPN*, the chapter on hegemony then looks to draw together strands from the previous chapters and present a synoptic account of how we might be able to understand Gramsci's most famous concept and its interrelations with the other key points of his thinking. Hegemony runs like a thread through Gramsci's notebooks and, in our argument, also forms the basis of Gramsci's understanding of history and of political strategy. We hope that the present volume, and in particular Part Two, might serve usefully as a companion to *SPN*, explicating some of Gramsci's most difficult concepts and placing them in tentative relation to one another.

The third part looks to apply Gramsci's thought to two contemporary questions: the possibility of a critical analysis of common sense in Political Theory (Chapter 6) and how to understand the diffusion of neo-liberalism in modern France and Britain from the standpoint of Political Economy (Chapter 7). In these chapters, we attempt to develop and extend Gramsci's thought by applying it to what we take to be problems of contemporary significance and interest. In so doing, we look to illustrate what we believe to be a 'Gramscian method' of philosophical and political analysis – both in the sense of following methodological precepts suggested by Gramsci and also in the sense of developing new theoretical insights (as Gramsci did) from the analysis of social relations as they exist and have developed historically. Finally, we intend Part Three to stand in support of a more general argument that Gramsci's thought is, crucially, *usable* today as a tool for those who want to think critically about society.

---

[1] Hoare and Nowell-Smith divide their selection of Gramsci's prison notes into 'Problems of History and Culture' (containing notes on Intellectuals, Education and Italian History), 'Notes on Politics' (The Modern Prince, State and Civil Society and Americanism and Fordism) and 'The Philosophy of Praxis' (The Study of Philosophy and Problems of Marxism).

The fourth part of the book attempts to map some aspects of Gramsci's legacy today (Chapter 8). First, we place Gramsci in the trajectory of twentieth-century Marxist thought and consider his influence on the Italian communist movement. We then look to chart Gramsci's relation to four intellectual fields particularly influenced by his thought: Cultural Studies, post-Marxism, Postcolonial Studies and International Political Economy. This exploratory 'map' of Gramsci's intellectual legacy suggests that Gramsci's influence on contemporary critical thought is a central one, especially for those concerned to think about the relations between historical context and the forms of domination in a given society, and ultimately between culture, politics, philosophy and power taken in their widest senses.

PART ONE

Life

1

Antonio Gramsci, 1891–1937

Introduction

Today the name of Antonio Gramsci is mainly associated with his *Prison Notebooks*. This vast and eclectic collection of fragmentary notes on an enormous range of topics continues to be studied in human sciences departments all over the world. Gramsci's remarkable academic popularity – particularly in Italophone and Anglophone academia – is no doubt justified, but it might serve to create a misunderstanding about Gramsci's life and work.

Gramsci, centrally, wanted to be a man of action as much as of thought. He was a political leader of high profile, at the head of the Italian Communist Party from 1924 to 1926 – the same party that for years, after the Second World War, was the largest communist party in the West. The exceptional circumstances of his incarceration cut him off from the world of action, and it was in a state of personal and political isolation that he wrote his *Prison Notebooks*.

Before his arrest, Gramsci wrote an enormous amount: he was an intellectual by temperament, a voracious reader and seemingly interested by all political events and cultural forms. He was a prolific journalist, who had a reputation for his panache and eloquence in writing. Nevertheless, when he was arrested in November 1926, he did not have a coherent *oeuvre* to his name.

As opposed to the authors of other 'classics' of the social sciences at the beginning of the twentieth century – such as Max Weber or Emile Durkheim – Gramsci did not belong to the 'academic' type, and in fact he did not acquire a higher education diploma or degree. He was, as we will explore below, a political organizer and militant by calling, and he conceived the *Prison Notebooks* as a *political* project, as much as an intellectual one. Moreover, his prison writings display a very strong strategic dimension and questions of political practice are never far from his mind, as we will see later with, for instance, the notions of 'war of position' (Chapter 3) and 'hegemony' (Chapter 5).

Crucially, Gramsci's thought developed on the basis of a life of political action and militancy. Gramsci's thought is thus inextricably linked to his biography.[1] This chapter aims to set out and contextualize the main events in Gramsci's life, and to explore some important texts that Gramsci wrote before he was imprisoned.

Sardinian origins: Antonu *su gobbu*

On the topic of his roots, Gramsci once wrote to his sister-in-law Tatiana Schucht from Turi prison in 1931: 'I myself am of no one race: my father was of recent Albanian origin…my mother is Sardinian on both sides'. 'Despite these things', he continues, 'my cultural formation is basically Italian and this is my world here'.[2]

Antonio Gramsci was born on 22 January 1891 in Ales, a small town in Sardinia. It has often been supposed that Gramsci had peasant origins, but this is not true. At the time of the birth of his son 'Nino', Francesco 'Ciccilo' Gramsci was in fact a bureaucrat in the local civil administration. However, in 1897 disaster struck the Gramsci family when Francesco, the *paterfamilias*, was accused of embezzlement, extortion and counterfeiting. These accusations were never proved, and it seems Francesco was the victim of a

---

[1] Giuseppe Fiori, *Antonio Gramsci: Life of a Revolutionary*, translated by Tom Nairn (London: New Left Books, 1970); Alastair Davidson, *Antonio Gramsci: Towards an Intellectual Biography* (London: Merlin Press, 1977).
[2] Letter to Tatiana Schucht, 12 October 1931; *LP*, p. 218.

local political vendetta aimed at punishing him for supporting the wrong candidate at a previous election.

Francesco was imprisoned from 1898 to 1904, and the consequences for his wife and seven children were nothing short of terrible. The home fell into a dire misery. Having sold the patch of land she had inherited from her family in order to pay the lawyer's fee, Gramsci's mother Peppina Marcias attempted somehow to ensure her children had sufficient food and a dignified life by working as a seamstress. The harsh trials of his childhood would leave a mark on Gramsci for a very long time. Among other things, he would develop a deep admiration for his mother, to whom he would often write letters from prison stamped with tenderness and respect.

It was also during this period of his childhood that the little Nino started to display symptoms of physical malformation. Seemingly due to Pott's disease (a variant of tuberculosis), his spine developed abnormally. In an attempt to cure him, the town's doctors ordered him to be suspended from a beam in the ceiling, regularly and for long hours. Nino thus endured the humiliation of this treatment – whose character is a sign of the relative social backwardness of Sardinia at the turn of the century in which Gramsci grew up – as well as the bullying of his schoolmates, as they threw stones at him in the schoolyard and called him 'Antonu *su gobbu*' (the hunchback).

However, Gramsci's childhood health problems did not stop at his spine, and his physical state was so precarious that until 1914 his mother kept ready in the house the small coffin and little dress in which he was supposed to be buried. In short, life did not exactly smile on the young Gramsci. But he reacted to adversity with a determination and a sheer strength of will that was to characterize him throughout his entire existence. Nino suffered without complaint the long sessions suspended from the ceiling and, in order to develop his muscles and be able to fight back the assaults of his schoolmates, he built makeshift dumbbells from stones and an old broom handle. In 1902, he was forced, along with his older brother, to work in the local municipality's offices. There Nino (who was 11 at the time) was compelled to carry heavy registers throughout the day, and spent his nights crying because the physical pain it caused him stayed with him long after he had returned home.

The fate of the young Gramsci, though, was being played out at school. In 1898, he was sent to school for the first time in Ghilarza, but he had to abandon his schoolwork at the end of his primary schooling to find a job and contribute to the family's income. The release of his father in 1904 allowed Gramsci to return to his studies. Nino then attended the small middle school of Santu Lussurgiu and, succeeding in his exams, went in 1908 to the Dettori high school in the provincial capital of Cagliari. There he moved in with his older brother Gennaro, who was already a political militant and had, since 1906, been sending socialist pamphlets back to Nino.

At this time, Sardinia experienced a wave of political rebellion targeted at the Italian central State. It should be borne in mind that the country had only been unified a few decades previously, through the unification process of the *Risorgimento* (a historical event of great interest to Gramsci that we discuss at length below, particularly in Chapter 3). Moreover, the largely agricultural Sardinian economy was the direct victim of the protectionist policies that the regime had put in place in the interests of Northern industrial production. When troops were dispatched from the continent to quell the movement, the rebels welcomed them with the cry of 'Continentals into the sea!' As a young Sardinian, Gramsci was receptive to this political cause and his first political adherence was to the regionalism of the island of his birth. He would soon renounce this, after his arrival in Turin, but throughout his life he retained a keen interest in analysing the regional specificities of Italy and the geographical elements of local and national political struggles.

Turin

Journalism and militancy

As a result of his diligence at school, Gramsci won a scholarship and entered the University of Turin in 1911. He selected a philology and linguistics curriculum, and his studies in these disciplines influenced some of the theoretical stances in the notebooks he would later fill up during his time in prison. However, Gramsci's true passion at this time – and for the rest of his life – was politics. Eventually his political commitments and his activity as a journalist led him to give up his studies and leave the university behind.

In 1912, Gramsci joined the Italian Socialist Party (*Partito Socialista Italiano*, PSI), which was affiliated to the Second International and in which Benito Mussolini was a prominent figure. Gramsci felt close to Mussolini at this time and notably sided with him in hostility to Italian imperialism in Libya. In 1914, at a point where the majority of the PSI advocated neutrality in the First World War, in one of his first published articles Gramsci defended Mussolini when the latter supported Italian participation in the conflict. Gramsci justified his stance in the name of the rejection of political passivity, of which 'neutrality' was in his eyes only one form, and one that he compared to Buddhist renunciation. A few years later, in the political pamphlet *La Città futura* ('The city of the future'), he explained that 'indifference is a powerful force in history. It operates passively but effectively'. Rejecting this, Gramsci wrote, 'I am alive, I take sides. Hence I detest whoever does not, I hate indifference'.[3] For Gramsci, indeed, living meant being partisan and taking sides.

In 1915, Gramsci joined the socialist weekly *Il Grido del Popolo* ('The cry of the people', a reference to Jules Vallès's paper of the Paris Commune, *Le Cri du Peuple*). Two years later, a wave of arrests hit Left-wing circles in Turin after an attempt at insurrection, and Gramsci was catapulted to editor-in-chief of the paper. At the same time he was also the theatre critic of another socialist newspaper, *Avanti!* This is perhaps an early demonstration of Gramsci's belief in the inextricable link between culture and politics.

Gramsci's experience as a political journalist instilled in him a talent and a taste for polemics. He was later to write to Tatiana, while imprisoned in Turi:

My entire intellectual formation was of a polemical nature, so that it's impossible for me to think 'disinterestedly' or to study for the sake of studying. Only rarely do I lose myself in a particular train of thought and analyse something for its inherent interest. Usually I have to engage in a dialogue, be dialectical, to arrive at some

---

[3] *La Città futura*, 11 February 1917.

intellectual stimulation. I once told you how I hate tossing stones into the dark. I need an interlocutor, a concrete adversary.[4]

In another letter to Tatiana, from 1931, he would refer to his journalistic output somewhat dismissively, commenting that 'these pages were turned out every day and should have ... been forgotten immediately afterwards'.[5] Gramsci's self-criticism here is excessive, since we can find in the accumulation of articles he wrote at the time, albeit perhaps in half-shaped form, many intellectual incursions that would go on to furnish some of the essential matter of the *Prison Notebooks*.

The Russian Revolution of 1917 radicalized Gramsci.[6] It was also the occasion for Gramsci to write one of his most famous pre-prison articles, the iconoclastically-titled 'The Revolution against *Capital*'. According to Gramsci, the conquest of power by the Bolsheviks demonstrated that a proletarian revolution could take place in a country whose capitalism was still 'primitive' or 'underdeveloped', such as Russia – or Italy. Gramsci sees this as in conflict with certain of the historical forecasts in Marx's *Capital* (1867), a work he sees as 'contaminated by positivist and naturalist encrustations'. The Second International, for Gramsci, ran the risk of hypertrophying these 'scoriae' into a dogma centred on economic determinism. However, Gramsci sees Lenin and the Bolsheviks as being able to 'live Marxist thought – that thought which is eternal' without falling into the trap of converting Marxism into a scholastic exercise divorced from political realities.[7]

For Gramsci, importantly, authentic Marxist thought:

sees as the dominant factor in history, not raw economic facts, but man, men in societies, men in relation to one another, reaching agreements with one another, developing through their contacts ... a collective, social will; men coming to understand economic facts, judging them and adapting them to their will

---

[4] Letter to Tatiana Schucht, 15 December 1930; *LP*, p. 193.
[5] Letter to Tatiana Schucht, 7 September 1931; *LP*, p. 203.
[6] See Domenico Losurdo, *Antonio Gramsci dal liberalismo al 'Comunismo critico'* (Rome: Gamberetti, 1997).
[7] 'The Revolution against *Capital*', Milan edition of *Avanti!*, 24 December 1917; *SPWI*, p. 35.

until this becomes the driving force of the economy and moulds objective reality, which lives and moves and comes to resemble a current of volcanic lava that can be channelled wherever and in whatever way men's will determines.[8]

These words suggest the extent to which the young Gramsci's perspective was removed from the conventional image we might have of Marxist doxa, although it is also clear that he is eager to assume the legacy of Marxism and to embrace (albeit critically) Marx's thought. In this passage Gramsci seems to want to find, within Marx's thought, a fundamentally *voluntaristic* kernel.[9]

In the *Prison Notebooks*, Gramsci would take his distance from such a radical voluntarism. However, he would at the same time continue to fustigate any form of crude economic determinism (as we will explore in Chapters 3 and 4) and remain an unfailing and merciless enemy of dogmatism of all stripes.

L'Ordine Nuovo

Perhaps Gramsci's most important formative political experience came during a period of intense political turmoil. A year after the October Revolution and the attempt at insurrection in Turin, the armistice was signed and the First World War came to a close. The Italian elites had finally chosen to enter the war on the side of the *Triple Entente*, but were unable to stabilize a society that was dislocated and scarred by the experience of an unprecedentedly destructive conflict.

Thus 1919 saw the unleashing of the *biennio rosso*, the 'two red years', centred around the revolutionary activism of the Turinese workers. In the wake of the failed Spartacist revolution in Germany and soon after the short-lived Republic of Councils in Hungary, it seemed

---

[8] 'The Revolution against *Capital*'; *SPWI*, pp. 35–6.

[9] It is also possible to discern in the above passage the influence of Giovanni Gentile's 'philosophy of action' as well as the *élan vital* of Henri Bergson; Gentile and Bergson were part of Gramsci's reading at the time and he was often taxed with 'Bergsonism' by his socialist comrades. We explore in more detail below the combination of Marxist and non-Marxist influences on Gramsci's thought.

that Italy was entering a period of unrest and potentially revolutionary activity. Panic spread among the 'owning classes' of the peninsula – a section of which would be only too happy, before long, to turn to fascism. Turin, together with Milan, was at this time the heart of the Italian industrial economy; a textile and metalworking centre, it was the seat of the FIAT (*Fabbrica Italiana Automobili Torino*) concern that employed 20,000 workers in the city in 1918. The workers, who were often female, went on strike and occupied their factories, demanding to direct production themselves. Giovanni Giolitti, the head of the Italian government, thought he might be able to defuse the situation if he could convince the FIAT managers to entrust the management of the firm to the unions. The Italian elites, in other words, were considering previously unconscionable measures.

The landscape of contestation at the time was marked by division within the Left. The national leaders of the PSI were hesitant, remaining a step back from the movement at a time when its most radicalized members in Turin, including Gramsci himself, were participating in it passionately. The unions, including the powerful *Confederazione Generale del Lavoro* (CGL, or 'general workers' union'), were also on the battlefield, but their leaders were mostly reformists. In effect, then, the main organizers of the struggle were the workers' councils, which took the form of 'enterprise committees' (*commissioni interne*) inspired by the structure of the 1917 Russian Soviets. Thus the *biennio rosso* importantly was not the production of a single Leninist political party or a single union organization, but rather the result of largely spontaneous 'councilistic' activism on the part of the workers.

There was, however, an organ of the press that embodied the political avant-garde of the movement: *L'Ordine Nuovo* ('The new order'), the very newspaper set up in 1919 by Gramsci and his comrades Palmiro Togliatti, Umberto Terracini and Angelo Tasca.[10] The new weekly made its first appearance in May 1919, after *Il Grido del Popolo* had already closed its doors. *L'Ordine Nuovo*'s subtitle was 'a review of socialist culture' and at first its ambition seemed quite

---

[10] Togliatti was to become secretary-general of the PCI from 1927 to 1964, Terracini would be imprisoned by the fascists from 1926 to 1943 before eventually becoming a communist senator, and Tasca, purged from the party in 1929, would emigrate to France and join up with the Vichy regime.

circumscribed, as witnessed by the fact that in the first issue Tasca mostly spoke in favour of an 'exercise in remembering' in the area of socialist culture. Yet as the surrounding protests grew in size, the paper started to sense the atmosphere on the streets. Gramsci, Togliatti and Terracini led a newsroom 'coup', thus marginalizing the Tascian line.[11] The unsigned editorial of the seventh issue of 21 June 1919 sets this new tone:

> The socialist State already exists potentially in the institutions of social life characteristic of the exploited working class. To link these institutions, co-ordinating and ordering them into a highly centralized hierarchy of competences and powers, while respecting the necessary autonomy and articulation of each, is to create a genuine workers' democracy here and now.[12]

They continue, 'the concrete and complete solution to the problems of socialist living can only arise from communist practice: collective discussion, which sympathetically alters men's consciousness, unifies them and inspires them to industrious enthusiasm'.[13] What is remarkable in these assertions is the expectation that all existing working-class organizations constitute together the embryo of the future socialist State. By contrast with the party-centric revolutionary model associated with Leninism, it also appears that at the time Gramsci and his comrades were rather looking to the *commissioni interne* instead of the party to play the chief coordinating role in the struggle. They urged, moreover, the participation of all workers – including non-union members and anarchists – in the *commissioni*. This in turn drew the ire of many in the PSI against *L'Ordine Nuovo*'s alleged 'spontaneist' and 'syndicalist' tendencies (although Gramsci actually never went so far as to deny relevance to the political party).[14]

---

[11] See Antonio Santucci, 'La perspective du communisme dans *L'Ordine Nuovo*', in: André Tosel (ed.), *Modernité de Gramsci: Actes du colloque franco-italien de Besançon, 23–25 novembre 1989* (Paris: Les Belles Lettres, 1992), pp. 191–206.

[12] Editorial titled 'Workers' Democracy', unsigned, written by Gramsci in collaboration with Palmiro Togliatti, *L'Ordine Nuovo*, 1:7 (21 June 1919); *SPWI*, p. 65.

[13] 'Workers' Democracy'; *SPWI*, p. 68.

[14] An in-depth study of Gramsci's often-overlooked relations to Italian anarchism and syndicalism is Carl Levy's *Gramsci and the Anarchists* (London: Bloomsbury, 1999).

L'Ordine Nuovo rapidly came to stand as the emblematic publication of the *biennio rosso*. Although it never reached a circulation above 5,000 copies per issue, it managed to exert a profound influence on the workers' movement of the time. It addressed topics that included socialism, council-based democracy, productive organization and the impact of Taylorism, working class education and the conditions of the emergence of a proletarian culture. The editorial line is slightly difficult to categorize briefly, as the small editorial team was influenced not just by Marxism but also by the Italian philosopher Giovanni Gentile and the French anarcho-syndicalist thinker Georges Sorel, and was not immune to a certain kind of what we might call 'revolutionary romanticism' (of which it would come to be more critical later). Looking internationally, *L'Ordine Nuovo* linked up with the small French cultural communist group *Clarté* associated with Henri Barbusse.[15]

The political-cultural turmoil of the *biennio rosso* was described by Togliatti as a 'proletarian *Sturm und Drang*'.[16] Rapidly, though, the fever fell. In April 1920, a month-long strike by the metalworkers of Turin failed as it not only encountered a huge armed force in the city but also did not manage to secure the support of workers outside Piedmont. After this, the autumn's strikes and occupations in Milan and Turin were mostly defensive in character, and the *biennio rosso* was in reflux. The *biennio rosso* ended as the industrial elites of Northern Italy eventually reached their goal of ending the situation of 'dual power' of capitalist management and workers' *commissioni interne* in factories.

The Communist Party

The editors of *L'Ordine Nuovo*, however, wanted to carry on the struggle. To them, the socialist revolution remained an imminent possibility in the Italy of 1921. Yet they had to acknowledge the failure of the attempt at council communism in Turin, which led them to reflect anew on the problem of political organization. Gramsci's

---

[15]See Christine Buci-Glucksmann, *Gramsci and the State*, translated by David Fernbach (London: Lawrence and Wishart, 1980).
[16]Cited in Marie-Antonietta Macciocchi, *Pour Gramsci* (Paris: Seuil, 1974).

articles at this time show a change in his thinking on the role of the political party; although he continued in the years immediately after the *biennio rosso* to stress the need for a plurality of working class institutions, he increasingly called for a leading role to be played by the party. However, he was clearly disillusioned with the PSI, since during the *biennio rosso* it was revolutionary in words only and its leadership made little attempt to coordinate the popular struggle during those years.

The solution to this problem of political organization came from the creation of a new party. At the Livorno Congress in January 1921 the Left of PSI, under the impetus of the Neapolitan Amadeo Bordiga, seceded and founded the Italian Communist Party (initially *Partito Comunista d'Italia*, or PCd'I, but later *Partito Comunista Italiano*, or PCI, which is how we will refer to it here). The four comrades from Turin – Gramsci, Togliatti, Terracini and Tasca – decided to join as, like Bordiga, they felt hostile to the PSI's indecision and impotence. However, there were strong disagreements between the four and Bordiga, whose theoretical perspective was a dogmatic economic determinism and whose practical stance was often marked by intransigence.[17]

After 1921, Gramsci decided to hide for the time being his disagreement with Bordiga, who emerged as the main figure of the PCI during its first years. Thus while the Comintern (the Third International) demanded of the PCI as a member party the establishment of a 'united front' with the PSI, Gramsci firmly supported Bordiga when the latter refused to compromise with the 'reformists' of the Left. Gramsci and Bordiga both saw such an option as 'liquidationist', risking the dissolution of the PCI's revolutionary identity, although Tasca (who came to embody the Right wing of the new party) was favourable to it.

The early life of the PCI was precarious. In October 1922, the 'March on Rome' led Mussolini to the presidency of the Council of Ministers. Compared to Hitler's regime in Germany, the fascists in Italy took comparatively much longer to suppress Left-wing organizations. Nevertheless, starting in 1922 the PCI endured successive waves of

---

[17] Bordiga was a target of Lenin's in the 1920 pamphlet, *Left-Wing Communism: An Infantile Disorder*.

repression and arrests, which drained its working class membership. The communist press eventually had to become clandestine, and the PCI cadres were forced to operate underground.

In 1922, Gramsci was nominated as a delegate of the PCI at the Comintern, and moved to Moscow. He stayed in the Soviet Union from May 1922 to November 1923. When he was being treated in a sanatorium, he fell in love with Julia Schucht, a violinist. This was an unexpected and unhoped-for source of happiness in Gramsci's life. Antonio and Julca ('Giulia') were married in 1923. They were to have two sons, born in 1924 and 1926, although Gramsci would never meet his younger son.

As he was about to be elected into the Chamber of Deputies (*Camera dei Deputati*, the lower house of the Italian Parliament) as a communist representative, Gramsci returned to Italy from Vienna (where he had moved from Moscow to be able to follow the activities of the PCI more closely) in May 1924. At this time, the rigidity of Bordiga's leadership was increasingly criticized, both within the PCI and the International, and the Neapolitan was eventually replaced by a 'centrist' leading group around Gramsci (who at the same time was the head of the communist parliamentary group of nineteen deputies). Gramsci only had one chance to give a speech at the National Assembly; Mussolini, present on the day, allegedly had difficulty following Gramsci, who was speaking quickly and in a low voice.[18]

With hindsight we can see that Gramsci failed to gauge the full dangers of fascism during these decisive years. Beginning in the autumn of 1920, fascist *squadristi* (militias) had started to proliferate in North and Central Italy, but Gramsci and his comrades at *L'Ordine Nuovo* saw this development as little more than a symptom of the failing bourgeois order badly shaken by the protests of the *biennio rosso*. Rather than seeing fascism as a fundamentally new or different threat, in other words, they interpreted it as a sign that the position of the owning classes was so desperate that they would consider doing without either legality or parliamentary constitutionalism. Even after the March on Rome, this interpretation remained the

---

[18] See Fiori, *Life of a Revolutionary.*

favoured one of the PCI; within Italian communist circles it was a commonplace to consider fascism as a noxious interlude bound shortly to be submerged by a revolutionary wave and then replaced by a genuinely popular democratic regime.

By the time of his arrest in 1926, Gramsci still saw fascism as essentially a contingent embodiment of the power of the bourgeoisie rather than as a threat in its own right. Thus neither Gramsci nor the PCI had ever proposed an anti-fascist alliance between Communists, socialists and anti-fascist liberals.[19] Nevertheless, Gramsci did write during those years several brief articles that carefully analysed some of fascism's facets, including the historical reasons for the support of the petty-bourgeoisie, the *squadristi* phenomenon and the supposedly 'Blanquist' instincts of Mussolini.[20] For Gramsci's analysis of fascism in the *Prison Notebooks*, see Chapter 3.

Shortly before his arrest, Gramsci began writing an essay, which remained unfinished, titled 'Some Aspects of the Southern Question' (*Alcuni temi della quistione meridionale*; hereafter *Alcuni temi*). In this important essay Gramsci puts forward a profound sociological reflection on Italian social and political space, setting out a comparative analysis of social organization in the North and the South. In this text, Gramsci establishes himself as a pioneer of spatial studies in Marxism.[21] *Alcuni temi* also gives Gramsci the opportunity to review the *biennio rosso* and to investigate why the movement ran into the indifference and even hostility of the Southern popular masses even though *L'Ordine Nuovo* was keenly aware of the need to overcome geographical cleavages and build a strategic alliance of all the country's subaltern elements. In addition, *Alcuni temi* develops the concept of hegemony more than any other pre-prison writing of Gramsci's, and we will have many chances to return to it in later chapters.

---

[19] The anti-fascist front in France and Spain was a product of the shift in Comintern policy at the Seventh Congress in 1935.
[20] Revealingly, the fascist newspaper *Il Popolo d'Italia* founded and edited by Mussolini had a quotation from Auguste Blanqui on its mast, '*Chi ha del ferro ha del pane*' ('He who has iron, has bread').
[21] See Bob Jessop, 'Gramsci as a Spatial Theorist', *Critical Review of International Social and Political Philosophy*, 8:4 (2005), pp. 421–37.

Prison and the *Notebooks*

On 5 November 1926, following an alleged murder attempt on Mussolini by a fifteen-year-old boy on 31 October, the Italian Council of Ministers put forward a series of emergency measures aimed at reinforcing the repressive powers of the State and eroding the democratic prerogatives of parliament. Some of Gramsci's comrades foresaw the authoritarian shift of the regime and exhorted him to flee to Switzerland. Gramsci, though, was reluctant to leave. As far as we know, he continued to believe in the protection of his parliamentary immunity, and at any rate he decided to stay in the country to participate in the parliamentary debates on the emergency measures (which were planned for 9 November). On 8 November, though, Gramsci was arrested and imprisoned, in flagrant violation of his immunity.

Gramsci's trial began eighteen months later, in May 1928, and he was sentenced to imprisonment for twenty years. Mussolini allegedly demanded 'we have to stop this brain from working for twenty years', and these words of Mussolini's were cited during the trial by the prosecutor. But *Il Duce*'s wish would not be fulfilled, as witnessed by the thirty-three notebooks Gramsci had written in prison by the time of his death.

Shortly after his arrest, Gramsci began to develop the ambition of engaging in a long-term intellectual undertaking during his time in prison. In 1927, he wrote to Tatiana, 'I am obsessed by the idea that I ought to do something *für ewig* [for eternity].' He continues, 'I want, following a fixed plan, to devote myself intensively and systematically to some subject that will absorb and concentrate my inner life.'[22]

The mention of doing something *für ewig* – a reference to Goethe – might be surprising coming from the pen of a revolutionary who had previously abandoned his academic studies to engage in political action. Yet it is possible to discern a change in Gramsci's state of mind following his arrest. As a response to the abrupt severance from the very political action that had defined his life, Gramsci foresaw the possibility of delving into 'disinterested' study and making this

---

[22] Letter to Tatiana Schucht, 19 March 1927; *LP*, p. 79.

the main thread of his new life in jail.[23] However, it is important that this did not amount, for Gramsci, to a renunciation of politics. The *Prison Notebooks* are inconceivable without their reflections on strategy and revolution.

The circumstances of Gramsci's imprisonment, though, were from the start very unfavourable to the completion of such an undertaking. It was only in January 1929 that he was granted permission to write something other than his correspondence (which was itself limited to one letter per fortnight, which Gramsci often sent to his sister-in-law Tatiana as she was in Italy while his wife was in Russia). Even after being allowed to write, Gramsci only had access to a fraction of the sources he requested. It is perhaps no surprise that Marx, Engels and other 'subversives' were out of the question. Gramsci had to fall back on quoting them from memory, or had to scour the work of the liberal philosopher Benedetto Croce for scattered quotations from Marx.

In addition, every page that Gramsci wrote was subjected to the examination of prison censors before being returned to him. In a 1936 letter to Julia, Gramsci explained that this humiliating practice had led him over the years to develop a 'prison style of writing' that would circumvent central concepts in a way bordering on self-censorship since he knew that every word he wrote would be read with 'acrimonious, suspicious pedantry' by the prison director.[24]

Gramsci was thus forced to resort to paraphrases and circumlocutions in place of certain 'sensitive' terms. For example, Marxism became 'the philosophy of praxis' and Marx 'the founder of the philosophy of praxis', while Lenin was 'Ilich' (since his real name was Vladimir Ilich Ulyanov). The subterfuge was often

---

[23]Nonetheless, Gramsci clearly found the isolation from political action and the outside world extremely difficult to handle psychologically, as can be seen from a letter to his mother (23 September 1929; *LP*, p. 153): 'Boredom is my worst enemy, although I read or write all day long; it's a special kind of boredom which doesn't spring from idleness … but from the lack of contact with the outside world. I don't know whether you've read the lives of saints and hermits; they were tormented by this special boredom, which they called the "noonday devil" because towards midday they were seized … by a longing for change, to return to the world, to see people.'
[24]Letter to Julia Schucht, 24 November 1936; *LP*, p. 267.

quite rudimentary, which suggests that the prison's agents were not overly familiar with the revolutionary thought of Marx and his successors.

Frosini has proposed dividing the writing process of the notebooks into three phases.[25] From 1929 to 1931, while incarcerated in Turi in the south of the Apulia region, Gramsci completed nine notebooks, which included translations – often from German – whose purpose was for Gramsci to retrain his hand and brain after being forbidden to work for three years. In 1932 and 1933, while still in Turi, Gramsci re-transcribed and amended some of these early notebooks in three 'special notebooks' (numbers 10–13 in the Italian critical edition). Finally, from 1933 to 1935, after having been transferred to the Formia clinic for medical reasons but still a prisoner, Gramsci continued his project both by furthering the reflections in past notebooks and by introducing some new themes (such as the idea of 'Americanism' in notebook 22; see Chapter 3).

Only a small proportion of the thirty-three notebooks aim for a single object of study or are based on a systematic mode of exposition. Instead, the pages of Gramsci's notebooks contain notes that are more or less brief, and of a disparate and heterogeneous character.[26] Frequently, the notes are simply incursions, leads, sketches or hypotheses – intellectual starting-points meant to be developed further, fleshed out and refined at a later stage. It is this essential openness of Gramsci's *Prison Notebooks* that has made them such an open-ended resource for critical thought, but which has also raised the challenge of interpreting and understanding them.

Shortly after his trial, there was an international campaign for Gramsci's liberation. However, it was only in 1933 that a gravely ill Gramsci was transferred to Formia, where he finally started to receive

---

[25] See Fabio Frosini, *Gramsci e la filosofia: Saggio sui 'Quaderni del carcere'* (Rome: Carocci, 2003).
[26] Revealingly, French scholars of Gramsci have converged in their refusal to use the term 'oeuvre' to describe the *Prison Notebooks* because this term is thought to imply misleading level of coherence; see for instance Robert Paris, 'Gramsci en France', *Revue Française de Science Politique*, 29 (1979), pp. 5–18; André Tosel, 'Modernité de Gramsci?', in: André Tosel (ed.), *Modernité de Gramsci: Actes du colloque franco-italien de Besançon, 23–25 novembre 1989* (Paris: Les Belles Lettres, 1992), pp. 7–16.

the medical care that he had desperately needed but that had been denied him previously.[27] He experienced a brief remission and started writing again. However, his health had already deteriorated too far, and by the time Gramsci was transferred to the *Quisisana* clinic in Rome in 1935 he was too weak to read and write. He became unable to digest and died, exhausted, on 27 April 1937. His sister-in-law Tatiana managed to smuggle his notebooks out of the clinic and send them to Moscow through diplomatic channels.

Gramsci's prison letters, together with reports from other inmates at the time, reveal the exceptional stoicism he displayed during his decade in prison. This is perhaps all the more remarkable given the bad health that plagued Gramsci his entire life. Writing to his mother from Turi, Gramsci stated, 'I don't want to be pitied. I was a soldier who had bad luck in the immediate battle.'[28] Despite his ill health, he adamantly refused any special treatment and criticized Tatiana when she attempted to obtain favourable treatment on his behalf. In another letter to his mother, Gramsci wrote, 'I've always refused to compromise my ideas and am ready to die for them, not just to be put in prison.'[29]

---

[27] In protest at his treatment, Gramsci's friend Romain Rolland wrote a short pamphlet entitled 'Antonio Gramsci, for those dying in Mussolini's jails', *L'Humanité*, 27 October 1934.
[28] Letter to his mother, 24 August 1931; *LP*, p. 202.
[29] Letter to his mother, 10 May 1928; *LP*, p. 133.

PART TWO

Thought

2

Culture

Introduction

The reader of the *Prison Notebooks* is immediately struck by the seeming omnipresence of cultural themes in Gramsci's prison writings. From Dante to Pirandello, Balzac to Sinclair Lewis, Gramsci comments on cultural works from a range of epochs. Gramsci's preoccupation with culture is perhaps not surprising given his personal trajectory. We have seen, for instance, that already by 1916 the young socialist militant – who had interrupted his studies in philology at Turin University – was the theatre critic of the *Avanti!* newspaper. The relative ease with which Gramsci had access to literary – as opposed to 'political' – writings may be significant but it is not sufficient to explain why he devotes so much space to cultural themes in the *Prison Notebooks*.

It is important to be clear what Gramsci means by the word 'culture'. Gramsci was not a 'standard' literary or artistic critic; even a short note of a seemingly anodyne or trivial nature, such as a reflection on a serial novel or a newspaper article, typically involves Gramsci developing a conception of cultural life that is highly original, at once *social* and *political*. However, Gramsci never provided a systematic definition or explication of his concept of culture that would be valid once and for all. What we attempt in this chapter, then, is to reconstruct Gramsci's understanding of culture through successive approximations.

First, we can note that for Gramsci culture is the antithesis of a *system*, and *a fortiori* of a 'value system', as it might perhaps be expressed today. This is an important point, because some strands in the history of anthropology have put forward precisely a paradigm of culture-as-system to elucidate modes of living of peoples once described as 'primitive'. Some of the weaknesses of a culture-as-system approach are immediately apparent: it tends to project the artificial coherence of a given culture while situating it in a sort of closed container; thought and practice, and thus culture and politics, are detached from one another; and perceiving (or explaining) change and history is extremely difficult.[1]

Against this approach, Gramsci allows us to see culture as a *succession of quotidian practices*. Culture for Gramsci denotes a certain way of living in society, or way of acting as a social being while thinking one's own action and the outside world. We will see in Chapter 4 the meaning and significance of Gramsci's assertion that 'everyone is a philosopher'. Here we can note that in Gramsci's view each individual participates in the culture of their society – in the maintenance, contestation or destruction of this culture – precisely to the extent that they have an original relation to the outside world that is constituted by their practice and thought on a daily basis.

Gramsci's understanding of culture goes radically against other common stereotypes about culture, such as the view that would associate 'culture' with some kind of encyclopaedic knowledge or would perceive behind the word 'culture' some surplus of intellectual refinement or sophistication to be found in the educated elite. In an article written in 1916, 'Socialism and Culture', Gramsci directly criticizes the latter position. The attitude of considering culture as the preserve of an educated elite, he writes, 'serves to create the kind of weak and colourless intellectualism that Romain Rolland has flayed so mercilessly, which has given birth to a mass of pretentious babblers who have a more damaging effect on social life than tuberculosis or syphilis germs have on the beauty and physical health of the body'. The young Gramsci concludes in a more humanistic vein, 'Culture is something quite different. It is organization, discipline of one's

---

[1] See Kate Crehan, *Gramsci, Culture and Anthropology* (London: Pluto, 2002).

inner self, a coming to terms with one's own personality; it is the attainment of a higher awareness, with the aid of which one succeeds in understanding one's own historical value, one's own function in life, one's own rights and obligations.'[2]

We can also note that for Gramsci culture is never fixed or rigid, but is always in flux as an object of historical becoming. Importantly, what is true for time also applies to space: cultures change spatially as well as historically. Thus Gramsci documents in the *Prison Notebooks* the ascendancy of specific national cultures at specific times (such as French in the nineteenth century and American in the twentieth), as well as the porosity of other national cultures (in the first instance Italian) in relation to the dominant world cultures.

For Gramsci, then, culture is accessed through the combined ways of acting, perceiving and feeling of all people. However, Gramsci recognizes that these quotidian cultural situations that concern everybody – along with the heterogeneous 'common sense' of an epoch and a society, Gramsci's understanding of which we will explore in more detail in Chapter 4 – are forged under the influence of the cultural production of elites. Thus literature, philosophical systems and fine arts stand in a set of important and irreducibly *political* relations to the 'everyday' or 'ordinary' culture to which everyone in a society contributes in their day-to-day lives. A crucial part of Gramsci's overall perspective on culture consists in thinking through the reciprocal relations between 'popular culture' and 'high culture', or between the culture of 'elites' and that of 'subalterns'.

Therefore, the issue of the relations between culture and social domination, and more generally between culture and politics, is at the very heart of Gramsci's thought. Before Bourdieu or Foucault, the *Prison Notebooks* offered one of the most thorough and sophisticated reflections of the twentieth century on the relation between knowledge and power, centred on Gramsci's concept of hegemony (which we will explore in Chapter 5). According to Gramsci, then, culture at all levels, and in each manifestation, has profound political implications: culture is for Gramsci a privileged site of *political struggles* and the terrain on which power is generated and exerted, but also struggled against and resisted.

---

[2] 'Socialism and Culture', *Il Grido del Popolo*, 29 January 1916; *SPWI*, p. 11.

In Gramsci's prison writings his constant preoccupation with the culture–politics relation is centred, we would argue, on the problematic of the *organization of culture*. Thinking about culture *organizationally* means thinking through how, where and by whom culture is produced, how it is diffused and distributed, and what structures, principles and constraints dictate its overall configuration. Thus Gramsci grapples with the following sorts of questions: what ensemble of institutions, including the press and 'popular literature', undergirds cultural life in a given society at a given time? What type of educational relation is required for the transmission and reproduction of a given culture? And, perhaps most importantly, what roles do intellectuals play in these processes?

Intellectuals

Defining the intellectual

As with many of Gramsci's investigations, his treatment of the question of the intellectual appears in a fragmentary form in his *Prison Notebooks*; it is only really possible to speak of Gramsci's 'theory of intellectuals' after a process of reconstruction that draws on material from the whole of the notebooks. Even then, it is important to bear in mind that such a theory could only exist at an exploratory stage. Nevertheless, many readers of Gramsci have seen in his reflections on the intellectual one of the most original aspects of his thought.

The first step in Gramsci's approach consists in rejecting any possible definition of the intellectual that makes reference to the content of their activities as 'cerebral' rather than 'manual'. As Gramsci notes, 'There is no human activity from which every form of intellectual participation can be excluded: *homo faber* cannot be separated from *homo sapiens*.'[3] Every human activity, that is, requires a certain amount of mental expenditure and effort on the one hand, and a certain amount of 'muscular-nervous' effort on

---

[3] Q12§3; *SPN*, p. 9.

the other. Against Frederick Taylor, who in his *Principles of the Scientific Organisation of Work* (1911) had lamented the fact that a warehouse worker would never reach the efficiency of a 'trained gorilla', Gramsci asserts that human intellectual power never ceases to be mobilized and drawn on in one way or another – including in the work of warehouse labourers. Thus, most basically, Gramsci states that 'although one can speak of intellectuals, one cannot speak of non-intellectuals, because non-intellectuals do not exist'.[4]

Thus for Gramsci the intellectual is not merely a 'thinking' person, or someone who can think 'more' or 'better' than others. The intellectual does not make herself – rather it is society that makes the intellectual. As Gramsci writes:

The most widespread error of method seems to me that of having looked for this criterion of distinction [for the definition of the intellectual] in the intrinsic nature of intellectual activities, rather than in the ensemble of the system of relations in which these activities (and therefore the intellectual groups who personify them) have their place within the general complex of social relations.[5]

A consequence of Gramsci's starting point, then, is that the intellectual is constituted by his or her social role. That role consists, for Gramsci, in the production and diffusion of knowledge in society. The intellectual's function is in this way distinguished from the workers and peasants (under the empire of capitalists and landowners respectively) who directly reproduce society's material resources.

At this point the originality of Gramsci's perspective begins to emerge. Whereas Marx and Engels in *The German Ideology* (1846) appeared to include the intellectual without qualification in the bourgeois class, Gramsci does not entirely assimilate intellectuals into the bourgeoisie. He tends to describe the intellectuals as one of the *ceti* of a society, or one of its 'layers' or 'strata'.

---

[4] Ibid., p. 9.
[5] Q12§1; *SPN*, p. 8.

The intellectual stratum, for Gramsci, is quite large and includes many types of people. For him, university professors, academics, journalists and writers are of course intellectuals, but so are artists, priests, technicians, politicians, civil servants, lawyers and even army officers. All of these groups, in one way or another, fulfil a certain cultural, political or technical function that exists apart from the immediate material reproduction of society. Specifically, all of these types of people participate in the process by which a certain cultural environment forms, and through which a certain vision of the world is created, diffused and reproduced in time and space. In referring to this 'vision of the world' Gramsci often uses the German word *Weltanschauung*, meaning literally 'world-perception' but with the connotation of the world view of an individual or group.

We should bear in mind that Gramsci was writing in the interwar period when the service sector, as it is understood today, occupied a far smaller economic share than it does in today's Western economies. Management and executive jobs were in Gramsci's day in their infancy, particularly in a country as unevenly developed as Italy. Gramsci, though, perceived capitalism's ongoing transformation, in the first place through the Taylorization of production methods, which tended to multiply administrative jobs within a firm. It is in the context of the changes in production led by Taylorism that he granted these emerging social positions the status of intellectuals, whether they were executives or administrators. Thus in his 1926 *Alcuni temi* essay Gramsci notes:

In every country, the layer of intellectuals has been radically modified by the development of capitalism. The old type of intellectual was the organising element in a society with a mainly peasant and artisanal basis. To organise the State, to organise commerce, the dominant class bred a particular type of intellectual. Industry has introduced a new type of intellectual: the technical organiser, the specialist in applied science.[6]

---

[6] *SPWII*, p. 454.

The organic intellectual and the traditional intellectual

For Gramsci, then, intellectuals represent a social stratum that is distinct from the classes that participate directly in the material reproduction of society. Gramsci's perspective has the merit of problematizing the degree of *relative autonomy* of intellectuals vis-à-vis the 'fundamental classes' in society (by which Gramsci means the capitalist class and the proletariat). Thus Gramsci asks, 'Are intellectuals an autonomous and independent social group, or does every social group have its own particular specialized category of intellectuals? The problem is a complex one, because of the variety of forms assumed to date by the real historical process of formation of the different categories of intellectuals.'[7]

Gramsci relates his response to this question to the two main interpretative models of the intellectual of his period. First, Gramsci wants to fight against the thesis according to which intellectuals are able to rise above the turmoil of history and reach a plane of thought somehow independent of social conflict and free from any sort of social bias. Gramsci considers such a perspective naïve at best, and intends to demolish it (as Marx had attempted previously). To adopt such a position, Gramsci notes, would be to take the 'eminent' intellectuals of the day at face value, since those intellectuals – like, perhaps, intellectuals of any epoch – are keen to found their legitimacy on contentions of impartiality and neutrality. Gramsci thus endeavours to demystify claims to the independence of 'pure thought'.

At the same time, Gramsci rejects the inverse thesis, associated at the time with 'vulgar' Marxism, that cultural life is no more than a mechanical reflection of economic forces. For Gramsci, any notion of 'reflection' cannot do justice to the decisive role that intellectuals play in the development of culture. For instance, Gramsci criticized the Russian revolutionary Bukharin for having straightforwardly reduced – and for that matter in an unrigorous way – Goethe's

---

[7] Q12§1; *SPN*, p. 5.

Prometheus (1789) to an unequivocal reflection of the situation of the bourgeois class of his day.[8]

Despite his consistent rejection of vulgar economic determinism, Gramsci stays faithful to Marx's original insight that intellectual life is always situated in a socio-historical field of forces in which class struggle is the primordial reality. Developing Marx's thought, Gramsci distinguishes between two different types of relations that intellectual social groups can have vis-à-vis the fundamental classes of society. These two different types of relations create 'organic intellectuals' on the one hand and 'traditional intellectuals' on the other.

Gramsci defines the organic intellectual as an intellectual-social type that is created alongside an *emerging* social class (meaning the bourgeoisie and, at a later historical period, the proletariat). This intellectual-social type is called on to play the role of an organizer in the advance of the new productive, legal and cultural system that develops in conjunction with the rising power of the emerging class. Thus the industrial bourgeoisie generated at its side organic intellectuals in the form of technicians, managers, economic advisers, lawyers and so on, all of whom were auxiliaries to the production process. In addition, the rising bourgeoisie, in the process of its gradual triumph over the older aristocratic classes during the European 'long nineteenth century', saw its ascension to the summit of society accompanied by several generations of writers, journalists and politicians who constituted the cultural and political elites of this incipient bourgeois world. These groups were organic intellectuals linked to the bourgeoisie, but were individually removed from the daily industrial production process and so were not part of the capitalist class *sensu stricto*. These elites, though, succeeded in transforming this relative detachment from economic life into their key asset, becoming in this way the 'cultural self-consciousness, the self-criticism of the dominant class'.[9] Far from being simple servants of particular economic interests or passive observers of history, the most advanced organic intellectuals are in

---

[8] The work referred to by Gramsci is Bukharin's *The Theory of Historical Materialism* (1921).
[9] Q5§105; *SCW*, pp. 278–9.

fact, according to Gramsci, the true organizers of a whole way of life that constitutes a society at a given point in time.

Gramsci refers to those intellectuals who exist prior to the ascendancy of the rising social class, and which the rising social class 'finds along its way', as traditional intellectuals. The first figure with which Gramsci illustrates the notion of the traditional intellectual is the man of the church – a product of feudal society who survived the supersession of that economic system as a caretaker of religion. In addition to religious figures, Gramsci also mentions certain State officials as traditional intellectuals, namely administrative types of high rank or diplomats who originated in aristocratic society but managed to reinvent themselves more or less successfully in the political world of the early twentieth century. More complexly, we could identify the figure of the academic as a traditional intellectual, particularly in certain national and historical contexts.[10] In his *Alcuni temi* essay of 1926 Gramsci identifies in addition two other groups of traditional intellectuals specifically associated with Southern Italy. First, there are the plethora of small rural intellectuals, such as notaries, bureaucrats and 'village pharmacy intellectuals', numerically quite considerable but always subordinate to the North-oriented State on the one hand and the landowners on the other.[11] Second, Gramsci refers to a handful of 'eminent' liberal intellectuals who enjoyed an immense cultural influence in the South during his day, such as Giustino Fortunato and, especially, Benedetto Croce (see Chapter 4).

Gramsci often uses the term 'elite' to describe organic intellectuals, and he turns to another French expression to describe the self-understanding of traditional intellectuals: 'Since these various categories of traditional intellectuals experience through an "*esprit de corps*" [the pride and loyalty shared by members of a group] their uninterrupted historical continuity and their special qualification, they thus put themselves forward as autonomous and independent of the dominant social group.'[12]

---

[10] See Perry Anderson, 'Components of the National Culture', *New Left Review*, 1:50 (1968), pp. 3–57 for a remarkable map of twentieth-century British academic culture.
[11] *SPWII*, p. 443.
[12] Q12§1; *SPN*, p. 7.

For Gramsci, then, a central characteristic of the traditional intellectual is the tendency to self-perceive as free and independent from the course of history and, particularly, as a custodian of a centuries-old cultural tradition that serves to confer legitimacy. Referring to the traditional intellectuals who had a political or administrative function in his day, Gramsci remarks that 'many intellectuals think that they *are* the State'.[13]

While at times traditional intellectuals are able to maintain a certain measure of autonomy – in particular when embodied in institutions specific to the traditional intellectual groups such as the Catholic Church – Gramsci rejects the notion of pure independence as an illusion. Even though they are the inheritors of a *longue durée* social reality, traditional intellectuals have for Gramsci only survived the vicissitudes of history as a social category by inserting themselves into contemporary social configurations. Here Gramsci mentions Benedetto Croce who, under the guise of a haughty detachment from the pettiness of political life, actually served before fascism to attract educated young Italians to Idealist philosophy and later to legitimize a stance of non-resistance to the fascist regime. This type of observation applies equally, according to Gramsci, to those traditional intellectuals who imagine they 'are the State': Gramsci notes that the aristocratic British members of parliament in the Victorian era, despite their self-perception as having a certain type of superiority, were in fact only the servants of the only existing dominant class, the bourgeoisie.

Intellectuals and political struggle

By denying the possibility of 'free thought' that stands independent of history and social contradictions, Gramsci takes away from intellectuals one of their traditional pedestals. Instead, he sees intellectuals as playing a key role in politics. Specifically, he calls upon the organic intellectual of the proletariat to produce a new culture, to diffuse a new conception of the world and to take on a directing role in political struggle: 'The mode of being of the new intellectual can

---

[13] Ibid., p. 16.

no longer consist in eloquence, which is an exterior and momentary mover of feelings and passions, but in active participation in practical life, as constructor, organiser, "permanent persuader" and not just a simple orator.'[14]

For Gramsci, intellectual activity, like manual activity, is a way the individual engages with the world and participates in its concrete transformation. The key difference here is that whereas the worker produces material objects, the intellectual produces knowledge and culture. In a way similar to the avant-garde of the bourgeoisie's organic intellectuals of the nineteenth century, the 'new' (i.e. communist) intellectual of the twentieth century for Gramsci has to become the *political organizer* of the proletariat.

Moreover, the revolutionary intellectual has to act as a catalyst for the historical process by which the proletariat homogenizes itself both politically and culturally. The notion of 'homogeneity', which Gramsci uses often in the *Notebooks*, refers to the decisive moment when a social group acquires self-consciousness and thus prepares to enter the historical stage as a collective actor. This idea of Gramsci's develops Marx's distinction between a 'class-in-itself' (i.e. a class that exists in objective material terms) and a 'class-for-itself' (which is subjectively committed to its historical mission). The revolutionary intellectual thus contributes to the development of the 'self-consciousness' of the proletariat as a class.

It is also necessary to situate Gramsci's notion of the communist intellectual in the context of his time. The figure of the communist intellectual was radically opposed to the conception dominant at one point in the Second International according to which the intellectual was an educated deserter from the bourgeoisie who could help the non-intellectual working masses at the theoretical level. By contrast, Gramsci's organic intellectual is defined neither by educational attainment nor by social origin, but instead by his or her function as a revolutionary leader and role as a political organizer. The primary source of inspiration here is probably Lenin, who demanded the abolition of any status distinction between workers and intellectuals as early as his *What Is to Be Done?* (1902).

---

[14] Q12§3; *SPN*, p. 10.

As Gramsci's organic intellectual is committed to serving the revolution, it might be tempting to draw an analogy with Jean-Paul Sartre's notion of *intellectuel engagé*. Such an analogy, however, is unconvincing. The Gramscian organic intellectual is not a 'fellow-traveller' to the cause but is rather, among other things, a political organizer within the party who at once lives the political struggle by the word as a permanent persuader and by action as a militant. A more convincing analogy has been made between Gramsci's organic intellectual and Mao Zedong's 'red and expert' cadre; for both Gramsci and Mao, working class hegemony needs its own (organic) intellectuals who are expert enough to lead and 'red' enough to retain their ties with the working class.[15]

Despite the political imperatives of the struggle, Gramsci is careful to emphasize that this new communist intellectual should never go as far as to doctor the truth in the name of revolution. Gramsci had written as early as 1919 in *L'Ordine Nuovo*'s 'Workers' Democracy' editorial: 'To tell the truth, to arrive together at the truth, is a communist and revolutionary act.'[16] We can see Gramsci's personal life as a revolutionary, indeed, as a model of intellectual probity.

Gramsci was also keen to historicize the intellectual struggles of his day by comparing them with the past. He thereby arrives at the conception of the 'popular intellectual', which he sees as having a wider range of historical applicability than the notion of the proletarian organic intellectual, which he recognizes as tied to the political imperatives of the interwar proletarian struggle. On the topic of the popular intellectual Gramsci remarks admiringly how Diderot and d'Alembert's *Encyclopédie* (1751–72) and more generally the 'Voltairean' atmosphere of eighteenth-century France prepared the cultural terrain for the 'Great Revolution' of 1789. He also notes how, across the nineteenth century, France gave to the world an image of society where, despite political turmoil, the intellectual life that was bourgeois in character was able to work for the positive development

[15] Arif Dirlik, 'The Predicament of Marxist Revolutionary Consciousness: Mao Zedong, Antonio Gramsci, and the Reformulation of Marxist Revolutionary Theory', *Modern China*, 9:2 (1983), pp. 182–211; Jerome Karabel, 'Revolutionary Contradictions: Antonio Gramsci and the Problem of Intellectuals', *Politics and Society*, 6 (1976), pp. 123–72.
[16] 'Workers' Democracy'; *SPWI*, p. 68.

of a wider part of society, specifically what he calls the 'people-nation' (see Chapter 3).

In a striking passage of the *Prison Notebooks* titled 'Passage from Knowing to Understanding and to Feeling and Vice Versa' Gramsci asserts that the 'popular intellectual' must have an emotive or feelings-based bond to the people. For Gramsci, it is this relation of sympathy or empathy that is the true spur towards the intellectual practice of the 'popular intellectual', and that produces the aspiration to make their intellectual efforts work for the lifting of the people's conditions: 'One cannot make politics-history without this passion, without this sentimental connection between intellectuals and people-nation. In the absence of such a nexus the relations between the intellectual and the people-nation are, or are reduced to, relationships of a purely bureaucratic and formal order; the intellectuals become a caste, or a priesthood.' He continues, 'The popular element "feels" but does not always know or understand; the intellectual element "knows" but does not always understand and in particular does not always feel. The two extremes are therefore pedantry and philistinism on the one hand and blind passion and sectarianism on the other.'[17]

Education

Defining education

While the intellectual is the central figure of the world of culture in Gramsci's account, another of his core preoccupations is the question of education. These two dimensions – intellectuals and education – are tightly linked for Gramsci, in particular in a specific progressive sequence whereby education trains and forms intellectuals, who are then able to educate the popular masses and raise their intellectual level, such that, finally, the people are increasingly able to self-educate and become actors in their own right in the new culture that is in the process of formation.

---

[17] Q11§67; *SPN*, p. 418.

Gramsci does not hesitate to call such a revolutionary transmission process, in which he envisaged everyone in society as participating, as a form of *work*. Gramsci sees the process of education not just as political and intellectual work, but also physical work: 'studying too is a job, and a very tiring one, with its own particular apprenticeship – involving muscles and nerves as well as intellect'.[18] It is perhaps not surprising that Gramsci (who himself had many occasions to teach in his life, both at the PCI school and in prison) emphasizes the labour of the teacher and insists that the knowledge transfer between teacher and student 'can only be realised by the living work of the teacher'.[19]

Gramsci begins, as he often does when setting out to examine a social theme, by taking the issue under investigation in its widest possible sense, and conferring to it a very wide domain. This might be termed Gramsci's 'maximal' framing of the question he is studying. Thus for Gramsci educational practice is not confined to the school and to the university; instead, it traverses and operates across all of society. In addition to the school system, Gramsci identifies a large number of public and private institutions as sites of educational activity. These include parliament and its legislative activity, and the penal system (which, according to Gramsci, has a 'negative educational function'). But also included here are political parties, unions, churches and popular clubs, along with more conventionally 'cultural' organizations such as the press, radio, theatre, museums, libraries, literary societies and even, Gramsci asserts, architecture and urbanism.

Although it might initially be unsettling, the true strength of Gramsci's perspective is that it makes it possible to discern the objective links between diverse social practices without denying the *differentia specifica* of each of those practices. For Gramsci, education is the 'live activity' of transmitting knowledge and culture, which must be both inherited from the conditions of the past and re-actuated by practice. All of the institutions mentioned above participate, for Gramsci, in this very activity.

Relatedly, Gramsci tirelessly advocated the education of adults, decades before expressions such as 'continuing education' and

---

[18] Q12§2; *SPN*, p. 42.
[19] Ibid., p. 35.

'lifelong learning' became common. Gramsci mainly had in mind, as might be expected, the working class population, and here we can see an interesting link to his biography. During the *biennio rosso* period of 1919–20 in Turin, the rise of the practices of the so-called 'scientific organisation of work' (notably at FIAT) led to demands on the part of the workers to reach a better understanding of the new production techniques and of technical and organizational changes. Although the management of a few large factories did provide some targeted 'technical' training to a few of the more qualified workers, *L'Ordine Nuovo* asserted that the training must combine professional training with education about the social reality – in both its historical and economic dimensions – underlying the scientific organization of work.[20] Gramsci and his comrades contended that it is only by intellectually mastering the context of the social relations in which their own work was embedded that the workers would be able to develop their own critical and revolutionary consciousness.

The school

Within the constellation of educational institutions that interest Gramsci, school in the strict sense has an essential role. An important context of Gramsci's reflections on education is the major change in education policy that Italy had experienced under fascism. In 1923, Giovanni Gentile, who was Minister of Education and an intellectual defender of the official policy of the fascist regime, oversaw a series of reforms intended to transform the traditional model of education centred on Latin and rote learning. Centrally, technical or professional teaching for children of working class or peasant backgrounds was included in the curriculum, and the 'spontaneity' of pupils was promoted at the expense of the supposedly overly mechanical transmission of knowledge that had previously predominated. Somewhat paradoxically this fascist education policy could perhaps be perceived as progressive today, as it aimed to replace what it took

---

[20] Attilio Monasta, 'Antonio Gramsci', *Perspectives: Revue trimestrielle d'éducation comparée*, 23:3 (1993), pp. 613–29.

to be formalism and theoretical aridity with communicative exchange between students and teachers. The advocates of the fascist policy at the time claimed a heritage from the 'Genevan pedagogy' inspired by Jean-Jacques Rousseau's *Émile* (1762).

In a note titled 'In Search of the Educational Principle' Gramsci takes a stance opposite to that of the Gentile reforms. He asserts, rather, that the experience of elementary and secondary schooling by necessity includes a share of suffering for the child, since it requires the imposition of a bodily and mental discipline to which there will initially be resistance. Despite their possible tediousness, Gramsci also sees in Latin and grammar a stepping stone towards the future capacity for free thinking, and considers that the capacity for abstract thought made possible by these subjects may also be converted at a later date into tools that will allow the fusion of theory and practice.

Gramsci also notes that a privileged social background is likely to nurture in a child dispositions that are favourable to learning, while children from a working class or peasant background might find these dispositions harder to come by – here it is possible to recognize aspects of Bourdieu's later theory of 'cultural capital'.[21] Therefore, to relegate intellectual discipline, as the Gentile reforms sought to do, is in fact to prevent students from working class and peasant backgrounds from attaining the sorts of dispositions necessary for the type of education practised in the school system. For Gramsci, the reforms aimed at promoting 'spontaneity' and developing technical secondary schooling curricula operate above all as a method of consigning generations of working class and peasant youth to subaltern manual positions. It is perhaps only superficially, then, that Gramsci appears in the *Prison Notebooks* to be a proponent of tradition or even authoritarianism in school. His aim is rather to illustrate the illusory character of Gentilean progressivism by demonstrating that what at first glance seems 'advanced' will in fact have reactionary social consequences.[22]

---

[21] See for instance Pierre Bourdieu, 'Reproduction culturelle et reproduction sociale', *Information sur les Sciences Sociales*, 10:2 (1971), pp. 45–99.
[22] Harold Entwistle, *Antonio Gramsci: Conservative Schooling for Radical Politics* (London: Routledge, 1979).

Gramsci also shows that in order for the school to be democratized, a completely different set of reforms would have to be adopted. We can mention here two of his prescriptions. First, he writes that a universal secondary curriculum has to be instituted and provided for the whole of society, as opposed to a bifurcated system channelling pupils towards either a technical-vocational track or an academic track at the end of primary schooling.[23] Second, looking forward towards a socialist form of education, Gramsci expresses the wish for a symbiosis of intellectual and manual teaching throughout the school system. Such a transformation would prevent the reification of pure mental activity that Gramsci sees as an 'intellectualism', and, perhaps as importantly, would also stand as a means for future organic intellectuals to be ever more engaged in concrete society, thereby inaugurating 'new relations between intellectual and industrial work, not only in the school but in the whole of social life'.[24]

The dialectic of conformity and spontaneity

Gramsci, then, conceives of education as a fundamental social process, present at every stage of human life and actuated by a whole range of diverse social activities that are both public and private, both collective and individual. At the same time, he puts forward a model of the school system that seems to include a traditional conception of education as discipline (although he does envisage transcending this traditional conception within an ideal of radical democracy).

---

[23] It is only in the post-war period that Western European countries moved towards the unification of the first stage of secondary education, thus partly fulfilling Gramsci's vision. In Italy, the 1962 reform turned the *scuola media* (middle school) into a unified, compulsory track for all pupils between 11 and 14. In France, similarly, a series of educational reforms between 1959 and 1975 established the *collège unique* as the compulsory stage between primary schools and *lycées* (upper secondary schools). Britain, by contrast, never achieved complete unification of lower secondary education, although the conversion into comprehensives of most secondary State schools in the 1960s and 1970s was very much part of the broader European dynamic at the time.

[24] Q12§1; *SPN*, p. 33. We can also note that Gramsci's proposals here are somewhat reminiscent of Chapter 15 of Marx's *Capital* (1867), which puts forward a similar idea of combining intellectual and manual training.

Although there may appear to be a tension, perhaps even bordering on inconsistency, between these two aspects of Gramsci's thinking on education, it is important to emphasize that there is a guiding thread in Gramsci's writings on education that allows us to reconcile these two parts. Gramsci sees education in its social context as a transition from learning as a form of *social conformity* to the achievement of *critical spontaneity*. Gramsci attempts to transform the opposition of these two poles – conformity and spontaneity – into a *dynamic* association. Although we may be tempted to see it as a simple progression from conformity to spontaneity, Gramsci makes it clear that the relation is in fact dialectical and the passage must therefore be a two-way one that transcends both poles taken separately and in their strictest senses.

Thus for Gramsci the education of young people rests on a first phase that is conformist or even almost coercive. In this stage the child has to assimilate and internalize the physical and psychological dispositions, as well as the form of sociality, that are necessary to a subsequent richer and more positive type of education. We can note here that Gramsci at one point describes studying as 'a process of adaptation, a habit acquired with effort, tedium, and even suffering'.[25] We might term this first stage 'conformisation', and it will perforce be painstaking and difficult, and additionally so to the extent that the child originates from a relatively uneducated social background. Indeed, if the child originates from the peasantry, then Gramsci takes it that one of the primary missions of elementary schooling will be to uproot superstitions and folkloric beliefs in magic that the child may have been exposed to in village life. However, as the child moves forward in the curriculum towards secondary and then tertiary education, Gramsci insists that the disciplinary dimension will progressively be replaced by the exercise of spontaneous critical reflection. In this way, conformism eventually generates its very opposite: the freedom of judgement.

Gramsci also applies a perspective centred on the passage from conformism to spontaneity to adult education. In discussing the phenomenon of 'Americanism' (see Chapter 3) he notes, apparently

---

[25] Q12§2; *SPN*, p. 42.

without disapproval, that the new Fordist production norms had surpassed all previous attempts to impose a sort of individual and physical-psychological discipline on the workers in the industrial production chain. Gramsci perceives in this conformization moment the fact that the Taylorized worker – the human product of the scientific organization of work – has the potential to overcome his or her existence as exploited labour power by reaching critical self-consciousness not just as an individual social actor but also as a member of a potentially revolutionary class.

Education is thus, for Gramsci, *political* as it is an important moment in the development of a critical understanding of society and ultimately of class consciousness. Accordingly working class unions and particularly the Communist Party are called on to play roles as educational sites animated by the activity of organic intellectuals. Gramsci's view of education in these contexts is completely removed from any project whereby party apparatchiks indoctrinate workers. On the contrary, Gramsci is interested in developing the critical consciousness of 'subaltern classes who want to educate themselves in the art of government and who have an interest in knowing all truths'.[26] In this way, he understands revolutionary consciousness as the precursor and outcome of the *self-education* of the working class.

Journalism

The press and the organization of culture

In. this chapter so far we have foregrounded the issue of the organization of culture as central to Gramsci's approach to understanding culture and its political dimensions, and have stressed that Gramsci sees the educational relationship central to the reproduction of culture as operating in a wide range of sites. The sites of the educational relationship, for Gramsci, include not just the school and university, but also the political institutions of the State,

---

[26]Q10II§41xii; *FSPN*, p. 396.

organizations of civil society (such as parties, unions and churches) and actors in the cultural market (including radio, the entertainment industry and publishing, for instance). It is worth emphasizing that Gramsci sees cultural life as made up of networks of institutions, with different parts having complex relations of interdependence with one another.

In the *Prison Notebooks* Gramsci asserts that the press can be considered as the 'most prominent and dynamic part' of the cultural universe made up of these reciprocal relations and interdependencies.[27] As a result, he devotes many pages to journalism in his notebooks. In contrast to his contemporary Walter Benjamin – who like Gramsci attempted to think about culture from a Marxist perspective – Gramsci does not focus on the audio-visual technologies of radio and cinema that were emerging at the time. From his prison cell Gramsci was not in the ideal situation to take stock of the increasingly propagandistic use of these newer means of communication by the fascist regime. Nevertheless, he did manage to grasp something of the nature of this cultural transmission, even if he did not fully grasp its political significance: 'spoken communication is a means of ideological diffusion which has a rapidity, a field of action, and an emotional simultaneity far greater than written communication … but [this action is accomplished] superficially, not in depth'.[28]

The bourgeois press

In the *Prison Notebooks*, Gramsci focuses mainly on the pre-fascist bourgeois press, which he had observed when he was himself a journalist in Turin. He notes that the greatest Italian newspapers before Mussolini's March on Rome in October 1922 (such as *Corriere della Serra* or *La Stampa*) fulfilled a crucial function that was at once both cultural and political: they homogenized the different points of view of the property-owning classes to express a supposedly universal and consistent 'public opinion'.

---

[27] Q3§49; *SCW*, p. 389.
[28] Q16§21; *SCW*, pp. 382–3.

On this issue he asserts, 'Public opinion is the political content of the public's political will that can be dissentient; therefore, there is a struggle for the monopoly of the organs of public opinion'.[29] Gramsci uses the expression 'public opinion', here as elsewhere, to refer not to the 'spontaneous' political disposition of subaltern classes, but precisely to the process whereby dominant social layers tend to project and reinforce their own particular and narrow perspectives through an apparently democratic media discourse ostensibly targeted at a universal readership. Thus 'public opinion', which the eminent bourgeois press purports to embody, serves to negotiate and smooth out the contradictions internal to the bourgeois class while also preventing the eruption of effective subaltern dissidence in the public sphere.

Despite a limited printing, the eminent newspapers of the post-*Risorgimento* decades enjoyed a form of cultural and political mastery over the destiny of the country. In Gramsci's opinion, their importance can barely be overstated: 'due to the absence of organized and centralized parties, one cannot overlook the newspapers: it is the newspapers, grouped in series, that constitute the real parties'.[30]

The *Corriere della Serra*, which was headed before the rise of fascism by Luigi Albertini, provides a clear illustration of Gramsci's argument. This great daily newspaper from Milan had a reputation for its consistent support for the industrial profits of North Italy, and in particular of Lombardy. Yet it managed to avoid limiting its identification only to such narrow and localized interests; on the contrary, the newspaper endeavoured to promote national-level political projects with the aim of unifying the country's industrial bourgeoisie without sacrificing any key part of that class. Thus Gramsci notes that in 1913 the editorship of the newspaper shifted political orientation and began to favour an alliance of Northern industrial profits with a 'Southern bloc' (mainly the landowning bourgeoisie) rather than with the industrial workers of the North.

At the same time, Gramsci acknowledges that the *Corriere della Serra* played a genuinely educational role in Italian society, through the professionalism of its journalists and the high quality of

---

[29] Q7§83; Antonio Gramsci, *Prison Notebooks*, Volume 3, translated and edited by Joseph Buttigieg (New York: Columbia University Press, 2007), p. 213.
[30] Q1§116; *SCW*, pp. 390–1.

its contents. The newspaper was thus a remarkable asset for the established cultural order, as it helped to diffuse throughout society – and particularly among the bourgeoisie – a specific understanding of political issues that encouraged ideological unity within the dominant groups of society. The *Corriere*'s influence was both direct, through its readers, and indirect, through the more general intellectual atmosphere it could promote in different parts of society, which could then be transmitted from one person or organization to the next. While the influence of a single publication should not be exaggerated, it seems that the *Corriere* did indeed fulfil a true pedagogical role in society, in the sense of performing an important socializing function.

'Integral journalism'

Gramsci's ambition was to see the revolutionary press embody such an educational role – or, in other words, for the communist press to do what the bourgeois press of the time was already managing to do. Gramsci's thoughts on the practicalities of fulfilling such an ambition are the subject of notebook 24, and are inspired in part by his own experience at *L'Ordine Nuovo*. Here Gramsci lays the foundations for a 'little handbook' (*manueletto*) for the creation of a party school for communist journalists. In the same way that the bourgeois press produced and disseminated the dominant culture, a communist publication would similarly have as its chief mission the illustration, diffusion and defence of the *Weltanschauung* of revolutionary socialism.

Gramsci writes a meticulous list of the various sections that a future communist publication would have to contain, including 'encyclopaedic monographs', 'politico-intellectual biographies', all manner of reviews, bibliographical resources, lexical appendices and so on.[31] The list is quite long, and might appear dated in certain respects.[32] Nevertheless, we can note that the sections mentioned

---

[31] See Q24§3 for the full list; *SCW*, pp. 414–16.
[32] Giuseppe Richeri, 'Réflexion sur Gramsci et le journalisme', *Quaderni*, 57 (2006), pp. 85–91.

above suggest that Gramsci had a very high intellectual level in mind, which is all the more remarkable given the publication's readership would be working class party members with little secondary schooling. Furthermore, the publication would have to carry out an intellectual and moral 'cartography' of the country in order accurately to identify existing and possible future cultural trends. Finally, Gramsci holds that the editorial staff must be disciplined, since the aim is to produce an 'intellectually homogeneous product' while also reflecting the differences in styles and literary personalities of the individual contributors.[33]

Generally speaking, what is striking in these pages of the *Prison Notebooks* is the level of ambition that Gramsci has for the communist press. He speaks of this project as 'integral journalism' (*giornalismo integrale*): a journalism that is at once activist and pedagogical, political and cultural, scientific and historical. Gramsci writes that integral journalism 'seeks not only to satisfy all the needs (of a given category) of its public, but also to create and develop these needs, to arouse its public and progressively enlarge it'.[34]

The communist press is, for Gramsci, not to be understood as an elitist educational project but rather as part of a wider revolutionary project carried out by the working class. The 'communist journalists' Gramsci has in mind to lead the development of the communist press are precisely the organic intellectuals produced by the proletariat itself.

Gramsci's conception of 'integral journalism' relies on a dialectic which begins with the newspaper emanating from the real and existing aspirations rooted in a given social configuration. The newspaper then develops these aspirations to knowledge while bringing about new ones, with the newspaper then reacting to new evolutions on the side of the readership, and so on. Moreover this dialectical movement has to operate in synergy with the educational dynamic between conformity and spontaneity mentioned earlier; in both cases Gramsci envisages the progress from hierarchical instruction to self-education.

---

[33] Q24§3; *SCW*, p. 413.
[34] Q24§1; *SCW*, p. 408.

Popular literature

In Gramsci's writing on 'popular literature' he develops a number of important ideas simultaneously: the importance of the intellectual as the organizer of culture; the need to investigate aspects and areas of cultural production that may otherwise be overlooked; and the necessity of examining culture historically. In the *Prison Notebooks*, we can see that the 'popular intellectual' of previous historical periods (which as discussed above he sees as more generally historically applicable than the category of the organic intellectual of the proletariat) is very often a novelist. For instance, Gramsci says of Dostoyevsky's work that it shows 'an awareness that the intellectuals have a mission towards the people'. Gramsci continues, 'The people may be "objectively" made up of the "humble" but they must be freed from this "humility", transformed and regenerated.'[35]

In a similar vein, Gramsci sees Honoré de Balzac, a monarchist by conviction, as important precisely because he 'perceived clearly that man is the complex of the social conditions in which he has developed and lives, and that in order to "change" man one has to change this complex of conditions'. Gramsci adds that the fact that Balzac 'is "politically and socially" a reactionary is only apparent from the extra-artistic part of his writing (digressions, prefaces, etc.)'.[36] By revealing to his readers the essential fluidity of social structures, Balzac unwittingly offers his readers the intellectual means to acquire awareness of society's potential to be transformed. At the same time, for Gramsci, an adventure story that might at first glance seem politically innocuous can reveal itself to be a sort of Trojan horse for revolutionary values. For instance, in *The Count of Monte Cristo* (1844) by Alexandre Dumas the hero Edmond Dantès grows up among the labouring classes of Marseille before disguising himself as an aristocrat such that his personal vendetta can be interpreted as a kind of 'social revenge'.[37] Gramsci notes that this kind of popular

---

[35] Q21§3; *SCW*, p. 293.
[36] Q14§41; *SCW*, p. 259.
[37] Pascal Durand, 'Culture populaire, culture de masse ou culture de mass-médias? Autour de cinq thèses moins une d'Antonio Gramsci', *Quaderni*, 57 (2005), pp. 73–83.

literature contains an essential ambiguity: it is caught between its deference to existing social traditions and its latent subversive aspirations.

Gramsci deplores that nineteenth-century Italy did not produce a popular novelist of the calibre of Balzac, Hugo or Dumas in France or Walter Scott in Britain. He sees this absence, importantly, as a symptom of the Italian nation's lack of cultural coherence and a legacy of its *longue durée* socio-political history (see Chapter 3). Gramsci also investigates the commercial literature of his own day, including serial novels, police stories, melodramas and other forms. He is often highly critical of the implicit *Weltanschauung* that he sees in these writings, but does not see in them simply another brand of 'opium of the people'.[38] Thus he remarks that 'the success of a work of commercial literature indicates (and it is often the only indication available) the "philosophy of the age", that is, the mass of feelings and conceptions of the world predominant among the "silent" majority'.[39] Furthermore, despite the inherent mediocrity of the greater part of this commercial literature Gramsci also sees in it a possible starting point from which an authentically revolutionary literature might be built. Such a 'new' popular literature, which Gramsci eagerly anticipates, will have to 'sink its roots into the humus of popular culture as it is, with its tastes and tendencies and with its moral and intellectual world, even if it is backward and conventional'.[40] Gramsci, then, did not contemplate a *tabula rasa* either for culture in general or for any particular cultural form. The cultural expression of the revolutionary project, for Gramsci, is not a complete negation or destruction of the inheritance of the past, but rather a critical embracing of that legacy that alters it from the inside and thereby transcends it by progressively lifting it to the level of revolutionary aspirations.

---

[38] André Tosel, *Le Marxisme du XXᵉ siècle* (Paris: Syllepse, 2009).
[39] Q5§54; *SCW*, p. 348.
[40] Q15§58; *SCW*, p. 102.

3

Politics

Introduction

Of all the great names of twentieth-century Marxist thought, Gramsci is perhaps the one who devoted the most attention to understanding politics as an essential moment of social life, with its own rules and modalities.

Gramsci's attention to politics as an independent realm of action stands in clear contrast to Marx's focus on the critique of political economy. Following the defeat of the 1848 popular revolution – when Marx was barely 30 years old – the prospects of a communist revolution in Europe were seemingly dimmed. As a result, Marx saw it as his priority to grapple theoretically with the *economic* contradictions of the capitalist mode of production. Marx's would be a long and somewhat tortured undertaking, resulting eventually in the first volume of *Capital* in 1867.

However, Gramsci's situation was fundamentally different from Marx's, which at least partly explains why Gramsci gave so much emphasis to the political moment. In the Italy of 1919–21, when society was dislocated by the fallout of the First World War and working class protest threatened the established order, revolution could easily have appeared imminent. Gramsci witnessed this revolutionary wave and its reflux while at *L'Ordine Nuovo* (see Chapter 1), before he saw his society's contradictions illusorily resolved in the so-called 'fascist solution' after 1922. We can restate here that Gramsci from 1924 to 1926 was at the head of the PCI, and so enjoyed the position of leadership of a working class party that

Marx and Engels did not. It is for Gramsci the revolutionary, above all, that the moment of the political takes on its crucial importance.

Gramsci drew on a wide range of sources of inspiration for his thinking about politics. These included not only Marx and Lenin, but also Ernest Renan, Georges Sorel and even Henri Bergson. The most important of these sources, though, is Machiavelli, who Gramsci clearly admires deeply. For Gramsci, *The Prince* (1532) is not a cynical work – it is not, that is, 'Machiavellian' in the most common sense of the word – and he rejects this shallow interpretation, instead discerning in Machiavelli's work 'a cry of passionate urgency' for the regeneration of Italy.[1] Most importantly, Gramsci finds in Machiavelli the sources of his own conception of politics as 'autonomous science' and 'autonomous art', that is as having rules and modes of operating distinct from other fields of social life.

At the same time as recognizing what we might call the 'specificity of politics', or the necessity of studying it and attempting to understand it in a way that moves beyond the direct reduction of politics to economics, Gramsci also understands politics in an extremely wide sense, just as he had with education and culture (see Chapter 2). Specifically, for Gramsci politics is constituted by *the contribution of each human being to the transformation of his or her social environment*. We can note immediately that this definition is not centred on the State but rather on the *human being*, and thus each person is *ipso facto* understood as a 'political being'. In a note from the *Prison Notebooks* titled 'Who Is a Legislator?' Gramsci elaborates, 'Every man, in as much as he is active, i.e. living, contributes to modifying the social environment in which he develops (to modifying certain of its characteristics or to preserving others); in other words, he tends to establish "norms", rules of living and of behaviour.'[2]

For Gramsci, therefore, politics is not a terrain monopolized by professionals (i.e. 'politicians') nor is it a specific social field within society, but it is instead a moment of almost every human activity right down to the most quotidian aspects of life. Politics is not, then, a means to an end, in the sense that the conquest of the State by

---

[1] Q13§1; *SPN*, p. 127.
[2] Q14§13; *SPN*, p. 265.

revolutionaries and the establishment of a communist society might abolish politics. On the contrary, for Gramsci politics is the foundation of any society, both in the present and in the future.

Central to Gramsci's account of politics are both his refusal to reduce politics to economics in his assertion of the former's 'autonomous' nature on the one hand, and his passionate affirmation of the political character of all social life on the other. The generative tension between understanding politics *sui generis* (and, as we shall see, with a strong tactical dimension to that understanding) and asserting that politics is ultimately grounded in a collective transformative relationship to the environment forms the basis for Gramsci's complex, sometimes difficult and immensely rich reflections on politics in his prison writings.

Civil society, political society and the State

Difficult definitions

The triangle of concepts 'civil society–political society–State' stands as the cornerstone of Gramsci's theory of politics. Although these terms, in various orientations, recur frequently throughout the *Prison Notebooks*, they are never defined by Gramsci in a systematic way. Sometimes it appears that the definitions of these terms fluctuate depending on their context and the historical period Gramsci is analysing, and their meanings seem to metamorphose from one passage to the next. Perhaps understandably, as a consequence of these seemingly fluid definitions, there have been almost ceaseless quarrels over the interpretation of these terms among commentators of Gramsci's work.[3]

---

[3] Jacques Texier, 'Gramsci, théoricien des superstructures', *La Pensée*, 139 (1968), pp. 35–60; Norberto Bobbio, 'Gramsci e la concezione della società civile', in: Pietro Rossi (ed.), *Gramsci e la cultura contemporanea: Atti del convegno internazionale di studi gramsciani* (Rome: Riuniti, 1969), pp. 75–100; Perry Anderson, 'The Antinomies of Antonio Gramsci', *New Left Review*, 1:100 (1976), pp. 5–78.

It is in his notion of civil society that Gramsci perhaps most clearly demonstrates his originality. Gramsci appropriates a concept that, until his time, had mostly been associated with the great liberal tradition that includes Locke, Hegel and Tocqueville. Civil society is understood by Gramsci to comprise all social relations and organizations that do not participate either in the economic reproduction of society or the life of the State. Thus, civil society is the 'private' institutions of a given society, including religious organizations (such as the Catholic Church), unions and political parties, cultural institutions (such as the media or publishing houses) and in general any freely formed association of citizens. Gramsci conceives of civil society as a social terrain on which rivalries and struggles of a cultural and ideological nature are played out and decided among social groups. We can note at this stage that there is a clear link between civil society and the intellectual as political organizer and permanent persuader (see Chapter 2).

As opposed to civil society, which is an open field for debate and the exercise of persuasion, political society is the domain of coercion, constraint, naked domination and the exercise of military, police and juridical-administrative force. Defined by its coercive nature, political society can be equated with a certain fraction of the State, namely that fraction embodied by the State's administrative and repressive functions (which are themselves made possible, in the last instance, by the State's 'monopoly on the legitimate use of violence', to use Weber's phrase). For instance, the State school system is not included in political society in this sense, as political society is instead equivalent to the practices of public coercive power, or to what Bourdieu has called the 'right hand' of the State (in contrast to its 'left hand' of education and welfare).[4]

The third term of the conceptual triad, the State, has the most unstable definition in the *Prison Notebooks*. Perry Anderson has argued that there are some detrimental 'slippages' in Gramsci's use of the term.[5] Despite this possible difficulty, it is possible to discern two relatively secure definitions of the State in Gramsci's work.

---

[4] See Pierre Bourdieu, *Counterfire: Against the Tyranny of the Market*, translated by Chris Turner (London: Verso, 2002).
[5] Anderson, 'Antinomies'.

First, Gramsci sometimes considers the State to be an organism that is strictly coextensive with political society as a pure administrative and repressive apparatus. There is no particular originality to this restrictive understanding of the State. In these cases, Gramsci uses the expression 'State-government' (*stato-governo*).

Second, and more interestingly, at other times in the *Prison Notebooks* Gramsci sees in the State the concrete unity of political society (domination) and civil society (consent). In these cases he writes of the 'integral State' (*stato integrale*), referring to the instances when the State embodies 'the entire complex of practical and theoretical activities with which the ruling class not only maintains its dominance but manages to win the consent of those over whom it rules'.[6] Such a conception of the State as comprising political society *and* civil society is contrary to established usage and might unsettle the reader of Gramsci's notebooks. It is important to note that with this second, integral definition of the State it becomes almost synonymous with *power* itself. The choice of the word 'State' by Gramsci is not arbitrary here, as it serves the purpose of pointing to the existence and importance of relations of power inside both 'private' civil society and 'public' political society. By his very choice of words, then, Gramsci rejects the liberal assumption of the political neutrality of civil society; Gramsci instead starts from an affirmation of the political substance of all social life.

Finally, a clarification is necessary. Gramsci does not attempt to convert his notions of 'civil society', 'political society' and 'the State' into permanent essences that somehow exist above or outside of history. His concepts, rather, are inherently *historical*, and he insists on the fact that these distinctions are of a 'methodological' and not an 'organic' character. By 'organic', an important term of Gramsci's, he usually means to suggest that something stands in a privileged or necessary relation to the economic structure of society. Thus, as we saw the 'organic' intellectual is the one tied to a class that is emerging in the field of production, and we will explore below the important distinction Gramsci draws between organic crises and conjunctural processes on the basis of different relations to society's fundamental economic development. Here, then, Gramsci means to

[6] Q15§10; *SPN*, p. 244.

suggest that his distinction between civil society, political society and the State is to be used methodologically rather than reified into a set of necessary and eternal categories that will be true for all types of societies. Rather, it is with a historian's mindset – we might plausibly see Gramsci as a historian of the present as well as of the past – that Gramsci elaborates and develops his concepts, and his concepts serve to illuminate society *at a specific point in time*, namely that of bourgeois liberalism. Bourgeois liberalism is precisely the historical form of society that institutes civil society as a sphere of individual civil liberties supposedly removed from the operation of the repressive and armed apparatus of political society. We can note that feudalism, fascism and, in its own way, communism, all involve radically different forms of political organization.

'East' and 'West'

Gramsci applies his distinction between political society and civil society to a comparison of the social structures in the 'East' and the 'West', by which he means Tsarist Russia before the 1917 revolutions and the Western Europe of his day, respectively. Through his comparative historical analysis, Gramsci addresses two crucial questions: why did the communist revolution take place in the East but not in the West, and how should the social reality of the West lead to the adoption of a revolutionary strategy different to that used successfully by the Bolsheviks? We can note that Trotsky, with whose writings Gramsci was familiar, had already raised the issue of the East–West contrast, but on this question – as on many others – Gramsci explicitly takes his distance from Trotsky.[7]

Gramsci outlines the distinction in the following way:

> In the East the State was everything, civil society was primordial and gelatinous; in the West, there was a proper relation between State and civil society, and when the State trembled a sturdy structure of civil society was at once revealed. The State was only

---

[7]On the Gramsci-Trotsky relation, see Frank Rosengarten, 'The Gramsci-Trotsky Question, 1922-1932', *Social Text*, 11 (1984–5), pp. 65–95.

an outer ditch, behind which there stood a powerful system of fortresses and earthworks.[8]

These few lines, in which the State is synonymous with political society, open the way to a radical reconceptualization of revolutionary strategy in the West by making civil society the favoured target of revolutionary activity. We can see that Gramsci takes the opposite stance to Lenin (whose work, and in particular *The State and Revolution* (1917), he greatly admired) by asserting that the conquest of the political power of the State might be considered a secondary objective for Western revolutionaries since the ultimate power of the bourgeoisie in the nations of the West resides in their civil societies.

War of movement and war of position

Gramsci pursues the military metaphor beyond 'outer ditches' and 'fortresses' by introducing the distinction between a war of movement and a war of position on the battlefield of political struggle. It is possible to perceive in Gramsci's choice of metaphor the still-recent memory of the First World War. At the beginning of the war, the German and French chiefs-of-staff had anticipated a quick war where the speed of manoeuvre would decide the victor, but they were soon confronted with the brutal reality of trench warfare that developed into a ruthless war of attrition lasting years.

Gramsci attempts to translate these military vicissitudes into the language of revolutionary struggle. He recognizes that the war of 'movement' was the appropriate revolutionary strategy for the Bolsheviks in 1917 because at that time the Tsarist State represented the concentrated force of a society that was otherwise little advanced or organized (or was 'gelatinous' in Gramsci's terminology). The Tsarist State was thus susceptible to collapse as a result of a 'frontal attack'. In Western Europe, though, Gramsci contends that a war of position and not a war of movement is the correct priority within revolutionary strategy, such that the latter does not disappear but

[8]Q7§16; *SPN*, p. 238.

becomes subsidiary and is instead converted into a moment within the former. Thus, the Communists in the West have, for Gramsci, to carry out a true 'siege war' on the terrain of ideological and cultural struggles in civil society before any attempt at the direct seizure of State power could be possible. Gramsci notes that this strategy is 'complicated, difficult, and requires exceptional qualities of patience and inventiveness'.[9]

The interpretation of modern politics

Gramsci's method of historical analysis

In reading the *Prison Notebooks* a defining trait of Gramsci's approach quickly becomes apparent: throughout his researches he demonstrates a remarkable sensitivity to historical processes, and his concepts always issue from historical inquiry rather than being formulated *in abstracto* and then only subsequently confronted with empirical reality. Gramsci's concepts, moreover, do not remain fixed and rigid but instead continue to be combined with one another, adapted and reformed in the light of the historical period he is studying. As noted above, the 'moving' or even 'slipping' character of Gramsci's conceptual constructions has attracted criticism.[10] However, the historical character of Gramsci's concepts demonstrates both a passion for concrete human history and the methodological premise according to which a concept must evolve to reflect the reality it seeks to unveil.

Gramsci's 'historical-political research' reveals an epistemological caution that is complementary to his theoretical audacity.[11] He rejects *a priori* propositions and *petitio principii* as well as dogmatism, both Marxist and liberal. We can describe Gramsci's approach to the analysis of politics as fundamentally *inductive*, with theory emerging from concrete discoveries. Interpreters of the *Prison Notebooks* have often stressed Gramsci's historicism, and there is a clear to-and-fro

---

[9]Q6§138; *SPN*, p. 239.
[10]Most influentially in Anderson, 'Antinomies'.
[11]Q19§24*; *SPN*, p. 60.

movement between history and theory in Gramsci's research. Gramsci himself laid claim to the word 'historicism', conferring on it a quite specific meaning that we explore in Chapter 4.

We now turn to the historically informed concepts that Gramsci develops from his concrete researches into politics. These concepts, such as 'national-popular', 'passive revolution', 'organic crisis' and 'Caesarism', together form the basic structure of Gramsci's innovative interpretation of modern politics.

The era of revolution-restoration

For Gramsci, the political universe of interwar Europe is the direct heir of the period of Western history that began with the French Revolution in 1789. He labels this era that of 'revolution-restoration'. Gramsci sees this period, which lasted over a century from 1789 to 1914, as especially historically rich and complex, as it witnessed profound economic, social and political rivalries between the aristocracy and the bourgeoisie and then between the bourgeoisie and the proletariat. Gramsci is particularly interested in the outcomes of these conflicts, and how they led to compromises or solutions that varied qualitatively from one national context to the next.

In Gramsci's opinion, the case of France stands as an exemplar of the era of revolution-restoration. France experienced the radical Jacobin dictatorship of 1793–4 in which the regime refused categorically any form of compromise with the old society and instead attempted to institute a fully novel social order. While in 1815 the *Ancien Régime* was seemingly re-established during the monarchical restoration, Gramsci notes that 'it is certain that in the movement of history there is never any turning back, and that restorations *in toto* do not exist'.[12] By 1848, the urban workers of Paris had entered history centre-stage, in opposition to the bourgeois order, and in 1871 the popular revolution of the Paris working population in the Commune was brutally eliminated by a coalition of neo-Royalists and bourgeois interests in the name of

[12] Q13§27; *SPN*, pp. 219–20.

a new restoration. Thus we can see that between 1789 and 1871 the terms 'revolution' and 'restoration' shifted meaning as the fundamental social contradiction underlying French society evolved from the conflict between the aristocracy and the bourgeoisie to the struggle between the bourgeoisie and the proletariat. Gramsci closely examines the French case of revolution-restoration and notes that similar social conflicts ended up in entirely different socio-political configurations in other countries (notably Italy, Britain and Germany). Hence Gramsci affirms, 'The question is to see whether in the dialectic "revolution/restoration" it is revolution or restoration which predominates.'[13]

The national-popular Jacobin revolution

Gramsci is a keen commentator on the French Revolution, and he considers its decisive episode to be the Jacobin Terror of 1793–4. He writes:

> the Jacobins … were the only party of the revolution in progress, in as much as they not only represented the immediate needs and aspirations of the actual physical individuals who constituted the French bourgeoisie, but they also represented the revolutionary movement as a whole, as an integral historical development. For they represented future needs as well, and, once again, not only the needs of those particular physical individuals, but also of all the national groups which had to be assimilated to the existing fundamental group.[14]

Thus despite the sometimes blind violence of the Terror, Gramsci takes the Jacobins to be heroic historical protagonists as they were able to project themselves beyond their immediate material interests – that is, those of the petty urban bourgeoisie from which they originated – and establish themselves as a representation of the revolution itself. In this sense, for Gramsci, they represented a

---

[13] Ibid., p. 219.
[14] Q19§24; *SPN*, p. 78.

'national-popular' revolution in which the bourgeoisie forged an alliance with other classes in society (namely the *sans-culottes* artisans and the peasantry) against all the surviving traces of the *Ancien Régime*.

Gramsci reads in Jacobinism, then, one of the great lessons of contemporary history: a rising social class must sacrifice its short-term material interests in the name of a class alliance that facilitates a 'national-popular' mobilization around universal social demands. It is therefore to the great historical credit of the Jacobins that they managed to mobilize the peasant masses in a war against the coalition of European monarchies. For Gramsci, the Jacobins thus united the political destiny of the city and the countryside, as well as of the bourgeoisie and the peasantry (at least in the short term), and thereby contributed to the formation of a modern 'people-nation'.

The notion of 'national-popular' is an important one in Gramsci's analysis of politics and it is important to make it clear that it is mistaken to see in it a kind of nationalism.[15] The essence of Gramsci's thought here is, rather, fundamentally strategic and democratic: a social class (whether the bourgeoisie or the proletariat) will be more legitimate and enjoy a greater historical efficacy to the extent that it can attract to itself other social groups by integrating their demands to its own. In this way a rising social group can thereby bring about the advent of an extended popular bloc. When Gramsci asserts, then, that the communist revolution will have 'to "nationalise" itself in a certain sense' he does not mean that it will have to promote particular national interests, but rather that it will have to fuse with popular elements of the nation in order to legitimize itself.[16]

The *Risorgimento* as 'passive revolution'

Gramsci's interpretation of Italy's unification in the second half of the nineteenth century – the *Risorgimento* – is that it represents a bourgeois revolution whose modalities were importantly different to that of the French Revolution. As with the French Revolution's

---

[15] Ernesto Laclau, *Politics and Ideology in Marxist Theory: Capitalism, Fascism, Populism* (London: New Left Books, 1977).
[16] Q14§68; *SPN*, p. 241.

Jacobins and Girondins, during the *Risorgimento* there were two rival bourgeois groups: Cavour's Moderates, centred on the court of the king of Piedmont-Sardinia, and the Action Party (*Partito d'Azione*) of Mazzini and Garibaldi, which tended to present itself as a romantic and voluntaristic alternative to the Moderates. However, Gramsci does not see in the *Risorgimento* a simple reiteration of the intra-bourgeois rivalry of the French revolutionary Convention. He notes that both the Moderates and the Action Party did not attempt during the wars of unification against Austria to mobilize the peninsula's peasant masses, who were the overwhelming majority of the population. Instead, they relied on the Piedmontese armies or on Garibaldian volunteers. Gramsci sees the absence of the mobilization of the peasant masses in the Italian case as explained by the fear shared by the Moderates and the Action Party that the peasantry could revolt in favour of agrarian reform. It is this fear that forestalled the formation of a national-popular bloc in Italy or any 'organic solidarity' between the city and the country. Although members of the Action Party claimed the legacy of the French revolutionaries of 1792, Gramsci saw in this only some 'Jacobin monkeying around' that obfuscated the national-popular substance of authentic Jacobinism.[17]

Differentiating it from the national-popular Jacobin revolution, Gramsci describes the *Risorgimento* as a 'passive revolution'. Gramsci takes this phrase from the Neapolitan thinker Vincenzo Cuoco (1770–1823), who defines it in a much more restrictive way than Gramsci. Two broad understandings of passive revolution can be identified in the *Prison Notebooks*.[18] The first can be understood in reference to the *Risorgimento*, and we discuss the second form of passive revolution below, with reference to the later 'transformist' period of Italian history. In the context of Italy's wars of unification from 1848 to 1870, then, the phrase 'passive revolution' denotes for Gramsci the paradox of a '"revolution" without a

---

[17] Macciocchi, *Pour Gramsci*.
[18] For a more in-depth treatment of the concept of 'passive revolution' see Peter Thomas, 'Modernity as "Passive Revolution": Gramsci and the Fundamental Concepts of Historical Materialism', *Review of the Canadian Historical Association*, 17:2 (2006), pp. 61–78.

"revolution"'.[19] By this Gramsci means a transformation of society – in this case the unification of the country under a bourgeois government – that lacks a corresponding popular movement or any sort of upheaval in the lives of the masses, and so does not involve the active political integration of the people in the new order.[20]

The thesis that the *Risorgimento* was a passive revolution in Gramsci's understanding of the term has been the subject of many historical debates, and historians of Italy have disagreed over whether the absence of a process of mobilization and subsequent integration hindered or favoured the development of Italian capitalism.[21] For Gramsci, though, it is clear that the passive revolution of the *Risorgimento* is responsible for the institutional fragility of the peninsula's socio-political order in the twentieth century. In particular, Gramsci discerns in the absence of a process of mobilization-integration the structural weakness of a society that is insufficiently 'coherent' and 'compact' – a weakness that would later be clearly revealed in the process of Italian society's fall into fascism.

Trasformismo, molecularity and scission

The Italian wars of unification ended in 1870, and Gramsci sees the next stage of Italian history, which lasted until the early twentieth century, as representing a second type of passive revolution. This phase has been termed *trasformismo* ('transformism'), referring to the increasing convergence of the political programmes of the Italian parliamentary Left and Right, which led to the disintegration of fundamental political oppositions and to the multiplication of unstable factions operating in a broadly consensual political framework.

---

[19] Q19§24; *SPN*, p. 59.
[20] Giuseppe Tomasi di Lampedusa's *The Leopard* (1958) and Luchino Visconti's 1963 cinematic version provide an illustration of the extent to which the events of the *Risorgimento* might have been experienced 'passively' by the majority of Sicilian peasants.
[21] See Rosario Romeo, *Risorgimento e capitalismo* (Bari: Laterza, 1959); Alberto Caracciolo (ed.), *La Formazione dell'Italia industriale: discussioni et ricerche* (Bari: Laterza, 1963).

Gramsci notes that the political cycle of *trasformismo*, which was criticized by many contemporary Italian writers, in fact represents the success on its own terms of the Italian parliamentary system: it managed – where the Piedmontese monarchy had failed – to integrate a range of diverse political personalities and interests. Although a part of the incorporation dynamics of *trasformismo* involved corruption and clientelism, Gramsci sees the process as a whole as demonstrating the internal flexibility of the ruling classes in attracting the required support among the elite (perhaps, though, at the cost of an increased distance between the elite and the people). Gramsci describes this process as 'molecular', by which he means a process in which social groups are incorporated into a given political order through the rallying of individuals (or small groups) to the established order. The 'molecule' here, then, represents the individual who comes to affirm their allegiance to the established order.

The *trasformismo* period represents a second sense of passive revolution for Gramsci, in which a population is collectively incorporated into a given social order through an accumulation of molecular processes. This second type of passive revolution is 'passive', then, in the sense that it is not accompanied by any mobilization of contesting (or revolutionary) forces. Although in the case of *trasformismo* the dynamic of incorporation worked on a relatively small scale – namely that of the Italian political elites – we can note that the molecular type of passive revolution has a very wide potential field of application.

Another example of a molecular passive revolution, which is not investigated in depth by Gramsci in the *Prison Notebooks*, is the joining together of the aristocracy and the bourgeoisie in England in the wake of the 'Glorious Revolution' of 1688. Gramsci writes of a 'fusion between the old and the new' in which the 'old aristocracy remained as a governing stratum, with certain privileges, and it too became the intellectual stratum of the English bourgeoisie (it should be added that the English aristocracy has an open structure and continually renews itself with elements coming from the intellectuals and bourgeoisie)'.[22] Individual members of the bourgeoisie, in this

---

[22] Q19§24; *SPN*, p. 83.

case, were molecularly incorporated into the traditional ruling class of the aristocracy. Gramsci's brief comments on England inspired the pioneering works of Tom Nairn and Perry Anderson in the mid-1960s, which in turn triggered a wealth of research that attempted to examine the long-term consequences of this 'fusion between the old and the new' for the political history of the country up to the twentieth century.[23]

For Gramsci, the antithesis of molecular incorporation is scission. By scission Gramsci means a situation in which the dominated group consciously embodies a political rupture that goes against the established institutional order. Thus, what we might call a 'counter-model' of *trasformismo* – which would also act as a counter-model to the British configuration after 1688 – is the Jacobin revolution. Gramsci sees this revolution as wholly 'active', and as founded on the scission enacted by the Jacobins as the most advanced part of the bourgeoisie. The Jacobin scission, then, for Gramsci affirmed the self-consciousness of the rising class as a historical actor, while simultaneously bursting open the institutional order of the old society. Gramsci defines the 'spirit of scission' as a group's 'progressive acquisition of the consciousness of its own historical personality', and looks forward to the Italian working class enacting a scission in opposition to the ruling class that will be comparable to that of the Jacobins.[24]

Conjunctural processes and organic crises

Gramsci also draws an important distinction between what he calls the 'conjunctural' and the 'organic'. *Organic* reality concerns the fundamental basis of a mode of production, and in particular the relations of domination and subalternity among the 'fundamental classes' (as we mentioned in Chapter 2, Gramsci sees the bourgeoisie and the proletariat as the fundamental classes of capitalist societies). Events in France from 14 July 1789 to the overthrow of Robespierre

---

[23] See Tom Nairn, 'The British Political Elite', *New Left Review*, 1:23 (1964), pp. 19–25; Perry Anderson, 'Origins of the Present Crisis', *New Left Review*, 1:23 (1964), pp. 26–53.
[24] Q3§49; *SCW*, p. 390.

and the Thermidorian reaction saw an organic change, in Gramsci's view, as the Jacobins destroyed the very foundations of the aristocracy's power. *Conjunctural* reality, on the other hand, refers to the concrete political relations between the existing social forces at a given point in time, which can be influenced by political tactics and immediate events. Accordingly, conjunctural reality exhibits a far greater level of historical contingence than organic reality. We can note here that Gramsci does not reify the organic-conjunctural distinction into two separate 'levels' or 'territories' of social life, not least because he recognizes that the organic manifests itself historically only as a conjunctural series of events. To illustrate, the specific events of the Terror in revolutionary France represented for Gramsci the political conjuncture of the period, as they were not organically determined as such. Importantly, rather than seeing the conjunctural as only an expression of the organic, Gramsci is careful to emphasize that the relations between the two – and between economics and politics – must be grasped in their full complexity (see Chapter 4). Gramsci's distinction here is not merely academic, as he considered that revolutionaries confusing the two dimensions would be led to a misguided and inappropriate revolutionary strategy (as we will see below).

Most instances of passive revolution and other 'molecular' social processes constitute moments, for Gramsci, of conjunctural history. In Italy, the *trasformismo* represented an alteration of the social features of the ruling group without a modification of the fundamental social relations underlying society. For Gramsci, the analysis of the conjunctural thus leads to an examination of transformation processes that are, in an important sense, *internal* to bourgeois society. Gramsci noted that such processes could at certain times be reactionary (for instance Boulangism in France in the 1880s) and at other times progressive (as with the Dreyfus affair). In the latter case, these processes have the potential to 'shatter stifling and ossified State structures in the dominant camp'.[25]

---

[25]Q14§23; *SPN*, p. 223. Boulangism was a reactionary militaristic political movement around General Georges Boulanger (1837–91), which attracted a heterogeneous group including royalists, conservatives and extreme nationalists in the late 1880s through Boulanger's advocacy of a military dictatorship and revenge on Germany.

However, in a situation where the very foundations of a social order begin to tremble, Gramsci talks of an 'organic crisis'. He writes, 'The crisis consists precisely in the fact that the old is dying and the new cannot be born; in this interregnum a great variety of morbid symptoms appear.'[26] For Gramsci, the failure of the Turin working class revolution at the turn of the 1920s and the conversion of bourgeois parliamentarianism into fascism were the 'morbid symptoms' of the changing political structures of the time. Gramsci thought he perceived the decadence of a decaying bourgeois civilization ('the old that is dying') and he anticipated a proletarian revolution ('the new that cannot be born') with the organic crisis that lay in between as a prolonged deadlock between existing social forces. He noted that such a stasis could last for decades.

Caesarism

A crisis, whether organic or conjunctural, can at times result in a phenomenon Gramsci calls 'Caesarism'. Caesarism is defined by the emergence of a 'great personality' who presents themselves as the solution to the uncertainty of the political moment, or even sometimes as a saviour or redeemer of the nation. Gramsci notes here that 'the immediate situation becomes delicate and dangerous, because the field is open for violent solutions, and for the activities of unknown forces, represented by charismatic "men of destiny"'.[27]

Gramsci uses the term 'Caesarism' to refer in the first instance to Mussolini, and to mock the commonplace fascist analogy between *Il Duce* and Julius Caesar. Gramsci also applies the term to the two Napoleons (I and III) and to Bismarck in a way reminiscent of Marx's construction of 'Bonapartism' in *The Eighteenth Brumaire of Louis Napoleon* (1852).

Gramsci is, though, careful to distinguish between different types of Caesarism.[28] Gramsci considers Napoleon I as an example of

---

[26] Q3§34; *SPN*, p. 276.
[27] Q13§23; *SPN*, p. 210.
[28] See Roger Simon, *Gramsci's Political Thought: An Introduction* (London: Lawrence and Wishart, 1991).

progressive Caesarism as he opened the way for the institutional strengthening of France's new bourgeois civilization at the turn of the nineteenth century. By contrast Gramsci sees Napoleon III, Bismarck and, of course, Mussolini as examples of a *reactionary* Caesarism that tries to go against the current of history and contain, albeit in different ways and in different contexts, working class contestation and prevent the revolution that this new (ruling) class is beginning to embody.

For Gramsci the roots of Caesarism are to be found in a 'crisis of authority', which is also a crisis of democratic representation as social classes cease to recognize the political parties that previously expressed their interests. In this sense, the parties of a liberal democracy can become 'anachronistic' as the groups previously attached to them start to detach. In these cases, entire sections of the population are then susceptible to separating themselves from the bourgeois elites who were, until that point, successful in incorporating them to the established order through the electoral mechanism. When this happens, parliamentary institutions lose their representative function and are then liable to fall into crisis as the organs of the State (the bureaucracy, the army and so on) lose their social underpinnings and give the impression of 'floating above' society. At this point, the diminished social basis of State organs makes them vulnerable to being seized by an arbitrary power. It is in precisely this type of conjuncture that Gramsci sees a Caesarist solution as likely to present itself.

The causes of such socio-political disintegration vary, for Gramsci, from one national context to the next. In the Italian case, Gramsci highlights the importance of the First World War as the country's peasant masses – who remained largely passive during the *Risorgimento* – were thrown onto the battlefield. In the war's aftermath, commentators at the time perceived that the peasantry had become noticeably more 'agitated', and more difficult for the elites to pacify and incorporate. In this context, relations between social classes take on an increasingly violent complexion, as witnessed in the Italian case by the rise of fascist militias.

We can finally stress that for Gramsci Caesarism must be understood as a social phenomenon: it emanates from a crisis that characterizes society as a whole, rather than deriving from the particular individual who has found themselves projected centre-stage. In other words, it is clearly not a 'Great Men' theory of history, since Gramsci sees Caesarism as fulfilling an important political function that can only be fully understood by examining society as a whole and the character of the antagonistic social relations that underlie it. Thus Gramsci mentions some cases of 'Caesarless Caesarism', in which Caesarism is put into practice by an elite collective rather than a single individual. An example he provides of this Caesarless Caesarism is the British National Government, set up in 1931 at the time of the Great Depression, which brought together Conservative and Labour politicians.

The analysis of fascism

In Gramsci's analysis of fascism, we can see many of the concepts discussed in this chapter so far come together. Of all the political investigations in the *Prison Notebooks*, the analysis of fascism is perhaps the most significant: it was the fascist coercive apparatus that was to defeat Gramsci during his life, and before his arrest in 1926 Gramsci and his comrades in the PCI crucially underestimated the solidity and coherence of the fascist project (see Chapter 1). At that time, Gramsci saw in fascism only a circumstantial embodiment of bourgeois power, and one that was very fragile and soon to be overthrown by socialist revolution.

At the time of Gramsci's arrest, though, Mussolini's regime was manifestly in the process of consolidating its power, and Gramsci was led during his time in prison to revise his past assessments in some crucial ways. However, due to prison censorship his treatment of the issue of fascism is 'unsystematic, abstract and elliptical'.[29] As such, it falls on the reader of the *Prison Notebooks* largely to reconstruct Gramsci's analysis from scattered and often elliptical comments.

Approaching the issue obliquely, Gramsci mentions the fable of the beaver, in which a beaver is chased by some hunters who are eager to obtain his testicles, which are known to have medicinal value. The

---

[29]David D. Roberts, 'Reconsidering Gramsci's Interpretation of Fascism', *Modern of Modern Italian Studies*, 16:2 (2011), p. 246.

beaver takes the initiative to tear off his testicles, leaving them to the hunters, in order to save himself. The beaver here represents the Italian bourgeoisie who had been on the back foot since the *biennio rosso*. In order to ensure its survival, it resorts to the fascist solution, jettisoning the liberal institutions of parliamentary democracy that it used to value so highly.

Gramsci understands fascism through the concepts of organic crisis and Caesarism, and in so doing deepens and develops the concepts themselves. In the context of Italy's deep social disintegration, due to the trauma of war and the threat of socialist revolution, no social force is in a position in the interwar period to build a hegemonic political project (namely one that combines coercion and consent; see Chapter 5). In the absence of such hegemony, a dictatorial regime, relying solely on coercion, emerges around a 'man of the hour'. At the first level, Gramsci concludes, fascism is thus a Caesarist reaction to the organic crisis of Italian society.

Gramsci is then led to ask whether the fascist regime might be able to transcend this crisis configuration and establish a new and more viable social order or whether it is fundamentally a transitional phenomenon that stands between bourgeois liberalism and proletarian revolution. From his prison cell, Gramsci still held on to a certain level of revolutionary hope, and therefore he tends towards the second alternative, although he does recognize that the first alternative accurately sums up fascism's ambition to become a perennial social order. Gramsci, we can note, gives little credence to a third scenario, namely that of the resurrection of liberal parliamentary democracy, which of course came to pass in post-war Italy.

On the basis of passages from the *Prison Notebooks* from the years 1930–3, we can see that Gramsci considered Mussolini's regime to be carrying out a 'war of position' on several fronts, aiming to undermine the potential sources of socialist revolution in Italy. Gramsci described the fascist strategy as 'totalitarian', in the sense that it aimed to unify society while eliminating the autonomous institutions that the bourgeois liberal regime had allowed to exist in civil society. Thus, opposition parties and the freedom to unionize were abolished, and the doctrinal liberal distinction between civil society and political society was rejected on the theoretical plane by the regime. Even private capitalist initiative was put into question by the State-led 'corporatist' productive model, or what Gramsci calls the 'programmatic economy'.

Yet Gramsci also stressed that fascist totalitarianism is largely an illusion: the organic crisis, which for Gramsci emanates from a profound contradiction between capital and labour and provided the conditions for the emergence of fascism, persisted under Mussolini's regime. Fascism, in short, was incapable of ending this fundamental social contradiction. Consequently, Italian society remained in a state of advanced disintegration, even of relative anarchy, despite claims to the contrary made by apologists of the regime. In this sense the suppression of parliamentarianism was unable to suppress political factions, such that social rivalries were not ended although their expression in the ideological sphere was forbidden. As a result, Gramsci contends, it is a symptom of fascism that the issues of politics are displaced into culture: 'polemics are unleashed and struggles are fought as in a game of blind man's bluff. In any case it is certain that in such parties cultural functions predominate, which means that political language becomes jargon. In other words, political questions are disguised as cultural ones, and as such become insoluble'.[30]

The modern Prince

What is a political party?

In the previous section we explored some of the core concepts of Gramsci's interpretation of modern politics. Although for Gramsci both the individual and the social group are key actors in politics, he sees a third actor as the historical agent *par excellence*: the political party.

Gramsci understands the political party as at once both the *representative* and the *organizing principle* of a social class. In Chapter 2 we saw the importance that Gramsci gives to a notion of organization in the cultural sphere, and it is also a guiding thread of

---

[30] Q17§37; *SPN*, p. 149.

his political analysis. Gramsci holds that any social class (including the landowning aristocracy, the bourgeoisie and the proletariat) must have a single, unique party, even if such a party does not exist formally as such. Therefore, Gramsci sees the rivalry between a multiplicity of disparate and small bourgeois organizations with divergent particular interests as a rivalry between different factions of a large, unofficial bourgeois 'party'. The litmus test of the underlying reality of the unofficial bourgeois party is for Gramsci the cycle of organic crisis, during which these factions suddenly join together. Gramsci concludes that the heterogeneity of the bourgeois class never prevents it from unifying in the face of serious threats against the established order.

For Gramsci, the political party is a 'live' interpretation of the social order, formulated and put into practice by a specific social group. In this sense, Gramsci believes that it is possible, when examining a political party, to decipher within it the whole range of social contradictions that exist in a given society at a given point, and accordingly one should always attempt to view it through the lens of society as a whole. Gramsci thus criticizes the studies of the sociologist Robert Michels (1876–1936) on the oligarchical tendencies of social democratic parties. Gramsci takes Michels to be incapable of fully understanding his object of study as he refuses to take into account the sociological composition and context of the political party.[31] For Gramsci, 'to write the history of a party means nothing less than to write the general history of a country from a monographic viewpoint, in order to highlight a particular aspect of it'.[32]

Furthermore, political parties will, for Gramsci, play an increasingly important role as capitalist society develops and complexifies. He notes how the Jacobins, despite their small numbers, had been able to take the lead in the bourgeois French Revolution and to indulge in a kind of maniacal voluntarism because the civil society of France at the time was still at a relatively unadvanced stage (or, as Gramsci puts it, civil society's 'gelatinous' character offered little resistance

---

[31] See for instance Robert Michels, *Political Parties: A Sociological Study of the Oligarchical Tendencies of Modern Democracy* (Leipzig: Verlag, 1911).
[32] Q13§33; *SPN*, p. 151.

to the initiatives of the Jacobins). However, from the second half of the nineteenth century onwards, Western political systems rested increasingly on civil societies that were organized on the principle of stabilized and institutionalized interests, and in which various forms of associations linked the individual to wider social groups. Within the vast and fundamentally politicized civil societies of modern States, it is for Gramsci the party that can feature as the decisive actor.

The modern Prince:
The incarnation of revolution

It is perhaps no surprise that of all the political parties that existed during his time, Gramsci was most interested in the Communist Party that he had led before his imprisonment. Many passages of the *Prison Notebooks* are devoted to thinking through the nature and strategy of the Communist Party, which Gramsci calls the 'modern Prince'.

The phrase 'modern Prince', which served to deceive the prison censors, is directly derived from Machiavelli. Machiavelli had appealed to the figure of the Prince – concretely, Lorenzo di Medici – to rescue the Italy of his time that he saw as vulnerable to foreign invasions and internal dissensions. Gramsci argues that the Prince of the twentieth century cannot be an individual, but rather has to take the shape of a social organization. He writes, 'History has already provided this organism, and it is the political party – the first cell in which there come together germs of a collective will tending to become universal and total.'[33] Thus the Communist Party is the modern Prince, and as such it is called upon to incarnate the proletarian scission that Gramsci sees as constituting the beginning of the overcoming of bourgeois civilization.

We can note here that for Gramsci the social class, taken as a purely economic entity, will always be short of autonomous historical action. In order to transform itself into a collective revolutionary subject, a class must first reach awareness of itself (become a 'class-in-itself') through the work of the party as organized by the organic

---

[33] Q13§1; *SPN*, p. 129.

intellectuals (see Chapter 2). In this transformative process the social class is politically and culturally homogenized, and is consequently able to generate and act on its collective will. In the words of Palmiro Togliatti, Gramsci's successor at the head of the PCI, the party itself will then become a 'collective intellectual'.

Gramsci's insistence on the crucial role of the organizational work of the party as led by the organic intellectuals is a way for him to reject the mechanistic and deterministic interpretation of history he associates with 'vulgar Marxism'. For Gramsci, the revolutionary class as such is not a direct and necessary product of capitalism, but instead must be actively *constructed* as a collective actor within the framework of the Communist Party. Gramsci's conception of the historical role and nature of the proletariat can thus be contrasted with the young Marx's assertion that the proletariat was *ipso facto* the universal class as it represents the negation of bourgeois society (in this case the revolution becomes, in a Hegelian turn of phrase, 'the negation of the negation'). For Gramsci, the proletarian revolution's universality is a concrete political project to be achieved, and the outcome of the party's practical work.

However, Gramsci's assertion that the Communist Party represents a collective will 'tending to become universal and total' requires some unpacking. It is possible to identify two main meanings of the potential 'universality' of the Communist Party in Gramsci's understanding. At the first level, it refers to the imperative of the Communist Party being 'national-popular', that is of sacrificing some of the interests of its own particular class in order to universalize its project by becoming the standard-bearer of the struggle of all the subaltern elements of society. Here we can see the centrality of the question of *class alliance* within the revolution. In his 1926 *Alcuni temi* essay, Gramsci writes, 'The proletariat can become the leading and the dominant class to the extent that it succeeds in creating a system of alliances which allows it to mobilise the majority of the population against capitalism and the bourgeois State.'[34] Indeed, Gramsci devoted a lot of energy prior to his arrest – and many pages of his notebooks after it – to defending a strategy of alliance between the Italian working class concentrated in the North of the

---

[34] *SPWII*, p. 443.

country and the rural masses of the South. In the early 1920 he had suggested as the PCI's revolutionary slogan 'a federal Republic of workers and peasants'.

At the second level, the Communist Party's 'universality' can also mean that even before the revolution it has to understand itself as the *embryonic State* of the future socialist society. It must, then, prepare itself to inherit the State, which in bourgeois society will necessarily be a political entity that disciplines society as a whole with its coercive apparatuses. Gramsci, after the revolution but before the achievement of communism, recognizes the utility of the State, including its repressive side. It is not, then, possible to say that Gramsci's is an anarchist strand of revolutionary thought. Gramsci in fact uses the Hegelian expression 'State Spirit' (*Staatsgeist*), and sees the modern Prince as its future custodian.

The party as living organism

The originality of Gramsci's thinking about the party is apparent in relation to his solution to the question of its internal organization. Gramsci repeatedly asserts in the *Prison Notebooks* the need for discipline and hierarchy within the Communist Party. He draws another military analogy: the organic intellectuals at the head of a party are its chiefs of staff, the masses of members are its soldiers and the immediate groups of local delegates are the non-commissioned officers who mediate between the first two elements. At the same time, though, Gramsci demands that the party be a 'living organism' centred on 'a continual adaptation of the organisation to the real movement, a matching of thrusts from below with orders from above, a continuous insertion of elements thrown up from the depths of the rank and file into the solid framework of the leadership apparatus which ensures continuity and the regular accumulation of experience'.[35]

It can be recalled here that for Gramsci the revolutionary intellectual must not only 'know' but also 'understand' and 'feel' (Chapter 2); what Gramsci believes can unite the heart and body of the party

---

[35] Q13§36; *SPN*, pp. 188–9.

is shared feeling (Gramsci goes as far as to write of 'passion') as much as political reason. For Gramsci, 'it is vital that there should be not passive and indirect consent but active and direct consent, the participation of individual members, even if this provokes an appearance of break up and tumult'.[36] Gramsci thus advocates a model of the party quite different from the kind of bureaucratic monolithism that predominated in Stalin's Soviet Union, but also holds that the 'tumult' within the party must not undermine the objective of the homogenization required for the development of the party's collective will.

Gramsci demands of the leaders of the party that they possess analytical capacities adequate to the political situation along with a capacity for understanding, and empathizing with, the 'people-nation'. Accordingly, he asserts that 'the active politician is a creator, an initiator; but he neither creates from nothing nor does he move in the turbid void of his own desires and dreams'.[37] Moreover, Gramsci repeatedly appeals to the 'intuition' of the political organizer, an idea he takes from Henri Bergson (who he had read enthusiastically in his youth). Although Gramsci does not give intuition the central place it enjoys in Bergson's philosophy, he does see in it a way for the leaders of the modern Prince to remain as close as possible to reality and to make vivid his insistence on the need to 'feel' as much as to know.

Two errors of revolutionary strategy

Lastly, the question of revolutionary strategy can now be addressed, a subject on which Gramsci tirelessly criticizes his contemporaries. He sees the confusion of the organic and the conjunctural as leading to two sorts of errors in revolutionary strategy. Gramsci introduces the dilemma: 'A common error in historico-political analysis consists in an inability to find the correct relation between what is organic and what is conjunctural. This leads to presenting causes as immediately operative which in fact only operate indirectly, or to asserting that

---

[36] Q15§13; *GR*, p. 244.
[37] Q13§16; *SPN*, p. 172.

the immediate causes are the only effective ones.' He continues, 'In the first case there is an overestimation of mechanical causes, in the second an exaggeration of the voluntarist and individual element.'[38]

The first error is based on the assumption that the proletarian revolution is *a priori* inscribed in the course of history through the operation of iron laws of history. In such a vision, the only factors that matter are economic ones, which are thought to be hidden behind the political events of the day. Such an approach can be described as an *economism* (the fetishization of economic relations), a *mechanism* (a belief that the course of history is followed in a machine-like way) and a *fatalism* (the assertion that socialism is the unavoidable fate of humanity). Gramsci uses these three terms frequently, in particular to criticize the positions of Amadeo Bordiga (who as we saw in Chapter 1 was the first leader of the PCI after its foundation congress at Livorno and then Gramsci's erstwhile rival in the party). Bordiga's attitude brought such an approach almost to the point of caricature, emphasizing the need to wait for economic events to resolve themselves and producing a deep form of political abstentionism in which the illusion of the inescapability of revolution and the purity of the revolutionary party were maintained only through the refusal to engage in the actual struggles of the day. This sort of abstentionism is a favoured target of Gramsci's.

The second error, which is a mirror image of the first, consists in purposely overlooking and ignoring the structural constraints that are inherent to any social configuration, and glorifying the moment of action as a result. If the first error is that of historical determinism, the second is that of revolutionary spontaneism. Here Gramsci criticizes the French anarcho-syndicalist Georges Sorel (1847–1922) for promoting, in his 1908 *Reflections on Violence*, the 'grand soir' of the general strike to the level of a myth.[39] Sorel sees in the 'grand soir' a revolutionary conflagration so sudden that no party can prepare for it or organize towards it. Gramsci characterizes such a

---

[38] Q13§17; *SPN*, p. 178.
[39] The idea of the 'grand soir' was very important in the French Left at the turn of the twentieth century, and although it was used by the communists and the anarchists in slightly different ways it refers to the 'great night' when the general strike suddenly comes about and capitalism abruptly collapses as a result.

position as a kind of 'Bergsonism', seeing it as reliant on an excessive faith in the 'vital impetus' (*élan vital*) that was so dear to Bergson. Gramsci also sees another illustration of this misguided revolutionary strategy in Rosa Luxemburg's 1906 pamphlet *The Mass Strike*, which in Gramsci's opinion also indulges in the mysticism of the 'grand soir' and accordingly overlooks the crucial organizational work that the party must undertake to prepare for the conquest of power.

Interestingly, Gramsci does not reject as such the role of the will or the power of action (as this is the exact error of 'mechanism'), and we have pointed out above that he does not deny the utility of intuition in the Bergsonian sense of the word for the leaders of the Communist Party. Importantly, it is rather that he sees in an excess of spontaneism an abandonment of the war of position and an exclusive focus on the war of movement. For Gramsci, to mythologize the conquest of the State and neglect all other dimensions of the revolutionary struggle is to indulge in a type of idolatry of the State, or 'statolatry' (*statolatria*, a neologism of Gramsci's). As we explained above, Gramsci begins his considerations on revolutionary strategy by examining the relation between civil society, political society and the State in the 'East' and the 'West'. In the latter, Western European case, Gramsci argues that the priority should be put on the war of position because the robustness of industrialized Europe's civil societies precludes revolutionary incursions of a purely voluntaristic character. For the myth of the 'grand soir', then, Gramsci substitutes the notion of the party's *revolutionary work* within civil society, which takes the shape of a long-term struggle through 'permanent persuasion' to form a 'national-popular' bloc.

Gramsci sees the ultimate function of revolutionary strategy not as to harbour illusions about the present state of things or to create myths of political change, but to understand the present as it is remains to be *transformed*. In Gramsci's famous words, here suitable as a maxim for the revolutionary strategist, 'It is necessary to draw attention violently to the present as it is, if one wants to transform it. Pessimism of the intelligence, optimism of the will.'[40]

---

[40] Q9§60; *SPN*, p. 175n75. We should note that Gramsci attributes his famous maxim 'Pessimism of the intelligence, optimism of the will' originally to the French author Romain Rolland.

4

Philosophy

Redefining philosophy: The individual, philosophy and politics

Theory, practice and philosophical anthropology

Gramsci's philosophical reflections rely on one essential postulate above all others: *the intimacy of theory and practice*. For Gramsci, theory is called on to provide a rational basis for practice, and practice is necessary to actualize theory: in every philosophy, and in each human being, one cannot be conceived without the other. Moreover, the concrete unity between thought and action is as an essential mission for individuals and for organized social classes.

Two aphorisms from the young Marx are worth recalling when situating the starting points of Gramsci's philosophy. In the introduction to *A Contribution to the Critique of Hegel's Philosophy of Right* (1843), Marx writes, 'The weapon of criticism cannot, of course, replace criticism by weapons, material force must be overthrown by material force; but theory also becomes a material force as soon as it has gripped the masses.'[1] Two years later, we find the following assertion in the third of Marx's *Theses on Feuerbach* (1845): 'The coincidence of the changing of circumstances and of human activity or self-change can be conceived and rationally

---

[1] Karl Marx and Frederick Engels, *Marx Engels Collected Works*, volume 3 (London: Lawrence and Wishart, 1975), p. 182.

understood only as *revolutionary practice*.[2] In the first of the *Theses on Feuerbach*, Marx rebukes Feuerbach for failing to understand the significance of revolutionary or 'practical-critical' activity.[3] Gramsci attempts to think through what it means to put human 'practical-critical' activity, or *praxis*, at the heart of Marxist philosophy.

A note titled 'What Is Man?' in notebook 11 provides a possible entry point into Gramsci's philosophy. Gramsci's answer to the question he poses himself is clear: there is no eternal human nature, and no fixed essence of the human being. Gramsci rejects both the idealist conception of a perfect Idea of man found in Plato and the notion of a human nature anchored within a fixed materiality that Ludwig Feuerbach develops. According to Gramsci man is above all a *social and historical animal* whose reality is constituted by the relations that tie the individual to others. These social relations, in turn, are the product of an accumulation of social practices.

This theory of man can be called Gramsci's 'philosophical anthropology' and is a keystone of the *Prison Notebooks*. Gramsci's philosophical anthropology is characterized by his rejection of naturalism, by his historicist understanding of 'the human' and above all by a relational ontology in which being can only be understood by reference to a set of *relations*. Here Gramsci's philosophical anthropology converges with the idea expressed by the young Marx in the sixth of his *Theses on Feuerbach* (1845): 'the essence of man is no abstraction inherent in each single individual. In its reality it is the ensemble of social relations'.[4] In accepting the idea that every human being is defined by the ensemble of his or her social relations, Gramsci attempts to trace a median ontological path between an 'individualism' that tends to detach the individual from their context and a 'holism' that reduces individual traits to characteristics of systems, which might be thought of as the Charybdis and Scylla of the social sciences.[5]

---

[2] Karl Marx and Frederick Engels, *Marx Engels Collected Works*, volume 5 (London: Lawrence and Wishart, 1975), p. 4.
[3] Ibid., p. 3.
[4] Ibid., p. 4.
[5] Étienne Balibar, 'Gramsci, Marx et le rapport social', in: André Tosel (ed.), *Modernité de Gramsci: Actes du colloque franco-italien de Besançon, 23–25 novembre 1989* (Paris: Les Belles Lettres, 1992), pp. 259–70.

Gramsci then asks what might be found on 'opening up' an individual. The answer, he believes, is a complex and stratified reality, combining collective culture and individual psychology. For Gramsci, then, 'personality is strangely composite: it contains Stone Age elements and principles of a more advanced science, prejudices from all past phases of history at the local level and intuitions of a future philosophy which will be that of a human race united the world over'.[6] Every epoch of history has thus handed down as its legacy to the individuals of the present a set of more or less consistent and compelling doctrines, beliefs and superstitions that survive as traces or 'sedimentations' in the human mind. Gramsci sees this essential historicity of the individual as generating a Socratic imperative. Embracing the famous inscription on the Delphi oracle, Gramsci writes, 'The starting-point of critical elaboration is the consciousness of what one really is, and is "knowing thyself" as a product of the historical process to date which has deposited in you an infinity of traces, without leaving an inventory. Such an inventory must therefore be made at the outset.'[7] Already in January 1916 Gramsci had written in *Il Grido del Popolo*: 'To know oneself means to be oneself, to be master of oneself, to distinguish oneself, to free oneself from a state of chaos'.[8]

We can note that for Plato the Socratic precept of the centrality of self-knowledge is situated in the context of a dialectical ascension towards the Idea performed through the philosophical dialogue. By contrast, for Gramsci the requirement to 'know thyself' requires the individual to look towards human society. We can only attain self-knowledge through social and historical awareness.

'Every man is a philosopher'

The relationship between 'philosophy' and everyday life is a central preoccupation of Gramsci's. Gramsci's position can be characterized by his bold assertion that 'every man is a philosopher'. Gramsci

---

[6]Q11§12; *SPN*, p. 324.
[7]Q11§12; *GR*, p. 326.
[8]'Socialism and Culture', *Il Grido del Popolo*, 29 January 1916; *SPWI*, p. 13.

contends, 'It is essential to destroy the widespread prejudice that philosophy is a strange and difficult thing just because it is the specific intellectual activity of a particular category of specialists or of professional and systematic philosophers. It must first be shown that all men are "philosophers."'[9]

What, then, does Gramsci understand by philosophy, if he takes it that every human being can participate in it? Referring to a definition Croce had applied to religion, Gramsci sees philosophy as a certain conception of life to which an ethical attitude is attached.[10] Every human, for Gramsci, is led to establish an original mental connection to his or her social environment and to the ways in which that environment is being transformed on a daily basis – a transformation that Gramsci sees every individual as contributing to in the irreducibly political dimensions of their everyday life (see Chapter 3). Within the reciprocal relations that tie each individual to his or her social milieu, Gramsci sees a certain conception of life as being developed, and it is this conception of life that emerges out of a concrete social context that Gramsci understands as philosophy. Importantly, Gramsci notes that such a philosophy usually remains at an implicit or fragmentary stage.

There is a clear link between Gramsci's assertion that everyone is a philosopher and his conviction that it is impossible to talk of 'non-intellectuals' (see Chapter 2): just as each individual, for Gramsci, uses his or her intellect, each individual also necessarily develops a conception of life – that is, a philosophy – by virtue of living and acting in society. However, in the same way that Gramsci recognizes the existence of professional intellectuals he is also aware that specialist or professional philosophers distinguish themselves from the 'everyday philosophers' that one finds within the mass of the people. Generally speaking the professional philosophers stand out from the everyday philosophers on the basis of the greater internal coherence or consistency of their reflections, their more fully developed capacity for logical argumentation and above all their cultural training that ensures them a fuller knowledge of the history of human thought. After having stated these differences,

---

[9]Q11§12; *SPN*, p. 323.
[10]See Jean-Marc Piotte, *La Pensée politique de Gramsci* (Montréal: Parti-Pris, 1970).

Gramsci notes that they are all, importantly, of a purely 'quantitative' character and that, *qualitatively* speaking, it is thus the case that all men equally are philosophers.

Having posited the essential correspondence between quotidian human thought and philosophy, Gramsci also sees an equivalence between philosophy and politics. As we explored above, politics for Gramsci refers to the transformative praxis that ties every human being to their environment (see Chapter 3). Thus philosophy and politics both originate in the most elementary reality of social life, and one cannot be actuated without the other: every political project that intends to act on and change society relies on a normative vision of collective life, and every conception of life germinates a praxis. Importantly, then, Gramsci contends that every conception of life and every *Weltanschauung* possesses – whether explicitly or in a hidden way – the will to reform social being, such that even the most seemingly ethereal and detached philosophy contains its own 'active ingredient'. At the same time, he believes that even the most apparently trivial and prosaic political demand cannot be expressed without an underlying ethical stance vis-à-vis the world and the society in which it is put forward. Here we can see that the unity of philosophy and politics corresponds to the unity of theory and practice that Gramsci takes as his starting point.

Gramsci thus ties together the notions of the individual, philosophy and politics in the following way:

> the real philosopher is, and cannot be other than, the politician, the active man who modifies the environment, understanding by environment the *ensemble* of relations which each of us enters to take part in. If one's own individuality is the *ensemble* of these relations, to create one's personality means to acquire consciousness of them and to modify one's own personality means to modify the *ensemble* of these relations.[11]

For Gramsci, if human praxis is the engine of history, then the bearer of that praxis – the individual – is socially, politically and historically

---

[11] Q10II§54; *SPN*, p. 352.

constructed. Practical-critical activity consists precisely in recognizing the historical limits of one's own individuality, and then acting to reform it.

Common sense

The 'folklore of philosophy'

The concept of *senso comune* – or common sense – is a central one in Gramsci's philosophical reflections.[12] Gramsci understands common sense as the 'most widespread conception of life and man' that can be found among different social groups at a given point in history.[13] Thus common sense is a form of popular philosophy or, more accurately, it is the 'mass' moment of philosophy. Gramsci goes as far as to call common sense 'the "philosophy of non-philosophers"'.[14]

What are the properties of common sense for Gramsci? First of all, Gramsci warns against simplification, as common sense is multiple and labile: '"Common sense" is a collective noun, like religion: there is not just one common sense, for that too is a product of history and a part of the historical process (*un divenire storico*).'[15] Further, 'common sense is an ambiguous, contradictory and multiform concept'.[16] The fragmentary or even inconsistent (*inconseguente*) aspect of common sense is manifest, writes Gramsci, 'even in the brain of one individual' who must live with the baggage of a set of contradictory thoughts, assumptions and presuppositions inherited from the past but lived out through the

---

[12]Thomas argues for retaining the Italian term over the English, both because of the difficulties of translating *senso comune* as 'common sense' and also to designate a genuinely new concept and mark the importance of Gramsci's addition to our philosophical vocabulary. See Peter Thomas, *The Gramscian Moment: Philosophy, Hegemony, and Marxism* (Leiden: Brill, 2009), p. 16n61.

[13]Q24§4; *SPN*, p. 326n5; *SCW*, p. 421.

[14]Q11§13; *SPN*, p. 419.

[15]Q11§12; *SPN*, pp. 325–6.

[16]Q11§13; *SPN*, p. 423.

prism of a singular individual biography.[17] Common sense is not, though, for Gramsci understood simply as the thought of a unitary or uniform 'man-on-the-street'; indeed, Gramsci writes of the 'average' man, in a letter to his sister-in-law: 'I doubt he is to be found in any anthropological or sociological museum'.[18]

Importantly, Gramsci takes common sense as seriously as he does the writings of professional philosophers. He sees these two aspects of 'philosophy' as mutually influencing and unconsciously fashioning each other throughout history. The 'savants' – the eminent thinkers and professional philosophers of the day – elaborate their systems on the basis of the philosophical humus of their epoch, which is composed of the recently discarded and decaying ideas of previous periods. At the same time, common sense renews itself by filtering through philosophical systems and incorporating some of their elements. As Gramsci puts it, 'Every philosophical current leaves behind a sedimentation of "common sense": this is the document of its historical effectiveness.'[19] Common sense, by embodying the dominant philosophical doctrines of its day, albeit it in a partial and refracted way, in turn endows those doctrines with a sort of historical potency. Linking philosophy and history, Gramsci writes:

> The philosophy of an age is not the philosophy of this or that philosopher, of this or that group of intellectuals, of this or that broad section of the popular masses. It is a process of combination of all these elements, which culminates in an overall trend, in which the culmination becomes a norm of collective action and becomes concrete and complete (integral) 'history'.[20]

Thus for Gramsci common sense and 'high philosophy' *together* compose the cultural reality of a given epoch; the cultural life of any period cannot be understood only in reference to its works of 'high' culture. A historian of society or culture who ignores or overlooks

---

[17] Ibid., p. 419.
[18] Letter to Tatiana Schucht, 12 October 1931; *LP*, p. 216.
[19] Q24§4; *SPN*, p. 326n5; *SCW*, p. 421.
[20] Q10II§17; *SPN*, p. 345.

common sense is thus, from Gramsci's point of view, committing a *scientific* mistake. In addition, as we stress below, the communist revolution that Gramsci anticipates must situate itself as a revolution of common sense, that is, as a revolution of quotidian philosophy. Consequently, the imperative to engage with common sense is for Gramsci simultaneously a methodological and political one.

Gramsci's methodological engagement with common sense starts with his recognition that common sense is the 'folklore of philosophy' and that 'like folklore, it takes countless different forms'.[21] During Gramsci's childhood in Ghilarza he became familiar with countless rural superstitions, and during the *biennio rosso* he was again confronted with the traditional beliefs of workers who were often from rural origins and with whom he tirelessly debated. Significantly, at the time of *L'Ordine Nuovo* many revolutionaries perceived the workers' common sense as a possible obstacle to the revolution and as a symptom of a conservative mindset.

While in prison Gramsci again grapples with common sense, but this time it is of course a theoretical engagement. He contends that common sense, including that held by the workers he had previously debated, is in one way like Janus: it displays two contrasting faces. One aspect of common sense is 'neophobic', centred on tradition and looking for indisputable truths and reassuring certainties. An illustration of this might be the usual turn of phrase or style of popular proverbs, which can set themselves up as a kind of 'wisdom of nations' meant to be valid at all times and in all places. With his deep historicist sensibility Gramsci is acutely aware of the ways in which such an attitude may consist in ignoring the historical character of the cultural world, and may thus be paralyzing for any sort of praxis that takes as its first assumption the changeability of society.[22]

---

[21] Q11§13; *SPN*, p. 419. Gramsci also notes that common sense as the 'folklore of philosophy' puts it 'always half-way between folklore properly speaking and the philosophy, science, and economics of the specialists'. He continues, 'Common sense creates the folklore of the future, that is a relatively rigid phase of popular knowledge at a given place and time.' (See Q24§4; *SCW*, p. 421; *SPN*, p. 326n5.)

[22] In his own way Roland Barthes, in his *Mythologies* (Paris: Seuil, 1957), also dissects the phenomenon by which the fantasies and collective images of a given epoch are manifest only in the fallacious guise of universal essences that naturalize history.

At the same time, though, common sense also contains the germs of potential resistance to the established order and a critical outlook on society from the point of view of the subaltern classes. Gramsci believes that the 'healthy nucleus that exists in "common sense"', which he calls 'good sense', 'deserves to be made more unitary and coherent', although he does not fully explicate how this nucleus can be identified and built upon.[23] Importantly, though, Gramsci does see common sense as in perpetual transformation and this makes it possible, at certain historical moments and through contact with revolutionary thought and praxis, to rationalize and reform it as a conscious critical *Weltanschauung*.

Whatever the political orientation of common sense in a given situation, it is for Gramsci importantly *constitutive of human subjectivity*. As such, common sense can be understood as a continuously operating reality, ceaselessly working at the 'pre-intentional' level where human agents are shaped as conscious subjects in society.[24] The anthropologist Kate Crehan has noted that Gramsci's notion of common sense is not only an accumulation of particular propositions, assertions and notions, but is the very *process* by which thought on a whole range of topics is itself generated.[25]

A pragmatist epistemology

Given that Gramsci postulates the qualitative equivalence of common sense and philosophy, it is important to clarify what he takes to be the truth status of a 'conception of life'. This is perhaps additionally significant given the importance of the notion of truth for philosophy (not to mention self-conceptions of philosophy as the search for, or love of, truth).

At this point in Gramsci's thought, two highly different intellectual traditions converge. First, there is the young Marx, particularly the second of the *Theses on Feuerbach* (1845): 'The question of whether objective truth can be attributed to human thinking is not a question of theory but is a *practical* question. Man must prove the truth – i.e. the

---

[23] Q11§12; *SPN*, p. 328.
[24] Guido Liguori, *Sentieri gramsciani* (Rome: Carocci, 2006).
[25] See Crehan, *Gramsci, Culture, and Anthropology*.

reality and power, the this-worldliness of his thinking in practice.'[26] Second, there are the American pragmatists of the early twentieth century, William James and John Dewey, who figured among Gramsci's prison reading and who enjoy a limited but real influence on his thought. Gramsci finds in Dewey in particular the idea that human thought is a tool in the service of situated, contextualized and concrete human action, such that the degree of truth of thought can only be accessed pragmatically.

Gramsci's critique of common sense or of philosophical systems of the past does not attempt to establish the inadequacy of those bodies of thought in terms of fixed and eternal truth categories. In contrast to a mathematical theorem or a law of physics, philosophy – whether specialized or popular – must be judged pragmatically, which for Gramsci means an appraisal that is primarily *historical*. Thus, a given *Weltanschauung* or fragment of common sense should not be understood as a series of propositions that are simply either true or false in the abstract, but rather as the accompanying element to the actions of human beings in society. The power of a given thought, in other words, is manifested as praxis.

The critical analysis of common sense must, then, proceed from an understanding that the propositions of common sense cannot be straightforwardly acknowledged as true or denounced as false. Gramsci, instead, sees the central aim of the critique of common sense as drawing on the Socratic 'know thyself' and applying it not to the individual but the collective being, or to the culture of the whole of society. While grappling with a given belief or saying, a piece of common wisdom, prejudice or habit, or a common attitude, Gramsci thus sees it as necessary to work as a sort of archaeologist in discovering the precise inventory of the strata of meaning that can be uncovered behind an apparently simple phenomenon. In investigating the multitude of 'palimpsests', then, that form common sense, one can begin to identify the traces of many past epochs of culture.[27] We attempt to develop a methodology of the critical analysis of common sense in Chapter 6, attempting to make such an inventory

---

[26] Marx and Engels, *Collected Works*, vol. 5, p. 3.
[27] The notion of 'palimpsest' is from Marcia Landy, *Film, Politics, and Gramsci* (Minneapolis: University of Minnesota Press, 1994).

of a specific fragment of common sense. We argue that one way of beginning to understand the complex truth status of common sense is by seeing it as composed of *narratives* that attempt to give a more or less compelling, rather than straightforwardly true or false, account of social reality.

Ideology

'Ideology' is another of the notions that, like philosophy, education or the intellectual, Gramsci redefines in his own way, granting it a much wider scope of application than conventional accounts might. In a note titled 'The Concept of "Ideology"', Gramsci retraces the history of the word. He notes that it first appeared in the materialist French school of the eighteenth century, where it denoted the science of ideas and the analysis of their origins. The meaning of the word had shifted towards the meaning of a 'system of ideas' by the time Marx and Engels used it in *The German Ideology* (1846). They there define ideology as a kind of collective illusion or, more specifically, as a deceptive veil that masks the conflictual and contradictory reality of the relations of production under the guise of various universalistic principles (such as 'liberty', 'equality' and 'fraternity'). *The German Ideology* was a key reference point during the twentieth century for Marxist critiques of the dominant ideology, although Marx himself rarely used the term 'ideology' in his works after 1846.

Gramsci consciously makes the concept of ideology central to his thought, regretting – in a way that might be surprising – that the Marxist tradition had assigned a 'negative' meaning to the word. He writes, 'The bad sense of the word has become widespread, with the effect that the theoretical analysis of the concept of ideology has been modified and denatured.'[28] Rather than seeing in ideology human thought degraded by bourgeois society, Gramsci identifies in ideology the very culture of society. In this sense the social surface of ideology is, for Gramsci, vast; similarly to 'high philosophy', ideology is intimately blended with and linked to common sense and to the

---

[28] Q7§19; *SPN*, p. 376.

everyday practices of everyone in society. Thus Gramsci writes that ideology is 'a conception of the world manifest implicitly in art, the law, economic activity, and all manifestations of individual and collective life'.[29]

Therefore, for Gramsci ideology is not simply a distorted 'reflection' of social or material givens, as this sort of reduction would deprive it of autonomous power in history. On the contrary, it is an active aspect of political praxis, and as such ideology exists in progressive as well as reactionary forms, depending on the objectives of the social groups whose struggles it accompanies. In political struggle, ideology is a crucial *factor of unity*, capable of joining together heterogeneous social coalitions under the rubric of shared or universalistic slogans or demands. As such, ideology must be an essential unifying ingredient in any 'national-popular' movement (see Chapter 3).

Gramsci illustrates the role of ideology in historical movements at various points in his *Prison Notebooks*. For instance, Gramsci comments on the ways in which the ideas of the Enlightenment philosophers diffused throughout eighteenth-century France, reaching beyond the bourgeoisie – albeit it in a refracted and unavoidably simplified form – to reform common sense and discreetly prepare the people for the French Revolution. Another example often mentioned by Gramsci, and which stands as a counterpoint to the French Revolution, is the Catholic Church, which we discuss in more detail below. Gramsci sees, in both cases and particularly in the latter, the *binding* or 'cementing' force of ideology, as it glues together diverse interests in pursuit of a shared goal.

As an instrument of political unification, though, Gramsci also understands ideology as a *terrain of struggle* within the world of culture. Here there is a direct link to Gramsci's formulation of the organic intellectual as permanent persuader (Chapter 2) and to his understanding of civil society as the site where attempts at persuasion are manifest (Chapter 3). As a producer of ideas and a diffuser of cultural critique, Gramsci sees the organic intellectual as a standard-bearer for the ideology they have embraced. Thus we can note here that for Gramsci the mission of the organic intellectual

---

[29]Q11§12; *SPN*, p. 328.

of the proletariat as a member of the Communist Party will be to develop, deepen and diffuse revolutionary ideology in the context of a struggle against rival ideologies.

Lastly, we might ask what, in Gramsci's opinion, can confer on a given ideology historical force and efficacy. Gramsci carefully distinguishes between 'historically organic ideologies, which are necessary to a given structure' and 'ideologies that are arbitrary, rationalistic, or "willed"'.[30] It is possible to recognize in this distinction the Marxist premise that Gramsci was never to renounce, namely that ideologies originating in the fundamental (economic) structure of society are the only organic ideologies and therefore the only ideologies truly essential to political struggle. As applied to the proletariat, this can only for Gramsci refer to Marxism. As we will see below, Gramsci develops his own specific conception of Marxism as 'the philosophy of praxis'.

Elsewhere in society, though, there may exist a plethora of ideologies, some of which may be the product of brilliant isolated thinkers. Whatever the profundity or sophistication of such intellectual constructions, Gramsci does not hesitate to describe these ideologies as 'arbitrary' since they are unable to tie themselves to the practice of the collective actors who make and unmake history. In other words, these secondary ideologies are condemned to remain purely intellectual products that are deprived of the activating and actualizing power of contact with human masses. Gramsci concludes, 'Only by this contact [with the masses] does a philosophy become "historical", purify itself of intellectualistic elements of an individual character and become "life"'.[31]

Religion and the Catholic Church

Gramsci sees religion both as a form of consciousness that necessitates understanding and critique from a standpoint within historical materialism and as an ideology actualized in a social

---

[30] Q7§19; *SPN*, pp. 376–7.
[31] Q11§12; *SPN*, p. 330.

movement. Gramsci's analysis of religion begins to bring together some of the themes we have explored in this chapter to this point. With regard to religion as a form of consciousness requiring critique, Gramsci contends that this critique must be carried out by philosophy: 'Philosophy is intellectual order, which neither religion nor common sense can be. It is to be observed that religion and common sense do not coincide either, but that religion is an element of fragmented common sense.'[32] Philosophy can, then, exhibit a greater level of coherence and a more logical structure than can religion, and the philosophy that Gramsci has in mind above all others here is the philosophy of praxis, or Marxism, which we will explore in more detail below. As Gramsci concludes, 'Philosophy is criticism and the superseding of religion and "common sense"'.[33] Another key affinity between religion and common sense is that every religion is in practice multiple and inconsistent, with different component groups holding different conceptions at the same time:

> Every religion, even Catholicism (indeed Catholicism more than any, precisely because of its efforts to retain a 'surface' unity and avoid splintering into national churches and social stratifications), is in reality a multiplicity of distinct and often contradictory religions: there is one Catholicism for the peasants, one for the *petits-bourgeois* and town workers, one for women, and one for intellectuals which is itself variegated and disconnected.[34]

Previous religions influence and remain parts of any contemporary religion, just as with common sense – with respect to Catholicism Gramsci mentions the influence of 'popular heretical movements [and] scientific superstitions connected with past cults'.[35]

Importantly, though, Gramsci maintains that religion can and must be differentiated from common sense and folklore on the basis of its organization: 'all religions, even the most refined and sophisticated, are "folklore" in relation to modern thought. But there is the essential

---

[32] Ibid., p. 325.
[33] Ibid., p. 326.
[34] Q11§13; *SPN*, p. 420.
[35] Ibid., p. 420.

difference that religions, in the first place Catholicism, are "elaborated and set up" by the intellectuals ... and the ecclesiastical hierarchy'.[36] The ways in which a religion is elaborated and set up necessitate, for Gramsci, analysing religion in terms of its history and social context, and not just as a set of ideas.

Gramsci, thus, is interested in religion not only as an ideology, but also as a *social movement*. Gramsci investigates, then, 'the problem of religion taken not in the confessional sense but in the secular sense of a unity of faith between a conception of the world and a corresponding norm of conduct'.[37] In this sense, religion falls under a more general question for Gramsci: how and when can ideologies provide rules for practical conduct? This is, of course, one of the central questions Gramsci seeks to answer on behalf of the philosophy of praxis.

The study of religion is thus interesting to Gramsci as he sees in it clues to the practical solution of uniting praxis and theory. Accordingly, Gramsci investigates the history and structure of the Catholic Church in search of concrete organizational lessons that can be applied to working class movements. Thus Gramsci writes that the organizational challenge facing any religious movement is:

> that of preserving the ideological unity of the entire social bloc which that ideology serves to cement and to unify. The strength of religions, and of the Catholic Church in particular, has lain, and still lies, in the fact that they feel very strongly the need for the doctrinal unity of the whole mass of the faithful and strive to ensure that the higher intellectual stratum does not get separated from the lower.[38]

Gramsci takes ideology here in its 'highest sense' of a conception of the world, and he is particularly interested in how it may play what we called above a binding role, bringing together a variety of social actors under a single, shared banner. It is important to be clear that the kind of organizational work Gramsci notes as

---

[36] Q27§1; *SCW*, p. 190.
[37] Q11§12; *SPN*, p. 326.
[38] Ibid., p. 328.

particularly important here – in this case the struggle over doctrinal unity within the Catholic Church – must be carried out in a concerted and organized way by dedicated actors within the institution itself. Gramsci continues, 'The Roman church has always been the most vigorous in the struggle to prevent the "official" formation of two religions, one for the "intellectuals" and the other for the "simple souls"'.[39] Gramsci has deep respect for the organizational capacity of the clergy in the cultural sphere and what he calls 'the abstractly rational and just relationship which the Church has been able to establish in its own sphere between the intellectuals and the simple', noting the particularly efficacious work of the Jesuits in this regard.[40]

Gramsci's study of the history of the Catholic Church is immensely rich and displays a great sensitivity to the specific role played by its cultural and organizational actors, including the Jesuits and the *Catholic Action* anti-secularization group (a study of the origins and development of which was included in Gramsci's central arguments in the opening of the first notebook). The central conclusion that emerges from his study relates to the relations between the church and the faithful:

> Religion, or a particular church, maintains its community of the faithful (within the limits imposed on it by the necessities of general historical development) in so far as it nourishes its faith permanently and in an organised fashion, indefatigably repeating its apologetics, struggling at all times and always with the same kind of arguments, and maintaining a hierarchy of intellectuals who give to the faith, in appearance at least, the dignity of thought.[41]

Gramsci notes that if a political event – such as the French Revolution – interrupts the organizational work of the church to a sufficient extent, then the losses can be irrevocable. Importantly, Gramsci sees the lessons of the importance of ideological unity as directly relevant to any cultural movement intending to replace

---

[39] Ibid., p. 328.
[40] Ibid., pp. 328–9.
[41] Ibid., p. 340.

common sense and old conceptions of the world. First, it must never tire 'of repeating its own arguments (though offering literary variation of form)' since 'repetition is the best didactic means for working on the popular mentality'.[42] Significantly, it must also – in direct contrast to Catholicism – aim to 'work incessantly to raise the intellectual level of ever-growing strata of the populace, in other words, to give a personality to the amorphous mass element'.[43]

Here we can see the central difference between Marxism and Catholicism: the former aims to work to lead the masses to a higher conception of life and a higher cultural state, whereas this is impossible for the hierarchy of the Catholic Church to do without losing the privileges directly derived from their superior position. We can note that Gramsci also criticizes Croce for his 'Malthusian attitude towards religion', or in other words one based on a contempt for the masses and a corresponding view that religion is suitable for the masses while the elite are able to comprehend a more rational conception of the world.[44] For Gramsci, thus, the position of the philosophy of praxis is antithetical to that of Catholicism on the basis of the type of educational relationship it envisages between the institution and its members: 'Whereas [the philosophy of praxis] maintains a dynamic contact and tends continually to raise new strata of the population to a higher cultural life, [Catholicism] tends to maintain a purely mechanical contact, an external unity based in particular on the liturgy and on a cult visually imposing to the crowd.'[45] The philosophy of praxis is inconceivable without the premise of engaging the masses in critical thinking through the whole range of cultural and educational institutions centred on the party and the organic intellectual.

Gramsci's understanding of religion is, therefore, driven by the question of how a unity between beliefs about the world and actions within it can be achieved by working class movements through organizational work based on an attempt to achieve ideological consistency. Gramsci sees the work of the party as central to this

---

[42] Ibid., p. 340.
[43] Ibid., p. 340.
[44] Q13§1; *SPN*, p. 132. See also *SPN*, p. 132n14.
[45] Q16§19; *SPN*, p. 397.

undertaking. In the context of criticizing Hitler's proclamation in *Mein Kampf* (1925) that founding or destroying a religion is more historically significant than founding a State or a party, Gramsci writes, 'The three elements – religion (or "active" conception of the world), State, party – are indissoluble, and in the real process of historico-political development there is a necessary passage from one to the other.'[46]

The economy: From economic base to historic bloc

Point of departure: The base/superstructure metaphor

We can now address the question of how Gramsci conceives of the place of the economic within society as a whole. The answer to this question involves tracing the development of one of his most important concepts, that of the 'historic bloc'. We can also note, in the context of an overall interpretation of Gramsci's work, that Gramsci's thought cannot be reduced to reflections on cultural and political themes, as the economy clearly plays a central role in the construction of his methodology for investigating social life.

The starting point of Gramsci's understanding of the economic is the distinction made by Marx between *Basis* and *Überbau*, usually translated into English as (economic) 'base' and (socio-political) 'superstructure'. The original framing of the distinction by Marx comes from the Preface to *A Contribution to the Critique of Political Economy* (1859). There one finds the famous assertion that the totality of the relations of production 'constitutes the economic structure of society, the real foundation, on which arises a legal and political superstructure and to which correspond definite forms of social consciousness'.[47] Thus, the political, legal, religious,

---

[46] Q17§51; *SPN*, p. 266.
[47] Karl Marx and Frederick Engels, *Marx Engels Collected Works*, volume 29 (London: Lawrence and Wishart, 1987), p. 263.

intellectual, artistic and even psychological realities of an epoch are, for Marx, dependent on the specific character of economic relations that preside over the material reproduction of society. Accordingly, for Marx a society with an economic infrastructure centred on slavery will have a political regime that tolerates or promotes slavery, a legal system that recognizes it, and a religious or moral ideology that justifies it.

The *Basis–Überbau* distinction, then, consists in applying to society a spatial metaphor based on the existence of 'levels'. For Gramsci, it is as a metaphor with heuristic value – rather than as an ontology – that these concepts must be appraised.

The critique of economism

In the period of the Second International the base–superstructure metaphor was, though, rigidified into a dogma. For some of the intellectual and political cadres of German social democracy and the PSI before the First World War, the base–superstructure model had become the pretext for the reduction of all social life to its economic dimension. Interpreted in a deterministic way, by positing the unequivocal priority of the base over the superstructure, the base–superstructure metaphor had become an easy way to negate the autonomy of the political and the cultural.

This context explains why many European Marxists tried to relativize or qualify the weight given to the base–superstructure distinction in the wake of the First World War and the Russian Revolution, two cataclysmic events that offered a resounding rebuttal to those who might have been tempted to deflate the role of politics in history. At the turn of the 1920s, Georg Lukács, in his *History and Class Consciousness* (1923), takes stock, as Gramsci was also to do, of the failures of revolution in Western Europe. Lukács attributes this defeat to the shortcomings of proletarian consciousness in Europe and considers that only a specifically *political* response would have a chance of developing that consciousness.

It is in the same historical conjuncture that Gramsci reached political maturity. As we have seen in Chapter 1, he showed himself to be a fierce critic of economic determinism as early as 1917 in his brief article 'The Revolution against *Capital*'. His critique of economic determinism is far more extensive in his *Prison Notebooks*, where he terms his target 'economism'. Economism consists, for Gramsci, in interpreting any political event or tendency as the unequivocal reflection of the economic base, a form of crude reductionism that Gramsci describes as a 'primitive infantilism'.[48] Rather, politics is for Gramsci both an autonomous science and an autonomous art (see Chapter 3), and thus requires serious and careful study in its own right.

Gramsci reproaches a number of Marxist authors individually for what he takes to be their economism, including Achille Loria (a 'materialist' economist and popularizer of Marx widely read in Italy at the turn of the twentieth century) and I. A. Lapidus and K. V. Ostrovitianov (perhaps less well-known today but the authors of the Soviet Union's standard economics reference textbook of the interwar period). Most importantly, though, Gramsci repeatedly criticizes Nikolai Bukharin, the 'Golden Boy' of the Bolsheviks in the 1920s – though executed in 1938 as a result of the Moscow trials – who had published in 1921 his *Theory of Historical Materialism*, which was subtitled 'A Manual of Popular Sociology'. Gramsci sees Bukharin's textbook, which was highly respected at the time, as characteristic of the sort of approach that would distort Marx's thought into an economism. Gramsci is keen to stress that Marx, despite his preoccupation with the critique of political economy, was 'an author of concrete political and historical works'.[49]

Gramsci's critique of economism is also politically situated – in Chapter 3 we explained that Gramsci saw the conversion of economism from an intellectual stance to a practical attitude as the source of the political disasters he terms 'fatalism', 'mechanism' and 'abstentionism'. Gramsci had been a first-hand witness to the embarrassing divisions within the PSI during the chain of events that led to Italian participation in the First World War. For Gramsci, the hesitations and clumsy passiveness of the PSI at this time were the fruits of a pernicious economism that undermined thought and paralysed action.

---

[48] Q7§24; *SPN*, p. 407.
[49] Ibid., p. 407.

Gramsci's attempt to move beyond economism is centred on his ambitious attempt – not always remarked on by those who would later interpret him – to lay the methodological basis of what he calls 'critical economics'. 'Critical economics' should aim, for Gramsci, to historicize the concepts of classical political economy, namely 'homo oeconomicus', 'market' and 'law of tendency'. With reference to the first of these three, Gramsci writes, 'Homo oeconomicus is the abstraction of the needs and of the economic operations of a particular form of society, just as the *ensemble* of hypotheses put forward by economists in their scientific work is nothing other than the *ensemble* of premises that are at the base of a particular form of society.'[50] Thus although Gramsci sees the concept of *homo oeconomicus* as an abstraction, he sees it as one that emanates from the very foundations of bourgeois society; within the historical limits of this society, it legitimately acts as a cornerstone of the science of the economy. In a similar fashion, several passages of the *Prison Notebooks* feature epistemological glosses on the notions of 'determined market' and 'law of tendency', which Gramsci sees as the decisive contributions of economics following David Ricardo (1772–1823). From his prison cell Gramsci is in frequent contact with his friend Piero Sraffa (1898–1983), a neo-Ricardian economist who had moved to Cambridge in 1927, and often in his letters to Sraffa he develops his intuitions on the economy. However, we follow Krätke in concluding that Gramsci's project of the development of a 'critical economics' remains at a very rough and exploratory stage, noting that it was extremely difficult for him to put his hands on the original texts of political economy while in prison.[51]

Americanism and Fordism

Despite lacking the textual resources to engage in the critique of political economy, at several points in the *Prison Notebooks* Gramsci demonstrates a genuine originality in his reflections on the economy, perhaps most clearly in his thoughts on the consequences

---

[50] Q10II§27; *SPN*, p. 400n39.
[51] Michael Krätke, 'Antonio Gramsci's Contribution to a Critical Economics', *Historical Materialism*, 19:3 (2011), pp. 63–105.

of changes in the world of production of American capitalism. Gramsci's notebook 22, titled 'Americanism and Fordism' and written in 1934, is remarkable in many respects, not least because it is one of the rare examples in the *Prison Notebooks* of a more or less structured and consistent text, focused on a single problematic. In addition, by focusing mainly on the evolution of the character of production in the United States, Gramsci focuses primarily on *economic* reality, somewhat contrary to the main pattern of the *Prison Notebooks*.

Gramsci starts his inquiry by questioning whether the transformations of industrial production in America represent a new organic cycle of capitalism or whether they are only conjunctural alterations that are incapable of 'constituting an epoch' (*fare epoca*). Gramsci did not have access to the full range of documentary sources he considered necessary to answer such a question fully and decisively, and consequently he is quite cautious and does not put forward a definite answer. Nevertheless, he seems to consider that the economic aspects of what he calls 'Americanism' constitute a major historical phenomenon with implications on the political, cultural and even anthropological planes.

Most basically, for Gramsci, the historical significance of Americanism is anchored in the specific changes to production methods that it has enacted. Chronologically, the cycle of Americanism starts with Taylorism. Taylorism was the scientific organization of work as pioneered by Frederick Taylor, centred on the rationalization of manual work by decomposing it into a series of minute movements that can then be optimized and performed in tight coordination with the operation of machines. Drawing on Taylorian innovations, Henry Ford succeeded in markedly increasing the productivity of his car factory by generalizing assembly-line work and intensifying the pace of production while paying his workers a wage that was generous for the time (the famous 'five dollar day'). Starting in the 1910s these innovations of American capitalism started to be discussed and debated in Europe, and some European entrepreneurs began to adopt them (for instance in Louis Renault's Billancourt factory). In the interwar period, Americanism diffused through Europe – including Lenin's Soviet Union – and it began to receive more consistent ideological backing.

The originality of Gramsci's perspective lies not in the perhaps commonplace observation of the universal spread of Americanism but rather in his perception of the consequences of Americanism beyond the productive sphere. Notebook 22 puts forward the powerful hypothesis that Americanism is 'the biggest collective effort to date to create, with unprecedented speed, and with a consciousness of purpose unmatched in history, a new type of worker and of man'.[52] For Gramsci the increased intensity of Fordist production methods requires of the worker 'the creation of a psycho-physical nexus of a new type'.[53] Gramsci's audacity here is remarkable: he is applying to the American economy a notion – 'to change man' – typically associated with Leninism.

Adopting a tone almost reminiscent of Nietzsche's *Genealogy of Morals* (1887), Gramsci suggests that the progress of the human species is only actuated through a succession of increasingly ruthless and painful struggles against the 'animality' that exists in each individual. The first Industrial Revolution imposed on the nascent proletariat, with what Gramsci calls 'incredible acts of brutality', a discipline of body and mind unimaginable in the context of traditional village modes of life.[54] Thus in the nineteenth century entire working populations were sacrificed on the altar of industrialism. Gramsci sees, in notebook 22, Americanism as a new phase in the secular process of 'anthropological reform' and although he does not deny its tragic aspects, he also emphasizes its 'inherent necessity'.[55]

According to Gramsci, Americanism demonstrates that the twentieth century is witnessing a new economic model, that of the 'planned economy' or the 'programmatic economy'. America, with its high degree of economic concentration, represents the avant-garde of this new economic form. In Gramsci's view the 'programmatic' nature of this sort of economy comes from the centrality of the coordination of public and private actions, and extends far beyond the economic sphere in the strict sense. Gramsci thus notes how prohibition (public policy) and the 'morality inspections' of the lives

---

[52] Q22§11; *SPN*, p. 302.
[53] Ibid., pp. 302–3.
[54] Q22§10, *SPN*, p. 298.
[55] Q22§1, *SPN*, p. 279.

of his workers carried out by Henry Ford (private action) both partake in a shared dynamic of the forced 'rationalization' of human life. Whereas the conventional interpretation of these events at the time saw in them the signs of an American religious moralism, Gramsci considers this surface analysis to be wrong, since a more deep-seated logic moves under the superficial layer of 'puritanism'.

Thus even though Gramsci takes in notebook 22 a set of innovations specific to the production process as his starting point, he engages in a much wider reflection centred on the economy. Moreover, one sees in Gramsci's analysis of Fordism an illustration of the notion of 'historic bloc' – that we discuss below – positing the organic solidarity of the economic, political and cultural dimensions of social life. In a sense Gramsci's reflections here are strikingly prescient: Fordism became a key term in the analysis of the Western world's socio-economic model only after the Second World War. Gramsci also perceives that the Great Depression would not end Americanism but rather that it would accelerate, particularly through Franklin D. Roosevelt's New Deal in 1933, the tendency towards the 'planned economy'.[56]

Perhaps more than any other section of the *Prison Notebooks*, Gramsci's thoughts on Americanism and Fordism have been the target of concentrated criticism (especially from French scholars). According to André Tosel, Gramsci here commits the sin of industrialism, putting his faith in the industrial economic system and, like Marx and Lenin before him, conflating the advance of the productive forces with the genuine progress of the human species. Thus Tosel concludes that Gramsci's belief in a 'civilizing mission of capitalism' leads him to fall into a 'socio-teleology' whereby the development of capitalism in history is equated with the development of humanity towards a final end state (of communism).[57] Jacques Texier, one of the pioneers of Gramscian studies in France, goes as far as to describe Gramsci's account of the repression of animality here as 'reactionary'.[58]

---

[56] Christian Barrère, 'Gramsci et la Troisième Internationale face à l'évolution du capitalisme', in: André Tosel (ed.), *Modernité de Gramsci: Actes du colloque franco-italien de Besançon, 23–25 novembre 1989* (Paris: Les Belles Lettres, 1992), pp. 123–46.
[57] André Tosel, *Marx en italiques* (Paris: Trans Europ Repress, 1991).
[58] Jacques Texier, 'Gramsci face à l'américanisme + Examen du *Cahier 22 des Quaderni del carcere*', in: André Tosel (ed.), *Modernité de Gramsci: Actes du colloque franco-italien de Besançon, 23–25 novembre 1989* (Paris: Les Belles Lettres, 1992), pp. 347–79.

Without necessarily rejecting these criticisms entirely, we can still stress that Gramsci does not depart from what he takes to be the perspective of revolution in his analysis of Americanism. Thus, when referring to Marx's *Capital* (1867), he writes that Fordism represents the 'ultimate stage in the process of progressive attempts by industry to overcome the law of the tendency of the rate of profit to fall'.[59] For Gramsci it is important to emphasize that American and European workers would be wrong to take Taylorism or Fordism as such as their enemies. A genuinely revolutionary project must, for Gramsci, consist at least in part in re-appropriating these methods, in the sense of building a future society where innovations in production of this type would no longer be the instruments for the exploitation of one class by another. However, Gramsci does note that under capitalism Americanism can only be imposed 'top-down' onto the masses of workers. Therefore, it constitutes for Gramsci a type of twentieth-century 'passive revolution' (see Chapter 3 on 'passive revolution'), since it is based on the necessity of imposing Fordist practices on the economy by fundamentally coercive means.

Point of arrival: The 'historic bloc'

Gramsci's reflections on economic questions – including his development of the starting points of a critical economics and his investigation of Fordist changes in production methods – can be seen as developing a conception of society that constitutes a decisive step beyond a crude reading of the base–superstructure metaphor. Although Gramsci refers frequently to the base–superstructure model in the *Prison Notebooks*, it is clear that for him the base does not 'determine' the superstructure in a straightforward and uniform way. A slightly iconoclastic reading of Gramsci – defended by Norberto Bobbio and Jean-Marc Piotte – goes as far as to hold that the superstructure is the pre-eminent and determining level of Gramsci's thought.[60]

---

[59] Q22§1; *SPN*, p. 280.
[60] See Bobbio, 'Gramsci e la concezione della societa civile', and Piotte, *La Pensée politique de Gramsci*.

A more plausible reading might be that for Gramsci the base and the superstructure instead constitute moments of equivalent importance in social life.[61] At any rate it seems crucial for Gramsci that these two levels are not understood as static realities with purely exogenous relations with each other; instead Gramsci contends that the *Basis* and the *Überbau* of any given society interpenetrate one other, with each level ceaselessly acting on and partly constituting the other. Gramsci calls the concrete unity between the base and the superstructure at any given point in history a 'historic bloc', asserting, 'Structures and superstructures form an "historic bloc" (*blocco storico*).'[62]

Although Gramsci does not use the expression 'historic bloc' frequently in the *Prison Notebooks*, it is an essential part of his thought.[63] In his discussion of the *Risorgimento*, Gramsci shows how the unification wars led by the kingdom of Piedmont-Sardinia generated a specific *historic bloc* founded on a series of traits: the economic domination of the Northern industrial bourgeoisie in objective alliance with the landowners of the South; the political dominance of Piedmont and of an elite that was molecularly assimilated by the new order through the subsequent process of *trasformismo*; the social passivity of the peasantry, which was at the scale of the villages absorbed into patronage networks controlled by local 'notables'; and the subalternity of the Northern industrial proletariat, which was at once too limited numerically and too privileged economically when compared to the peasantry not to engage in particularist, 'corporatist' demands and aspirations.[64]

While the social situation of Italy in the wake of the *Risorgimento* is perhaps Gramsci's central example of a historic bloc, Gramsci discerns another historic bloc in the political struggles of the French Revolution, as we will discuss in more detail in Chapter 5. Beyond the interaction of economic and political variables we should also stress that a historic bloc must be understood in relation to the

---

[61] See Hugues Portelli, *Gramsci et le bloc historique* (Paris: Presses Universitaires de France, 1972); Thomas, *The Gramscian Moment*.
[62] Q8§182; *SPN*, p. 366.
[63] Portelli, *Gramsci et le bloc historique*.
[64] See Chapter 5 for a full account of the significance of 'corporatism' for Gramsci and its role in his theory of hegemony.

ideological landscape of society, that is by reference to the state of philosophy and the nature of the common sense that predominates at the time. The notion of a historic bloc serves for Gramsci to denote the aspect of unity that can obtain at the level of the whole of society, such that the unity of that society becomes operative through the solidarity of its parts. Simon argues that the notion of historic bloc indicates the situations in which a hegemonic class is able to combine leadership in the sphere of production with its leadership of a block of interests in civil society.[65] This is one of Gramsci's most complex concepts, and in Chapter 7 we attempt to place it into an extended historical context, arguing that it may also be possible to see a historic bloc in situations where there is no hegemony.

The notion of a historic bloc also, for Gramsci, has historiographical and methodological implications. First, seeing society as a historic bloc implies putting into question a notion of historical science divided into separate subfields such as 'economic history', 'social history', 'political history', 'history of ideas' and so on. The point for Gramsci is not to devalue detailed and rigorous historical inquiry, or to deny the *relative autonomy* of each individual dimension of social life, but rather to pay attention to the social whole in order to move from analysis to synthesis. It is only by comprehending the relations between all of the parts within the whole that any one part can be fully understood.

With respect to the base–superstructure metaphor and its possible place within the methodology of Marxism, the historic bloc also appears to represent an overcoming or moving beyond (as opposed to a simple negation) of the levels metaphor. Although the heuristic value of the *Basis–Überbau* coupling may endure, its explanatory power is reduced to the extent that the goal of historical inquiry is seen as thinking through the dynamic unity of the levels of base and superstructure within the historic bloc.

Here Gramsci converges with the other Marxist thinkers of the twentieth century who have attempted, with quite different theoretical tools, to relativize or qualify the base–superstructure metaphor in

---

[65] See Simon, *Gramsci's Political Thought.*

order to emphasize a notion of *social totality*.[66] It is no coincidence that Althusser simultaneously accused Gramsci, Lukács and Sartre dissolving the base–superstructure distinction into historicism.[67]

The philosophy of praxis

Materialism, idealism and Croce

Gramsci's philosophy reaches its conclusion in his understanding of Marxism as the 'philosophy of praxis'. Although the circumlocution serves to thwart prison censorship (see Chapter 1), it also, importantly, expresses Gramsci's distinctive *conception of Marxism*.[68] It is also significant that the phrase appears increasingly frequently in later notebooks, suggesting the maturation of Gramsci's thought on this point.

The starting point of the philosophy of praxis is the rejection of the two philosophical traditions that are anterior to Marx's thought: materialism and idealism. Gramsci observes that the Marxist tradition, and Marxist thought in his own day, is itself torn between these two poles, either converted into the vulgar materialism of the Second International and Nikolai Bukharin or transfigured into a vehicle for the renaissance of idealism among, for instance, the Italian neo-idealists led by Benedetto Croce and Giovanni Gentile. The young Marx's original intention, as explicated in the *Theses on Feuerbach* (1845), was to put forward a superior dialectical synthesis of these two schools, and almost a century later Gramsci attempts to carry through this project in order to renew Marxist thought.[69]

Here Gramsci relies in part on the thought of Antonio Labriola (1843–1904). In his *Essay on the Materialist Conception of History*

---

[66] In particular, Georg Lukács's *History and Class Consciousness* (Berlin: Malik-Verlag, 1923), Franz Jakubowski's *Ideology and Superstructure in Historical Materialism* (Danzig: Fooken, 1936), and Jean-Paul Sartre's *Search for a Method* (Paris: Gallimard, 1957) and *Critique of Dialectical Reason* (Paris: Gallimard, 1960).

[67] Louis Althusser, 'Marxism is not a Historicism', in: Louis Althusser and Étienne Balibar, *Reading Capital*, translated by Ben Brewster (London: New Left Books, 1970).

[68] See Tosel, 'Modernité de Gramsci?'; Thomas, *The Gramscian Moment.*

[69] See Tosel, *Marx en italiques.*

(1896) Labriola had revealed himself to be a pioneer of the critique of materialism from within the Marxism of the Second International. From Gramsci's perspective philosophical materialism consists in the translation of economism into the realm of ontology, as it posits that material phenomena constitute the foundational reality of the universe and wholly determine the contents of human consciousness and the movement of history. Finding its modern origins in the thought of eighteenth-century philosophers such as Denis Diderot, materialism was reformulated as a critique of Hegelianism by Ludwig Feuerbach that was then submitted to the decisive critique of the young Marx.[70]

Although materialism aimed to be the 'antidote' to metaphysics, Gramsci – not without irony – draws an analogy between the two. 'Vulgar materialism', he writes, '"divinises" a hypostasis of matter'.[71] Gramsci, in his typically historicist vein, defines metaphysics as 'any systematic formulation that is put forward as an extra-historical truth, as an abstract universal outside of time and space'.[72] Materialism, then, is for Gramsci a religion of matter, which in its Marxist version expects revolution as the Christian believers in predestination anticipated the grace of God. Gramsci had little time for this vulgar 'necessitarianism', which he located in Bukharin's 1921 *Popular Manual*. Bukharin's tendency to present a Marxism adorned with the trappings of a positivist sociology is not at all what Gramsci will come to mean by the philosophy of praxis.

The critique of philosophical idealism presented Gramsci with a greater intellectual challenge, not least because he confronts two worthy adversaries: Croce and Gentile. These two thinkers had read and absorbed Marx, eventually rejecting him at the turn of the twentieth century to promote their own neo-idealist syntheses.[73] Gentile, who would later become an intellectual figurehead of fascism and whose education policy we discussed in Chapter 2, had made his reputation with his *Philosophy of Marx* (1899). In this text, Gentile argues for a radically subjectivist reading of Marx's thought,

---

[70] Although Marx and Engels later embraced the term 'materialism', Gramsci seems sceptical of this decision since he holds it to encourage a relapse into economism.
[71] Q11§32; *SPN*, p. 469.
[72] Q11§14; *SPN*, p. 437.
[73] Tosel, *Marx en italiques.*

one inspired by Fichte and giving a privileged place to the notion of praxis. At one point Gramsci was highly influenced by Gentile's philosophy, as was a large section of the Italian revolutionary youth. However, Gentile's thought can be seen to lead to 'actualism', that is the consecration of the act as a philosophical absolute without adequate consideration of the *social* environment of the subject. In Gentile's neo-idealist conception of praxis, it becomes detached from society, turning inwards and leading to a 'mystique of the subject'.[74]

Although Gentile clearly influences the development of Gramsci's conception of the philosophy of praxis, Croce stands as one of the central figures in the whole of the *Prison Notebooks* and one of the most important of the 'concrete adversaries' that Gramsci had noted he needed an engagement with to develop his thought (see Chapter 1). Today, although the name of Benedetto Croce (1866–1952) may be reasonably well-known within philosophy, his works are not widely read. In the first half of the twentieth century, though, Croce was one of the foremost intellectual authorities in Europe. Coming from the Abruzzo region of Southern Italy, Croce was a student of Labriola and was influenced by the latter's attempt to put forward an anti-scientistic interpretation of Marxism against the mechanistic materialism that dominated the Second International of the time. While Croce was initially attracted to a sort of Labriolan socialism, by the time of a 1899 letter to Giovanni Gentile he was in a position to assert that 'the sound, realistic core of Marx's thought should be freed' from Marxism.[75] He later denounced 'rigid orthodox Marxism' for seeing the economy as the 'hidden God' of human history.[76]

Having settled in Naples and left Marxism behind, Croce set out in the early decades of the twentieth century to elaborate, following Hegel, a neo-idealist philosophical system centred on a 'dialectic of distincts'. By this he meant a network of overlapping conceptual oppositions that he was to devote his career to reworking time and

---

[74] Domenico Losurdo, 'Gramsci, Gentile, Marx et les philosophies de la praxis', in: André Tosel (ed.), *Modernité de Gramsci: Actes du colloque franco-italien de Besançon, 23–25 novembre 1989* (Paris: Les Belles Lettres, 1992), pp. 381–412.
[75] Cited in Tosel, *Marx en italiques.*
[76] See Benedetto Croce, *Storia della Storiografia Italiana nel Secolo Decimonono* (Bari: Laterza, 1921).

again.[77] At the same time, Croce conceived history as the progress of the idea of freedom, ultimately manifesting the perfectibility of mankind. Croce was a prolific thinker, and in publishing works of history, political philosophy, ethics, aesthetics and logic, he eventually rose to become the most visible intellectual in Italy. In contrast to Gentile, he refused to rally to Mussolini, although he remained in Italy during fascism and continued to publish without being troubled by the regime.

The young Gramsci was an enthusiastic reader of Croce, and in the 1917 pamphlet *La Città futura* described him as the 'greatest European thinker of the age', while a letter from prison cites a description of Croce as 'Italy's greatest prose writer after Manzoni'.[78] Although Gramsci was to distance himself from Croce on the issue of socialism, he did embrace in particular two aspects of Croce's thought: the critique of the kind of positivism that had been in fashion in post-*Risorgimento* Italy, and the emphasis on the 'ethical-political' dimension of human action that provided an important contrast to the 'vulgar determinism' of some Marxist thinkers of the time.[79]

Although Gramsci's admiration for Croce would not disappear, as the *Prison Notebooks* develop it becomes increasingly counterbalanced by acerbic criticism of Croce's philosophical and political positions. It is precisely because Croce's thought exercised such a cultural influence on educated Italians – for whom Gramsci thought him to be the 'secular Pope' – that Gramsci takes him as a favoured target while in prison.[80] In the *Prison Notebooks* Gramsci even sketches the outlines of an 'anti-Croce', modelled on Engels's famous *Anti-Dühring* (1878). For Croce's idealist and speculative historicism Gramsci aims to substitute a fully 'terrestrial' philosophy: the 'absolute historicism' that we discuss

---

[77] Tosel, *Marx en italiques.*
[78] Letter to Tatiana Schucht, 25 April 1932; *LP*, p. 233. The description is from a French account of contemporary Italian literature, written by Benjamin Crémeiux and published in Paris in 1928. Gramsci continues the letter, though, by arguing that Croce's prose in fact derives more from the great Italian writers of scientific prose, centrally Galileo, than it does from Manzoni.
[79] Losurdo, *'Comunismo critico'.*
[80] Letter to Tatiana Schucht, 7 September 1931; *LP*, p. 203.

below. Moreover, Gramsci denounces Croce's attitude of haughty aloofness from the events of 'real' history, seeing it in a 'political morphinism' that is all the more pernicious given that Italy was experiencing the horrors of a fascist regime.[81]

Croce was in fact later to write of Gramsci, in a 1947 review of a collection of the latter's *Prison Letters* published after the Second World War: 'As a man of thought, he was one of us'.[82] The post-war period was to be the twilight of Crocean thought since reaction against neo-idealism within Italian philosophy and the rapid diffusion of Marxism in Italy after 1945 combined to eclipse Croce's previously towering figure. Nevertheless, we can note that Croce's neo-idealism remained a key point of reference for Gramsci in his development of the philosophy of praxis as the attempt to achieve a dialectical synthesis of materialism and idealism.

'Absolute historicism'

Thus rejecting Gentile and Croce, Gramsci looks to consolidate the intellectual basis of a 'philosophy of praxis' able to avoid materialism and idealism, and also able to escape falling entirely either on the side of the object (thereby creating an objectivism of matter) or on the side of the subject (leading to a subjectivism of action). Gramsci's solution to this philosophical problem is what Tosel calls 'situated praxis', which displays the dialectical unity of society (as historic bloc) and human critical-practical activity (as praxis).[83] Thus although human beings are subject to the influence of social circumstances, they are themselves able to modify these circumstances. While it is true, then, that the social environment is the 'educator' of men, it is equally true that, in a phrase of the young Marx's from the third of the *Theses on Feuerbach* (1845) of which Gramsci was fond, 'the educator must himself be educated'.[84]

Gramsci's conception of the philosophy of praxis thus allows an escape from metaphysics, in the sense that neither matter nor

---

[81] Q15§62; *SPN*, p. 114.
[82] Cited in Losurdo, *'Comunismo critico'*.
[83] Tosel, *Le Marxisme du XXᵉ siècle*.
[84] Marx and Engels, *Collected Works*, vol. 5, p. 4.

human subjectivity are converted into absolutes, which for Gramsci can only happen to one of these terms to the detriment of the other. Gramsci takes matter and human subjectivity to be in relations of co-constitution in an environment of an entirely historical character. Thus the philosophy of praxis also represents for Gramsci a philosophy of history, a *Weltanschauung* that is exclusively anchored in the real world, and a fully terrestrial or 'earthly' discourse that rejects any notion of transcendence in favour of absolute immanence.[85]

Gramsci's thought here implies, among other things, that any intellectual construction – including the philosophy of praxis itself – is tied to concrete history and expresses a specific moment of that history. The knowledge of human beings, whatever its nature, emerges for Gramsci from historical becoming, even if it is then converted into praxis and thereby affects history. Therefore we can agree with Christine Buci-Glucksmann that Gramsci's philosophy is a 'gnosiology', that is a theory of knowledge that above all *historically* grounds the products of human thought.[86]

If it is true, then, that no philosophy can escape history, then the philosophy of praxis is the only system of thought fearlessly to accept this fact and fully to embrace its implications. As Gramsci writes, the 'philosophy of praxis not only claimed to explain and to justify all the past, but to explain and justify historically itself as well. That is, it was the greatest form of "historicism", total liberation from any form of abstract "ideologism", the real conquest of the historical world, the beginnings of a new civilisation'.[87]

Thus we can see the true breadth of Gramsci's conception of the philosophy of praxis: it constitutes nothing less than the beginnings of a 'new civilization' and 'the result and crowning point of all previous history', and that it is a 'new culture in incubation, which will develop with the development of social relations'.[88] Gramsci's reference to the development of Marxism with the development of social relations suggests that Gramsci sees Marxism as a philosophy that is able to move past petrifying dogmatism and inherit from Marx's thought by

---

[85] See Q11§27; *SPN*, p. 465.
[86] Buci-Glucksmann, *Gramsci and the State*.
[87] Q16§19; *SPN*, p. 399.
[88] See Q15§61; *SPN*, p. 417; Q16§19; *SPN*, p. 398.

continually reaching beyond it. The process of the elaboration of the philosophy of praxis is, for Gramsci, a continuous task that must be carried out in tight conjunction with revolutionary activity.

Gramsci also considers the philosophy of praxis to be a 'humanism': it is based on the centrality of human critical-practical activity in history. The world is for Gramsci neither the slave of matter nor of the Idea, nor particularly of the divine. Rather, it belongs in full to the human species to the precise extent that it is forged by collective human praxis. To avoid any misunderstanding, it is important to clarify here that Gramsci's humanism is not the same as that of the Renaissance 'men of letters'. Instead, Gramsci's humanism rests on a very specific conception of what man is, centrally defined by anti-naturalism (and explored in more detail in the first section of this chapter).

We can conclude with a famous passage from the *Prison Notebooks* in which Gramsci brings together many of the elements that we have discussed: 'The philosophy of praxis is the absolute "historicism", the absolute secularisation and earthliness of thought, an absolute humanism of history. It is along this line that one must trace the thread of the new conception of the world.'[89] The striking phrase 'absolute historicism' inspired many later polemics, perhaps most influentially in the work of Louis Althusser. Althusser, in his 1968 essay 'Marxism is not a Historicism', sees in this expression of Gramsci's a serious and distorting 'blunder'. Nonetheless, the idea of the philosophy of praxis as an absolute historicism is the logical conclusion of Gramsci's philosophy, and it is clear that he believes this interpretation to be the only viable one of Marxist philosophy.

The revolution of common sense

For Gramsci, the philosophy of praxis is synonymous with revolution in a number of ways. First, it entails a revolution in the area of ideology: absolute historicism, as discussed above, requires the simultaneous critique of all past philosophical doctrines. For Gramsci, though, this critique should not take the form of an indiscriminate

---

[89] Q11§27; *SPN*, p. 465.

denunciation (which Gramsci criticizes Bukharin and other Marxists for having done in their writings on culture), but rather the grasping of the rationality of every conception of the world in the very limits of its historicity. 'Of the past let us make a clean slate', as *The Internationale* puts it, is thus not a Gramscian precept; Gramsci instead contends that it is only historical becoming that can enact the overcoming of movements of ideas, and thus any philosophy aspiring to be revolutionary must recognize the importance of history in systems of thought of the past. The philosophy of praxis is thus based for Gramsci on the critical absorption of a number of intellectual currents of the past, including the Renaissance, the Protestant Reformation, the French Enlightenment and German classical philosophy. The question of the appropriate relation to the cultural and philosophical heritage of the past is a problematic that underlies much of Gramsci's thought.[90]

The philosophy of praxis, though, first and foremost spells revolution in the sphere of concrete political activity: 'The philosophy of praxis...does not aim at the peaceful resolution of existing contradictions in history and society but is rather the very theory of these contradictions.'[91] Gramsci's understanding of the historic bloc is based on what he takes to be the fundamental truth of the class struggle. The proletariat, with the Communist Party at its head and armed with the theoretical weapon of the philosophy of praxis, will for Gramsci be the collective subject of a revolution that will put an end to social contradictions by abolishing capitalism.

At this point, Gramsci raises the question of how to 'operate' the link between, on the one hand, the philosophy of praxis as the doctrine of absolute historicism and, on the other, the mass of the 'subalterns' for whom Marxism is not a 'spontaneous' thought product. Gramsci understands this question as concerning the possible relation between the philosophy of praxis and common sense; he cannot accept the idea that the philosophy of praxis would be the specific culture of an elite of professional revolutionaries whose mission would be to lead a proletariat deprived of a full understanding of the historical process to the 'grand soir' of the

---

[90] Losurdo, *'Comunismo critico'*.
[91] Q10§II§41xii; *FSPN*, p. 395.

revolution. Gramsci asserts instead that the subaltern classes must be the genuine, conscious subject of revolutionary praxis.

Gramsci responds to this practical challenge by formulating the notion of 'the revolution of common sense'. The common sense of the dominated classes in society – which is also for Gramsci, as we have seen above, their own philosophy and *Weltanschauung* – must be worked on tirelessly in view of making it a favourable soil for the growth of the philosophy of praxis. In turn, the philosophy of praxis must be transformed into a new common sense through direct contact with the subaltern classes. The authentic intellectual support of the proletariat for Marxism validates, in Gramsci's view, the historicity of the philosophy of praxis and thus constitutes a necessary step towards revolution.

It is perhaps no surprise that the key figure in this long-term process of ideological work is the organic intellectual, who Gramsci sees as the 'permanent persuader' of the revolution. The intellectual's mission is to build in conjunction with the dominated classes in society an educational relation that is founded on consent while also being able to enact the progressive passage from conformity to spontaneity (see Chapter 2). Gramsci here applies the idea that the educator must always in turn be educated, and describes the *reciprocal* movement between the organic intellectuals and the proletariat as 'living philology', which enables the revolutionary leaders and militants to merge in a collective organism.[92]

Using an expression that he takes from Georges Sorel, and which originates in Ernest Renan, Gramsci calls this great upheaval of the mind 'intellectual and moral reform'.[93] This intellectual and moral reform is a direct consequence of the interrelation Gramsci sees between the philosophy of the masses and the philosophy of the elite. As Gramsci concludes, the 'relation between common sense and the upper level of philosophy is assured by "politics"'.[94] Ultimately, then, for Gramsci politics and philosophy are most intimately joined through the revolution of common sense.

---

[92] Q11§25; *SPN*, p. 429.
[93] Q13§1; *SPN*, p. 132.
[94] Q11§12; *SPN*, p. 331.

5

Hegemony

Introduction

In this chapter we move to a discussion of Gramsci's most famous concept, that of hegemony (*egemonia*). We attempt to reconstruct Gramsci's understanding of hegemony in all its wealth and depth, arguing that it constitutes the main philosophical and political thread of Gramsci's thought.

If hegemony has such a central place in Gramsci's thought, then the question may be raised of why we are only addressing it in the fifth chapter. Our argument is that Gramsci's concept of hegemony not only relies on but deepens and furthers his other major theoretical innovations: the intellectual as the organizer of culture or politics; the distinction between civil society and political society; the theory of crisis as a situation of the dissolution and constitution of the political; ideology as a mobilizing and binding factor in social movements and as a terrain of philosophical and political struggle; and the revolution of common sense as intellectual and moral reform. Thus, it is only after having encountered the other key concepts in Gramsci's thought that a reader, in our opinion, is fully able to understand the way in which hegemony is applicable to all the other topics that Gramsci reflects on in his prison writing.

Gramsci's notion of hegemony, in this way, confers on his seemingly fragmentary theoretical incursions a new degree of coherence and consistency. At the same time, we argue, Gramsci's reflection on hegemony is the key to understanding his *theory of power* – that is, the theory of the conditions of power's emergence, of its modalities of operation, and of its historical and political consequences.

Hegemony: The exercise of leadership

Origins

Hegemony, for Gramsci, serves to stress the cultural and moral dimensions of the exercise of political power. This is not, though, the original meaning of the word, either in Ancient Greece or among the Russian revolutionaries of the late nineteenth century who resuscitated the term in the modern context.

In Ancient Greek the word derives from *eghestai*, which means to direct or to lead. This word later produced *eghemon*, which by the time of the Peloponnesian War was used to designate the city in a leading position within the alliance of Greek city-States. In the discipline of International Relations the term 'hegemony' is still used in a sense directly borrowed from this period of antiquity, naming a situation in which a single State is dominant on the military, economic and diplomatic planes.

In the 1880s, though, the meaning of the word was modified by Marxist Russian revolutionaries, particularly Georgi Plekhanov.[1] They argued that the working class should form an alliance with the peasantry to overthrow the bourgeoisie, and described this alliance as one in which the workers would exercise 'hegemony' while the peasantry would be an ancillary force. In this case, then, hegemony served to denote a *class alliance* under the leadership of the proletariat (and an alliance that was understood as a stepping stone towards revolution). In the following decades, references to hegemony grew more common in revolutionary newspapers and pamphlets in Russia, with Lenin himself using the word in Bolshevik polemics against the Mensheviks before the October Revolution.[2]

---

[1] See the account in Anderson, 'Antinomies'.
[2] Derek Boothman, 'The Sources for Gramsci's Concept of Hegemony', *Rethinking Marxism*, 20:2 (2008), pp. 201–15.

Moreover, we can see that Lenin and the Bolsheviks attempted to put hegemony into practice during this period: their political programme was based on the incorporation of the aspiration for land redistribution among the peasantry, the desire for peace among soldiers and the demands for national autonomy on the part of the Finnish, Ukrainian and Baltic peoples.

Both the experience of 1917 and the presence of the word in Lenin's writings are factors that led Gramsci to use 'hegemony' in his *Prison Notebooks*. However, as we will see, the term for Gramsci has entirely new implications. First, it no longer serves to designate solely the activity of the working class in its struggle against the bourgeoisie, but instead can be applied to any form of 'directing' political action on the part of one social group vis-à-vis others, theoretically at any point in history. Second, Gramsci's use of hegemony stresses the cultural, moral and cognitive aspects of that leadership, and it is in this way almost completely redefined. Lastly, while we might say that hegemony was a means (to revolution) for Lenin, it is transmuted to an end (of politics) for Gramsci.

Political projects

Importantly, Gramsci does not offer a single definition of hegemony that would be valid for all times and places. Instead, in the same way that we observed with his use of the word 'State', Gramsci's understanding of hegemony evolves across the concrete historical situations that are described and analysed. We can term this Gramsci's *methodological historicism* – that is, we can note that Gramsci's historicism is methodological as well as philosophical (see also Chapter 3). Typically, the concepts that Gramsci uses in his analyses of politics appear for the first time in the context of a specific historical inquiry, and then are widened and refined as he applies them in subsequent passages to new objects of study.

It is therefore important to try to identify Gramsci's uses of the word 'hegemony' in some of the specific historical periods he investigates in the *Prison Notebooks*. Gramsci uses the concept of hegemony in his notebooks on the Italian *Risorgimento* (see Chapter 3), where he writes of the hegemony of Cavour's Moderates vis-à-vis the Action Party of Garibaldi and Mazzini, as well as in relation to the rural and urban bourgeoisie and petty bourgeoisie of the peninsula. It is important to bear in mind that the Moderates were only a fraction of the bourgeoisie, a numerically limited stratum of political actors that can be thought of as the 'intellectuals' of the court of the kingdom of Piedmont-Sardinia. Their 'hegemony', which also represented the hegemony of Piedmont over the rest of Italy, was continued after unification in the process of *trasformismo* by which Italian political elites were molecularly incorporated into the parliamentary system.[3]

Gramsci's study of the *Risorgimento* illustrates an important point: although the Moderate party's hegemony relied partly on military pre-eminence (through its backing by the Piedmontese army), it also operated through a 'power of attraction' that refers to the general ability of a social group to attract others to identify with, and rally towards, its struggles and causes. The *Risorgimento* thus saw the success of the Moderates' political project as they made war against some (Austria and the Pope), obtained the consent of others (the Action Party and the bourgeoisie) and neutralized the subaltern groups who were cast aside from the process (the peasantry and the urban working class).

In the case of the *Risorgimento*, then, four different sorts of entities co-existed: the directing group, the auxiliary groups, the subaltern groups and the 'enemy' camp. Hegemony, formally, denotes the relation, consented to on both sides, that the leading entity has to the auxiliary group or groups.[4] Gramsci's criticisms of the *Risorgimento*, as we have already seen, are focused on the partial or limited character of the hegemony that presided over Italy's unification; Gramsci sees in the *Risorgimento* a non-national hegemony, and specifically a *subnational* one that reduced the majority of the population to a passive state and thus relegated it to a subaltern position.

Gramsci is particularly careful to draw a contrast between the *Risorgimento* and the Jacobin phase of the French Revolution. According to Gramsci, the ambition of the Jacobins was to incorporate

---

[3] Pierre Laroche, 'Gramsci et le *Risorgimento*', *Italies*, 6 (2002), pp. 313–23.
[4] Portelli, *Gramsci et le bloc historique*.

the entirety of the underprivileged groups of the country within the revolutionary project as allies in the struggle against the aristocracy. To this end, importantly, the Jacobins were willing to sacrifice some of the immediate material interests of their class – or their 'corporatist' interests – in order to include in their programme some demands that emanated from the popular classes. Gramsci describes the situation as follows:

> The representatives of the Third Estate initially only posed those questions which interested the actual physical members of the social group, their immediate 'corporate' interests (corporate in the traditional sense, of the immediate and narrowly selfish interests of a particular category).... Gradually a new elite was selected out which did not concern itself solely with 'corporate' reforms, but tended to conceive of the bourgeoisie as the hegemonic group of all the popular forces.[5]

Thus 'Jacobinism', which as we have already seen in Chapter 3 was for Gramsci a 'national-popular' phenomenon, refers to a project of total or whole hegemony, rather than the partial hegemony of the sort that characterized the process of the *Risorgimento*. Jacobinism thus denotes the ambition on the part of the fundamental group (in this case the bourgeoisie) to hegemonize all the popular elements of society through concrete concessions, thereby achieving their *active* – and no longer passive – political support. Importantly, the power of attraction of the fundamental group in relation to the auxiliary strata operates through specific intermediary agents: the organic intellectuals, who in this instance are the Jacobins.

Gramsci envisages the Jacobin politics of the French Revolution as reproduced in twentieth-century Italy, only this time in a new configuration of forces in which the urban proletariat of the North would be the leading group and the peasants of the South the auxiliary group, with the industrial bourgeoisie as the adversary to overthrow. This is the main theme of Gramsci's *Alcuni temi* essay, written in 1926 just before his arrest. In this text Gramsci

---

[5] Q19§24; *SPN*, p. 77.

insists on the fact that the Communist Party's organic intellectuals must persuade, through their ideological activism, the traditional intellectuals of rural Italy of the benefits and political rationality of an alliance with the proletariat. Gramsci sees these members of the countryside petty bourgeoisie as pivotal actors, halfway between the landowners and the peasants and therefore in the position to promote support for the working class cause among the peasantry.

Consent and coercion

For Gramsci, hegemony is thus constructed through the power of attraction of the leading group and also through compromises and concessions aimed at the conscious rallying of auxiliary forces. The essential condition of hegemonic politics is the consent of the auxiliary groups. We have already covered the notion of consent in relation to the civil society–political society dichotomy (Chapter 3), the first term of which is associated with private initiatives, private actions, intellectual debates and consensual mobilization, while the latter refers to the domain of coercion enacted through administrative or military constraint. Hegemony, then, is forged in the context of civil society where the political party and its organic intellectuals (the 'permanent persuaders') rally to their cause various disparate social groups.

The consent–civil society coupling is thus central to Gramsci's conception of hegemony. However, the role of coercion is less clear, and the question of whether consent can be conceived of without coercion – such that hegemony would be a purely consensual process – is a difficult one to answer. The conceptual difficulty here is compounded by the fact that Gramsci seems to alternate between two definitions of hegemony in different passages of the *Prison Notebooks*.

A first type of understanding of hegemony can be sketched in the following way: 'hegemony = consent + coercion = civil society + political society'. Hegemony would in this case 'walk on two legs', namely those of free choice and constraint. Other passages, though, seem to run against this first definition. For instance, we find, in a famous passage, Gramsci schematizing his thinking algebraically, as we have just done above, and stating, 'State = political society + civil society, in other words hegemony protected by the armour of coercion'.[6] This would imply a second definition or formula: 'hegemony = consent = civil society'.

Is it possible to overcome this definitional ambiguity? We can note, first, that it is almost impossible to find in Gramsci's notebooks a reference to a hegemonic configuration in which the 'moment of force' is completely absent. Thus whatever the exact definition of the word 'hegemony', the combination and dynamic interaction of consent and coercion is the recurrent characteristic of the situations described by Gramsci. In the historical examples above, then, we can note the decisive action of the Piedmontese army during the *Risorgimento* and the constant threat of the guillotine during the Jacobin Terror.

Similarly, for the proletarian revolution that Gramsci anticipates in the West, the active adherence of all the underprivileged groups in society to the working class cause will lead to an assault on the State, which is likely to be violent, even if only for a brief period. These two steps in the revolutionary process – the building of alliances and the assault on the State – correspond for Gramsci to the war of position and the war of movement, respectively (see Chapter 3). Referring to an expression used in 1925 by the then head of the Comintern Grigory Zinoviev, Gramsci mentions here the need for a 'double perspective': revolutionary strategy must be able to theorize both consent and coercion, both the war of position and the war of movement, as well as the relations between these terms.

Gramsci's historical investigations are in this way an invitation to think through the *interpenetration* of consent and coercion. The example of present-day Western democracies might illustrate the fact that these modalities of power tend to be closely connected and mutually reinforcing: modern States enjoy the 'monopoly of legitimate violence' (in Weber's phrase) exerted through the coercive element of the police and the army, but they are also constituted by the electoral mechanism as the consensual and democratic expression of a political community made up by the whole body of

---

[6]Q6§88; *SPN*, p. 263.

citizens. The coercive apparatuses of the State are, then, the means to implement public policies that have been sanctioned by elections, while the electoral mechanism itself contributes to ensuring the durability and stability of the violence of the State by making that violence, in another of Weber's terms, 'legitimate'.

It is highly likely that the most solid and stable hegemonic system is precisely the one in which brute force is least visible because its daily exercise has been made unnecessary by the logic of consent. In such a system the ubiquity of consensual institutional mechanisms will tend to conceal the coercive apparatuses that can remain off-stage, held back 'just in case'. It is only in a situation of crisis, whether organic or conjunctural, that hegemony crumbles away and political violence may resurface. Following Gramsci's logic, we can see that the resort to a range of coercive apparatuses in response to such a crisis situation is not a sign of the power of the established order, but rather a symptom of its weakness. The repressive apparatuses of contemporary States stand ready and waiting, in 'anticipation of moments of crisis of command and direction when spontaneous consent has failed'.[7] In order to describe a political landscape that is essentially coercive Gramsci uses the terms 'domination' (*dominazione*) and 'dictatorship' (*dittatura*) rather than 'hegemony' (*egemonia*) or 'leadership' (*direzione*).

The centrality of the dialectic of coercion and consent for Gramsci's understanding of hegemony can be traced to the influence of Machiavelli's writings. In *The Prince* (1532) we find the image of the centaur – half beast and half man, thus half force and half reason – as a metaphor for politics. Machiavelli asserts that a successful political operator must at times behave like a ferocious beast and at other times as a human being. Gramsci adopts in his thinking about hegemony a fundamentally Machiavellian problematic of power, which puts as central the nature and balance of the relation between force and reason (or, for Gramsci coercion and consent).[8]

It might at first seem surprising that a Marxist revolutionary of the twentieth century such as Gramsci has chosen to extract from

---

[7]Q11§12; *SPN*, p. 12.
[8]Joseph V. Femia, *Gramsci's Political Thought: Hegemony, Consciousness and the Revolutionary Process* (Oxford: Oxford University Press, 1981).

the world of the Renaissance some of the most decisive categories for his reflections on politics. In particular, it might be questioned whether the modalities of 'consent' and 'coercion', fundamental as they undoubtedly are, exhaust the full range of the realities of the operation of power in a modern society. The conceptual couplet of consent and coercion – as arising from the distinction between civil society and political society – might be thought to risk neglecting more strictly economic power, including the specific constraints that force those who do not own the means of production to sell their labour power to those who do. The theme of 'economic power', which is so central in Marx, is much less prominent in Gramsci.[9] In addition, Gramsci himself acknowledges that between consent and coercion one can identify a third term, namely corruption or fraud. For Gramsci, these forms of power will predominate 'in certain situations when it is hard to exercise the hegemonic function, and when the use of force is too risky'.[10]

Hegemony: A cognitive and moral process

A culture in formation

In the previous section, we discussed a number of the major components of Gramsci's theory of hegemony, but one of the most influential and original aspects of Gramsci's reflections on hegemony concerns the ramifications of the hegemonic process on the very consciousness of social subjects. For Gramsci, hegemony constitutes a *form of knowledge* and signifies an *ethical renewal*. In this section, we will attempt to unpack these two dimensions in which Gramsci sees hegemony not just as the exercise of leadership but also as a fundamentally cognitive and moral process.

Gramsci recognizes that hegemony is constructed through mechanisms of political negotiation and intellectual persuasion. In this sense, it is Gramsci's riposte to the theoretical and practical

---

[9] Anderson, 'Antinomies'.
[10] Q13§37; *SPN*, p. 80n1.

economism we discussed in Chapter 4. For Gramsci, then, a given economic landscape, including the actual or potential pre-eminence of a particular social class in the sphere of production, represents only a precondition of hegemony rather than being sufficient for its realization. To be clear, if the bourgeoisie monopolizes and becomes the master of capital in a given epoch, this only makes hegemony *possible* rather than *necessary*. Similarly, then, if the working class has the reasonable hope of expropriating the capitalist class in the future, this allows it to anticipate a future hegemony but does not mean that hegemony is in any way guaranteed. Economic facts are thus only premises and first steps for Gramsci and they do not 'determine' any set outcomes; Gramsci remains here keen to avoid any sort of crude 'necessitarianism'.

The privileged – though not exclusive – terrain on which hegemony is built and actively defended is that of *ideology*. Hegemony thus operates chiefly at the level of the superstructure. Accordingly, the agents of hegemony are the intellectuals, whose responsibility it is to make sure hegemony and the revolution of common sense coincide. It is through the conjunction of these elements, which we discussed in Chapter 4, that hegemony corresponds for Gramsci to nothing less than a *recomposition of culture*.

Referring to Lenin and the 1917 Revolution, Gramsci writes that the 'realisation of a hegemonic apparatus, in so far as it creates a new ideological terrain, determines a reform of consciousness and of methods of knowledge: it is a fact of knowledge, a philosophical fact'.[11] It should be borne in mind that, for Gramsci, 'philosophy', 'ideology' and 'common sense' stand in close relation to one another. The October Revolution, by overturning both the political order and the economic relations of society, thus also implied an intellectual and moral upheaval among the popular classes (and so reformed common sense) as well as among the elites (by changing the arts, science and the 'upper level of philosophy'):

However, it is necessary to guard against an overly subjectivist interpretation of hegemony. Gramsci's use of the expression 'hegemonic apparatus' suggests that any renewal of human

---

[11] Q10II§12; *SPN*, pp. 365–6.

consciousness caused by a hegemonic process is undergirded by a structure of *concrete institutions* both in political society (the administration, tribunals, courts and so on) and most crucially in civil society (including the school system, publishing houses, the press, radio and a number of other cultural institutions). In other words, intellectual and moral reform can only, for Gramsci, result from praxis since the culture of human beings can only be actuated through *material practices*.[12]

The ethical State

For Gramsci, hegemony serves less to describe a state of fact than to denote a *process*, namely a socio-political project that is in the course of being realized and enacted. For Gramsci, then, an expression such as 'the hegemony of the bourgeoisie' does not imply the limitation of the field of inquiry to the fact of the politico-cultural pre-eminence of a specific social group at a particular point in time. Rather, the expression also simultaneously refers to the process by which the hegemony of the bourgeois class is reproduced on a daily basis while being altered, extended, retracted or weakened in that process through the struggle with rival hegemonic projects.

The key to hegemonic reproduction is the *educational relationship* we discussed in Chapter 2; there we saw that Gramsci does not take this relationship to be reducible or limited to the site of the school or to traditional questions of schooling. Instead, as Gramsci writes, 'this form of relationship exists throughout society as a whole and for every individual relative to other individuals. It exists between intellectual and non-intellectual sections of the population, between the rulers and the ruled, elites and their followers, leaders [*dirigenti*]

---

[12]We can note that Gramsci's notion of the 'hegemonic apparatus' served as a direct inspiration for Louis Althusser's article of 1970 in which his influential theory of 'ideological State apparatuses' (ISAs) is developed; see Louis Althusser, 'Idéologie et appareils idéologiques d'État', *La Pensée*, 151 (1970), pp. 3–38. On the difficult issue of the intellectual relationship between Gramsci and Althusser, see Buci-Glucksmann, *Gramsci and the State* and Pierre Macherey, '*Verum et factum*: les enjeux d'une philosophie de la *praxis* et le débat Althusser-Gramsci', in: Stathis Kouvelakis and Vincent Charbonier (eds), *Sartre, Lukács, Althusser: Des marxistes en philosophie* (Paris: Presses Universitaires de France, 2005), pp. 143–55.

and led, the vanguard and the body of the army. Every relationship of "hegemony" is necessarily an educational relationship'.[13]

We have already seen that time and again the central individual political actor in Gramsci's thought is the intellectual, and in particular the organic intellectual of the Communist Party, and this is certainly the case in Gramsci's analysis of the educational relationship. Embedded in civil society, the intellectual must work tirelessly on the 'matter' of common sense in order to introduce and to disseminate through common sense the philosophy of praxis. This educational work opens the way to a mass revolutionary engagement with the philosophy of praxis on the theoretical level and with the practice of the Communist Party. To the ruling educational relationship that accompanies and conditions bourgeois hegemony the proletariat must, for Gramsci, struggle to counterpose an original counterhegemonic project founded on the enactment of this new educational relationship.[14]

What we might call 'education towards hegemony', referring both to the process of reforming common sense and to the proletariat's self-training in the exercising of hegemony, entails for Gramsci a fundamental principle: the overcoming of *eco-corporatist* demands in order to reach the *ethical-political* plane. These key terms of Gramsci's thinking on hegemony need to be unpacked carefully. By 'eco-corporatist' Gramsci means a group ambition that is limited to particular economic interests. Gramsci uses 'ethical-political' to designate the situation when eco-corporatist demands have been transformed into a universalistic outlook that takes into account the complex interrelations of the interests of a group with the demands and aspirations of the other groups in society – and in particular those groups that could stand in an auxiliary relation to a potentially hegemonic group. It is, of course, such a universalistic political outlook that must characterize any hegemonic or national-popular political project.

It can further be noted that the eco-corporatist cycle can, according to Gramsci, be itself divided into two stages. The first stage in this cycle is the defence of a given job or station and

---

[13] Q10II§44; *SPN*, p. 350.
[14] Entwistle, *Conservative Schooling for Radical Politics*.

the promotion of interests that are directly attached to a particular economic activity. This stage corresponds to the defence of the interests of the banker, miner, or metalworker taken as a specific occupation within society. The second stage of the cycle involves the promotion of *class-based* economic interests, namely the interests of the bourgeois class or the working class. The passage from the first to the second stage represents, in Gramsci's view, a process of *distancing* the interests of a group from particularism or localism, but he also asserts that this dynamic of universalization must be extended even further in order for a class to build a hegemonic project. In his 1926 *Alcuni temi* essay, he writes, 'The proletariat, in order to become capable as a class of governing, must strip itself of every residue of corporatism, every syndicalist prejudice and incrustation.'[15] Put differently, in order to claim hegemony the working class must learn genuinely to embody the people as a whole. Only then will the proletariat reach what Gramsci calls the 'sphere of hegemony and ethical-political relations'.[16]

Gramsci takes the term 'ethical-political' from Croce, using it to signal the fact of 'reaching beyond' the economism in which the eco-corporatist state of mind remains unavoidably stuck. For Gramsci, the dynamic of universalization required to move from eco-corporatist demands to the ethical-political plane implies, importantly, the possibility of a new *ethical State*. This, for Gramsci, would be a State that, like Machiavelli's centaur, is able to work both in the 'human' realm of morals and consent and with the 'animal' means of naked force. As Gramsci writes, positioning the educational relation as central to the production of the ethical State, 'the State must be conceived of as an "educator", in as much as it tends precisely to create a new type or level of civilisation'.[17] Moreover, he contends:

> the most reasonable and concrete thing that can be said about the ethical State, the cultural State, is this: every State is

---

[15] *SPWII*, p. 448.
[16] Q13§18; *SPN*, p. 167.
[17] Q13§11; *SPN*, p. 247.

ethical in as much as one of its most important functions is to raise the great mass of the population to a particular cultural and moral level…. The school as a positive educative function, and the courts as a repressive and negative educative function, are the most important State activities in this sense.[18]

Thus, we can see that the educational relationship defines the ethical State and as a result the dynamic of hegemonic reproduction penetrates the whole social body. The bourgeois ethical State, then, is the one that attempts to justify morally and to put into practice universalistic principles in the political realm (such as civil and political rights) without questioning the economic contradiction between capital and labour. The project of creating a proletarian ethical State as a hegemonic alternative with which all the popular elements of society are called to identify themselves must be based on enacting 'scission' (see Chapter 3) vis-à-vis this bourgeois historic bloc.

Hegemonic consciousness as catharsis

In order to realize the ambition of constructing a proletarian ethical State that can act as a hegemonic alternative to the existing bourgeois ethical State, the revolutionary social class must, according to Gramsci, experience the realization of its hegemonic potential. In order to realize this collective potential the individual members of the revolutionary class must achieve *self-consciousness* through sudden moments of self-recognition. In other words, it is necessary for a mutation of class consciousness to come about. Specifically, the change in class consciousness required must correspond to the passage from the eco-corporatist stage to the ethical-political plane. Gramsci sees this process as psychological as much as political, and terms it *catharsis* – a term borrowed from Aristotle's *Poetics* (c. 335 BCE) that suggests Gramsci sees this change as a moment of rare intensity resulting

---

[18]Q8§179; *SPN*, p. 258.

in the intellectual liberation of the subject. Through this process the subject of the process comes to understand that his or her economic demands are not enough in themselves and that they must instead be inscribed within a wider and more encompassing political project. Crucially, Gramsci concludes, the members of the proletariat ready themselves to construct and govern the ethical State only through such a process:

> Critical understanding of self takes place... through a struggle of political 'hegemonies' and of opposing directions, first in the ethical field and then in that of politics proper, in order to arrive at the working out at a higher level of one's own conception of reality. Consciousness of being part of a particular hegemonic force (that is to say, political consciousness) is the first stage towards a further progressive self-consciousness in which theory and practice will finally be one.[19]

We can recognize here the centrality of Gramsci's problematic of knowledge to his thinking on the relationship between class consciousness and self-awareness on the part of individual members of a class. This is a key stage in the process of self-knowledge that comes from the Socratic injunction to 'know thyself' (Chapter 4). A process of *catharsis* is therefore for Gramsci the catalyst of the revolution of common sense whereby the popular classes seize on and take possession of the knowledge that is created by the philosophy of praxis. This knowledge, specifically, sheds light on social contradictions by historicizing them while indicating to each individual his or her place in society and the very history of those social contradictions. It is at the point at which this knowledge – of the historical character of social contradictions and the inherent mutability of the social forms currently embodying those contradictions – has been spread through the members of the revolutionary classes that they are in a position to translate theory into 'critical-practical activity' or praxis (see Chapter 4).

---

[19] Q11§12; *SPN*, p. 333.

The historical stages of hegemony

The pre-hegemonic State

Hegemony is thus for Gramsci a truly multidimensional concept. It serves to denote not just the political leadership of a social group, but also the strategy of alliance vis-à-vis the auxiliary group or groups, the symbiosis of coercion and consent as the fundamental mechanics of power, the recasting of the ideological landscape and of cultural life, the formulation, expression and construction of a political project in a universalistic and 'ethical' form, an original educational relationship and the moral and cognitive mutation of consciousness.

The implications of the theory of hegemony are, accordingly, exceptionally wide and numerous. However, it is also important to bear in mind that Gramsci developed his theory without ever losing sight of concrete history. We have already mentioned the historical events of the *Risorgimento*, the French Revolution and the October Revolution, analyses of which are central to Gramsci's thought. In this section we try to illustrate the trajectory of hegemony in a more synoptic way, interpreting it as developed implicitly throughout the overall movement of Gramsci's thought in the *Prison Notebooks*. In this historical trajectory we can identify the key moments of the pre-hegemonic State of the medieval commune, the hegemony of the bourgeoisie and the hegemony of the proletariat in a communist society (or what Gramsci calls the 'regulated society').

Gramsci is particularly interested in the Italian medieval commune as a particular type of political unit that represents the very antithesis of the bourgeois hegemony of his time. On the subject of the commune, he writes, 'It is necessary to determine what significance the "State" had in the Communal State: a limited "corporative" significance'.[20] In the Middle Ages the communal city was thus for Gramsci the direct expression of particular economic interests as no social group was able to 'universalise' itself in the framework of a successful hegemonic project. Thus Gramsci explains that in the medieval case:

---

[20]Q5§123; *SPN*, p. 54n4.

The State was, in a certain sense, a mechanical bloc of social groups, often of different race. Within the circle of political-military compression, which was only exercised harshly at certain moments, the subaltern groups had a life of their own, institutions of their own, etc., and sometimes these institutions had State functions which made of the State a federation of social groups with disparate functions not subordinated in any way.[21]

The notion of a 'federation of social groups' suggests a relatively static collection of social categories between which a central authority then acts as a more or less brutal arbiter. To this extent, pre-modern political society tends to leave social stratification unaffected since it does not embody a radical transformative project with the ambition of overturning existing social relations.

Bourgeois hegemony

The bourgeoisie is for Gramsci the first social class in history to embrace such a transformative ambition of upturning the social relations with which it finds itself initially confronted. Thus Gramsci sees that the bourgeoisie politically expressed its newly acquired place of pre-eminence in the economic realm in the 1688 'Glorious Revolution' in England; a century later it was also the bourgeoisie that was the motor force behind the French Revolution. The bourgeoisie was also able to institute economic liberalism, secure political and civil rights, develop the modern State and ultimately to uproot the surviving relics of feudalism and absolutism in Western Europe. As Marx and Engels famously put it as early as 1848 in Chapter 1 of *The Communist Manifesto*, 'The bourgeoisie cannot exist without constantly revolutionizing the instruments of production, and thereby the relations of production, and with them the whole relations of society. Conservation of the old modes of production in unaltered form, was, on the contrary, the first condition of existence for all earlier industrial classes.'[22]

---

[21] Q25§4; *SPN*, p. 54n4.
[22] Karl Marx and Frederick Engels, *Marx Engels Collected Works*, volume 6 (London: Lawrence and Wishart, 1976), p. 487.

In the *Prison Notebooks* Gramsci attempts to understand the implications of this political project through the prism of his theory of hegemony. He asserts, 'The modern State substitutes for the mechanical bloc of social groups their subordination to the active hegemony of the directive and dominant group, hence abolishes certain autonomies, which nevertheless are reborn in other forms, as parties, trade unions, cultural associations.'[23] He continues:

> The revolution which the bourgeois class has brought into the conception of law, and hence into the function of the State, consists especially in the will to conform (hence ethicity of the law and of the State). The previous ruling classes were essentially conservative in the sense that they did not tend to construct an organic passage from the other classes into their own, i.e. to enlarge their class sphere 'technically' and ideologically: their conception was that of a closed caste. The bourgeois class poses itself as an organism in continuous movement, capable of absorbing the entire society, assimilating it to its own cultural and economic level.[24]

Gramsci thus follows Marx and Engels in recognizing that the historical force specific to bourgeois civilization, which constitutes the spring of its development and the source of its resilience, is its dynamic capacity for perpetual movement. The hegemony of the bourgeoisie has thus manifested itself in multiple forms, such as the Jacobin revolution in France, the Victorian era in Britain, or the *Risorgimento* in Italy, and each form is for Gramsci tied to the specific economic and political conditions that obtained in that national context at that point in time.

Furthermore we can note that Gramsci sees all national societies as continually experiencing processes of internal recomposition and contestation. The 'passive revolution' enacted through molecular processes of incorporation is the essential manner, for Gramsci, through which the phenomenon of hegemonic recomposition

---

[23] Q25§4; *SPN*, p. 54n4.
[24] Q8§2; *SPN*, p. 260.

occurs.[25] The bourgeois political order is never as strong, or as assured of its own future, as when its material resources and its cultural and moral power of attraction allow it to assimilate a great number of disparate social elements and to make them its auxiliaries. 'Scission', as the very opposite of 'incorporation', is conversely the major threat hanging over the social power of the bourgeoisie. To repeat, it is the scission of the working class vis-à-vis the established order, as actuated by catharsis and by the revolution of common sense, that marks the birth of a rival hegemonic project.

Between the extremes of maximal incorporation into the established order and effective scission in opposition to it, it is possible to identify various stages of what we might call *hegemonic disintegration*. On the subject of interwar society, Gramsci writes, 'The bourgeois class is "saturated": it not only does not expand – it starts to disintegrate; it not only does not assimilate new elements, it loses part of itself (or at least its losses are enormously more numerous than its assimilations).' Thus 'the conception of the State as pure force is returned to'.[26]

It should be borne in mind that for Gramsci the aftermath of the First World War triggered a profound 'crisis of authority' on the European continent and especially in Italy (see Chapter 3). The parliamentary political system born out of the *Risorgimento* would, of course, not survive this crisis: as the social strata that used to be auxiliary to parliamentarianism (i.e. the urban and rural petty bourgeoisie) withdrew their support and the subaltern classes started to display their antagonistic potential, the system fell into fascism in the early 1920s. The 'Caesarism' of Mussolini is thus the symptom of a hegemonic system that has fallen into a 'decadent' state.[27] In the years following the March on Rome, the fascist regime then began to substitute coercion for consent and dictatorship for hegemony.

---

[25] Thomas, 'Modernity as "Passive Revolution"'.

[26] Q8§260; *SPN*, p. 260.

[27] Evelyne Buissière, 'Gramsci et le problème du chef charismatique', in: André Tosel (ed.), *Modernité de Gramsci: Actes du colloque franco-italien de Besançon, 23–25 novembre 1989* (Paris: Les Belles Lettres, 1992), pp. 207–22.

From proletarian hegemony to the 'regulated society'

Although in the mid-1920s Italian Communists – including, as we have seen in Chapter 1, Gramsci himself – were apt to see in fascism only a last-ditch and reactionary embodiment of bourgeois power before the workers' revolution, Gramsci's conception of revolution deepened during his time in prison as it evolved in conjunction with his development of the concepts of war of position and hegemony.

We have already seen (in Chapter 3) that the war of position tends to relativize – as opposed to negate – an understanding of revolution as 'rupture' or as a 'grand soir' that embodies a single radical break-up of existing conditions. The conquest or seizure of the State – that is, the assault on bourgeois political society – of the war of movement can only follow a long-term hegemonic struggle of an ideological and cultural character carried out on the terrain of civil society. Revolution as a single event is then reconceptualized as the completion of a longer process, as opposed to a single and isolated cataclysm.

The theory of hegemony allows us to think further beyond the revolution as rupture: in the *Prison Notebooks* Gramsci asserts that the communist hegemonic project will have to continue *after the conquest of the State*. Thus he notes that a social group 'becomes dominant when it exercises power, but even if it holds it firmly in its grasp, it must continue to "lead" as well'.[28]

Having seized the repressive apparatuses of political society the working class will have to constrain itself to rule the post-revolutionary society through consent as much as coercion. The contrast between Lenin and Gramsci on the topic of hegemony can be stressed once again: for the former hegemony is a means to the end of seizing the State, whereas the latter sees hegemony as the essential way in which power itself is exerted and operates.

It might therefore be asked whether it is as a consequence impossible to think anything *beyond* hegemony, or whether the hegemonic form of power can be overcome in the process of

---

[28] Q19§24; *SPN*, pp. 57–8.

the movement of history. It is important to bear in mind that in the tradition of Marxist theory 'communism' does not describe the social situation the day after revolution; instead, a transitional period between the fall of capitalism and the reaching of communism is to be expected (often termed 'socialism'). In the few (very brief) of Marx's writings in which he addresses it explicitly, communism tends to be described in terms of the free organization of work by the producers, with communist society appearing at the end of a process of the gradual disappearance, or 'withering away', of the State. These are perhaps the few fragments of Marx's thought that seem to be utopian, with communism depicted as an almost anarchic state.

Gramsci devotes only a few brief passages of the *Prison Notebooks* to the communist stage of history, which he calls the 'regulated society' to escape prison censorship. Thus he contends Marx 'initiates intellectually an historical epoch which will last in all probability for centuries, that is, until the disappearance of political society and the coming of a regulated society. Only then will his conception of the world be superseded, when the conception of necessity is superseded by the conception of freedom'.[29] Communism as a historical prospect is thus so remote for Gramsci that it might be 'centuries' away. It might be possible to consider this cautiousness of Gramsci's regarding the proximity of communism as a laudable sign of realism on Gramsci's part.[30] Nevertheless, we can probably discern a note of utopianism in Gramsci's contention taken as a whole, and one that seems to run against Gramsci's deep historicist convictions.

Elsewhere in the *Prison Notebooks* Gramsci writes in relation to the State and regulated society: 'It is possible to imagine the coercive element of the State withering away by degrees, as ever-more conspicuous elements of regulated society (or ethical State or civil society) make their appearance.'[31] Here the 'regulated society' is defined in reference to the Gramscian couplet of civil society and political society such that the regulated society corresponds to the

---

[29] Q7§33; *SPN*, p. 382.
[30] Losurdo, *'Comunismo critico'*.
[31] Q6§88; *SPN*, p. 263.

suppression or disappearance of political society. The expression 'regulated society' might suggest the centrality of a rule or regulation, but we can see here that Gramsci intends it to be a rule consented to by the political community. It thus converges with the notion of 'free organisation' as the central principle of communism. In a different register, we might conclude, it is at the stage at which education mutates into 'self-education' that external constraints to individual and collective development begin to disappear.

PART THREE

Applications

6

Thinking through Gramsci in Political Theory: Left/Right and the Critical Analysis of Common Sense

Introduction

At this point it might be useful to summarize the argument so far. In Part One we gave a brief overview of Gramsci's biography and his intellectual development, and discussed some of his most important pre-prison writing. In Part Two we offered a reading of Gramsci's thought, particularly as developed in his *Prison Notebooks*. We structured our reading of Gramsci around the concepts of culture, politics, philosophy and hegemony. Specifically, we contended that the concept of hegemony forms the basis of Gramsci's account of history and political strategy, and that it is important to understand his other key concepts in terms of their relation to hegemony. In our reading, it is necessary to place Gramsci's thought in the context of his understanding of Marxism; crucially, the parts of his thought that may at first appear disparate and unconnected are in fact tightly joined together as different but complementary aspects of a unified project of the renewal of historical materialism.

In Part Three we attempt to illustrate what we take to be Gramsci's distinctive method of social analysis, namely the development of new concepts and theoretical insights from historical inquiry. It is therefore necessary to focus on two relatively narrow case studies; in this sense the aim of Part Two to provide a systematic account of the basic structure of Gramsci's thought is replaced with the aspiration of Part Three to show what 'thinking through' Gramsci today might look like in practice. As a consequence of this change in the aims of the argument, we have often found it necessary to move from an exposition of Gramsci's concepts to a detailed examination of historical reality. In both this chapter and Chapter 7, therefore, we depart some distance from the reading given in Part Two, but we aim to do so following a consistently Gramscian methodology.

We hope that the two case studies of Part Three – the notion of Left/Right as part of the 'common sense' of modern politics and the spread of neo-liberalism in Britain and France in the 1980s – also support two further arguments. First, that Gramsci's thought is useful and usable in the twenty-first century, even in fields as traditionally distant as Political Theory and Political Economy. Second, that Gramsci's thought is unfinished but it is also flexible. By this we intend to mean that it is necessary but possible to supplement the conceptual framework that Gramsci developed in his *Prison Notebooks* with new concepts that emerge from the empirical inquiries that take his concepts as their starting points. Accordingly, in this chapter we propose the concept of political narrative as a way to develop Gramsci's understanding of common sense, while in Chapter 7 we suggest a distinction between coherent and split historic blocs as a development of one of Gramsci's most important but difficult concepts.

The present chapter is structured so as to develop what we take to be a possible Gramscian methodology for the investigation of *senso comune*, or common sense. This is one of the central concepts of Gramsci's philosophy (see Chapter 4). The argument of this chapter develops through an extended examination of the history, meaning and function of the commonsensical assertion that 'politics is about a battle between a Left and a Right', which we summarize as 'Left/Right'. As we will see, this is a widespread but deceptively complex way of 'making sense' of the social field of politics. We analyse Left/Right along a number of dimensions, then, which we take to represent the steps in a Gramscian methodology for the analysis of given pieces or 'fragments' of *senso comune*. First, we contextualize Left/Right by situating it in relation to everyday life and seeing how it might 'make sense' of social life outside of the political sphere. Second, we 'historicize' Left/Right by tracing its history and origins. Third, we analyse the formal and linguistic characteristics of the Left/Right metaphor. Fourth, we attempt to uncover the 'conception of the world' contained in Left/ Right; in other words we look at the understanding of politics on which Left/Right is premised. Fifth, and most tentatively, we take Left/Right as a story about politics, and relate it to class struggle as a competing narrative of political conflict. We develop the concept of 'political narrative' to capture how commonsensical stories about politics gain some of their efficacy not by being true or false but by being compelling or 'successful' narratives (according, that is, to the criteria we might want to begin to think about for the assessment of the success of narratives). We would propose that our methodology could be used by those who would wish to investigate fragments of *senso comune* in other contexts (such as assertions about gender relations or our relation to the environment).

The focus on Left/Right in this chapter is justified, we would assert, because it stands as a fragment of common sense like any other. If it is possible to show how complex and important is the ideological work that it performs, then this opens the possibility that other fragments of common sense might be susceptible to similar sorts of analyses. It is also important for us to make it clear to the reader that existing studies of Gramsci's thinking on *senso comune* focus on three fundamentally theoretical tasks: establishing the place of common sense in Gramsci's wider revolutionary project; theorizing the relationship of common sense and the concept of ideology; and asserting the formal and abstract characteristics of common sense.[1] What is required truly to follow up and extend Gramsci's researches on *senso comune* is for us to 'get our hands dirty' by analysing common sense *as it actually exists* in all its contradictoriness and complexity, rather than theorizing it in the abstract. It is in this spirit of following Gramsci's thought that we attempt to develop some pointers for what Gramsci might have called the 'critical analysis of the philosophy of common sense'.[2]

Contextualizing common sense: Left/Right in politics and everyday life

We select 'Left/Right' as the fragment of common sense to analyse in this chapter because it is one of the most widely held and easily recognized common sense accounts of politics. Research in political sociology finds consistently high rates of European voters recognizing Left/Right and placing themselves on the scale.[3] This result is also repeated, with variation, across the world.[4] In one study, almost all of the 1,500 experts – academics, political analysts, think

---

[1] See Kate Crehan, 'Gramsci's Concept of Common Sense: A Useful Concept for Anthropologists?', *Journal of Modern Italian Studies*, 16:2 (2011), pp. 273–87; Landy, *Film, Politics and Gramsci*; Guido Liguori, 'Common Sense in Gramsci', in: Joseph Francese (ed.), *Perspectives on Gramsci: Politics, Culture and Social Theory* (London: Routledge, 2009), pp. 112–33; José Nun, 'Elements for a Theory of Democracy: Gramsci and Common Sense', *Boundary 2*, 14:3 (1986), pp. 197–229; Andrew Robinson, 'Towards an Intellectual Reformation: The Critique of Common Sense and the Forgotten Revolutionary Project of Gramscian Theory', *Critical Review of International Social and Political Philosophy*, 8:4 (2005), pp. 469–81. A partial exception from this pattern is Evan Watkins's 'Gramscian Politics and Capitalist Common Sense', *Rethinking Marxism*, 11:3 (1999), pp. 83–90. There Watkins attempts to investigate the common sense of economic relations in the United States in late 1990s, although he does not look either to analyse in detail the common sense he outlines, or to develop a systematic methodology for the analysis of common sense.

[2] Q11§13; *SPN*, p. 419.

[3] Peter Mair, 'Left-Right Orientations', in: Russell Dalton and Hans-Dieter Klingemann (eds), *The Oxford Handbook of Political Behaviour* (Oxford: Oxford University Press, 2007), pp. 206–22.

[4] Russell Dalton, 'Social Modernization and the End of Ideology Debate: Patterns of Ideological Polarization', *Japanese Journal of Political Science*, 7:1 (2006), pp. 1–22.

tank workers and so on – asked found it possible to apply Left/Right to the parties in their country.[5] A notion of Left/Right is one of the most intuitively accessible and pervasive accounts of the political universe, and has been described as the equivalent of 'political Esperanto'.[6] It is a commonplace political item: 'few notions, indeed, are as ubiquitous as the idea of a division between the left and the right in politics'.[7] Thinking historically, Left/Right has been called the 'great bipolar' of Western European politics prior to 1989 and the 'grand dichotomy' of twentieth-century political thought.[8] As Bobbio puts it, Left and Right are 'two antithetical terms which for more than two centuries have been used habitually to signify the contrast between the ideologies and movements which divide the world of political thought and action'.[9] Finally, at the aggregate level, we might conclude that 'left and right have defined the broad space of political antagonism in modern Western societies'.[10] In political sociology, the model of Left/Right is 'an enduring element in comparative analysis'.[11] It is not an overstatement to say that Left/Right is one of the most common ways of making sense of politics.

However, it is not the case that Left/Right is the *only* possible way of making sense of politics. We must remember that common sense is a heterogeneous mass of propositions about a given domain of social life, and is undergoing constant change (see Chapter 4). In particular, Left/Right might have been seriously questioned since

---

[5] Kenneth Benoit and Michael Laver, *Party Policy in Modern Democracies* (London: Routledge, 2009).
[6] Juan Laponce, *Left and Right: The Topography of Political Perceptions* (Toronto: University of Toronto Press, 1981).
[7] Alain Noël and Jean-Philippe Thérien, *Left and Right in Global Politics* (Cambridge: Cambridge University Press, 2008), p. 10.
[8] Ferenc Feher, '1989 and the Deconstruction of Political Monism', *Thesis Eleven*, 1:42 (1995), pp. 87–112; Steven Lukes, 'Epilogue: The Grand Dichotomy of the Twentieth Century', in: Terence Ball and Richard Bellamy (eds), *The Cambridge History of Twentieth-Century Political Thought* (Cambridge: Cambridge University Press, 2003), pp. 602–26.
[9] Norberto Bobbio, *Left and Right: The Significance of a Political Distinction* (Cambridge: Polity Press, 1996), p. 1.
[10] Steve Bastow and James Martin, *Third Way Discourse: European Ideologies in the Twentieth Century* (Edinburgh: Edinburgh University Press, 2003), pp. 23–4.
[11] Mair, 'Left-Right Orientations', p. 206.

1989.[12] Today, Left/Right might be challenged by an understanding of politics that promotes a kind of apathy or detachment on the basis that 'there is no alternative' to liberal capitalism.[13] Alternatively, there might be an important commonsensical understanding that politics is a realm dominated by venal, unscrupulous and hypocritical politicians who look to con rather than represent the electorate. Nevertheless, Left/Right is a widely recognized understanding of politics, and plausibly forms part of contemporary common sense.

The first step in the 'critical analysis' of Left/Right as a fragment of common sense, as following the methodology specified above, is to ground Left/Right as a part of the contested common sense of politics in the wider context of other ways of making sense of the world using a spatial metaphor based on a split between a left and a right.

The significance of the division of reality into a left and a right extends far beyond their usage in modern politics. The design theorist David Crow, in his *Left to Right: The Cultural Shift from Words to Pictures* (2006), presents Left/Right as the key dichotomy through which to understand contemporary visual culture in the bold red double-page spread with which his book opens (see Table 6.1).[14]

Crow contends that we are witnessing a societal transition from his list of 'Left' characteristics to those he associates with 'Right', in much the same way we read English text from left to right. We may disagree with Crow's understanding of visual culture in late capitalism, but his choice of presenting the transition through the heuristic of Left/Right suggests the assumption of a deep familiarity with the symbolic division on the part of his readers. Left/Right here provides the master division relevant to the explanation

---

[12] Schwarzmantel argues that the period in which Left/Right was the dominant model of politics can be clearly identified: the 'age of ideology' from the revolutions of 1776 and 1789 to the end of modernity. The division of political conflict along Left/Right lines is thus related to difficult and important questions of the periodization of contemporary history, and in particular whether we have reached a period beyond the modern in which traditional identities and maps such as those based on the Left and the Right need to be discarded. See John Schwarzmantel, *The Age of Ideology: Political Ideologies from the American Revolution to Postmodern Times* (Basingstoke: Macmillan, 1998).

[13] See Mark Fisher, *Capitalist Realism* (London: Zer0 books, 2009).

[14] David Crow, *Left to Right: The Cultural Shift from Words to Pictures* (London: Thames and Hudson, 2006).

Table 6.1 Associations of Left and Right in visual culture

Left	Right
Word	Image
Male	Female
Verbal	Non-Verbal
Analytical	Holistic
Adam	Eve
Apollo	Dionysus
Yang	Yin
A.D.	B.C.
Science	Sorcery
Page	Screen

Source: Crow, *Left to Right.*

of visual culture in whose terms other divisions – such as between Apollo and Dionysus or Page and Screen – can be understood. We may also disagree with Crow's choice of left and right categories; perhaps, though, this disagreement is only possible due to the strong collective set of associations between left or right and a set of other concepts or ideas.

Indeed, anthropologists have long been interested in the symbolic division between left and right. The recognized starting point of anthropologists' interest in Left/Right was Robert Hertz's 1909 essay 'The Pre-eminence of the Right Hand'. Hertz died in the First World War, and much of the influence of the essay in Anglophone anthropology came through its promotion by E. E. Evans-Pritchard while the latter held the Chair of Social Anthropology at the University of Oxford. Hertz's essay pointed to three elements of relevance here. First, Left/Right was seen to be virtually a cultural universal: a dualistic spatial classificatory metaphor, with *symbolic* differences between the left and the right, was pointed out by Hertz and found by every subsequent anthropologist who has searched for it. More recent studies have if anything extended this finding, with Left/Right seeming to be applicable to virtually all areas of social life and research. James Hall, in an interesting account, traces the history of Left/Right dualism in the history of Western art, noting that especially since the Renaissance there has been a consistent and clear connection between left and the overtly or 'femininely' emotional, perhaps as a consequence of the belief of the physiological connection of the left side to the heart.[15]

Second, in Hertz's account – and again as found by later anthropologists – right is privileged over left. The political theorist Steven Lukes interprets the anthropological evidence as suggesting 'the pre-eminence of the right is virtually a cultural universal'.[16] In Needham's fascinating account of 'Right and Left in Nyoro Symbolic Classification', included in a collection of responses to Hertz's essay, we can see the sheer range of Left/Right associations that concern many dimensions of everyday life, as shown in Table 6.2.[17]

Other contributions to the collection of responses to Hertz's essay also find a Left/Right symbolic classification to be important, among other cases, in Southern India, China, Africa and Greek philosophy.[18] As McManus puts it, 'Wherever one looks, on any continent, in any historical period or in any culture, right and left have their symbolic associations and always it is right that is good and left that is bad.'[19]

Third, Hertz also argues that the ultimate root of Left/Right symbolic classifications is religious. Three examples may be given from the Bible: in Matthew 25.33, God sets the sheep on his right hand, with the goats on his left; in Matthew 26.64, the association is made between sitting on the right hand of God and power; and, in Genesis 1.28, God makes Eve out of Adam's *left* side. While the assessment of the religious origins of Left/Right is not a key

---

[15] James Hall, *The Sinister Side: How Left-Right Symbolism Shaped Western Art* (Oxford: Oxford University Press, 2008).

[16] Lukes, 'Epilogue', p. 603.

[17] See Rodney Needham (ed.), *Right and Left: Essays in Dual Symbolic Classification* (Chicago: University of Chicago Press, 1973).

[18] See Rodney Needham, 'Right and Left in Nyoro Symbolic Classification', in: Rodney Needham (ed.), *Right and Left: Essays in Dual Symbolic Classification* (Chicago: University of Chicago Press, 1973), pp. 299–341.

[19] Chris McManus, *Left Hand, Right Hand* (London: Weidenfeld and Nicolson, 2002), p. 39.

Table 6.2 Associations of Left and Right in Nyoro society

Left	Right
Hated	Normal
Girl	Boy
Cooking	Brewing
Woman	Man
Subject	Chief
Bad omen	Good omen
Hunter	Owner of land
Sickness	Health
Sorrow	Joy
Barrenness	Fertility
Poverty	Wealth
Earth	Heaven
Black	White
Danger	Security
Death	Life
Evil	Good
Impurity	Purity
Odd	Even
Soft	Hard
Diviner	Princess
Mystical office	Political rank
Illegitimacy	Legitimacy
Twin birth	Normal birth
Chickens	Cattle
Hunting	Milking
Naked	Clothed
Nature	Culture
Disorder	Order
Anomalous	Classified
Long hair	Shaven hair

Source: Needham, 'Nyoro Symbolic Classification'.

focus here, this reinforces the point that Left/Right as a *political* classification only emerged in the modern period, so we must be aware that other classificatory systems may have existed before it and indeed competed with it as an heuristic through which to understand politics.

In assessing this evidence, McManus talks of 'a universal human desire to treat left and right as symbolically different'.[20] However, following Gramsci, we might rightly be wary of claims to universal human traits. Nevertheless, the ubiquity of Left/Right and the pre-eminence of the right do seem to be robust findings. It seems sensible to follow Ignazi in concluding that

> the term Right displays both an amazing stability over time and large diffusion in the Indo-European languages; on the contrary, the term Left is highly unstable and undifferentiated.... Right is associated to positive adjectives such as honest, reliable, straight, even lively, to the juridical right and to political rights; while the term Left is linked with malicious, dangerous, unaccountable, untrustworthy, incapable, and even deathful.[21]

We might contextualize Left/Right as part of common sense in the following way: Left/Right as part of the common sense of contemporary politics is situated in the context of the presence of left/right frames in a wide variety of symbolic systems. In these systems, the right seems to be consistently privileged.

Historicizing common sense: Left/Right since the French Revolution

The second step in the methodology for investigating common sense that we are proposing here is to examine as closely as possible the origins and historical development of the individual fragment of common sense under investigation. Thus, in this section we trace

---

[20] Ibid., p. 17.
[21] Piero Ignazi, *Extreme Right Parties in Western Europe* (Oxford: Oxford University Press, 2003), p. 7.

the emergence of Left/Right as part of the common sense of politics. Again, we attempt to be illustrative rather than exhaustive in our account.

Left/Right is commonly thought to have entered political vocabulary in the context of the French Revolution. Importantly, the horizontal metaphor of Left/Right is contended to have replaced a *vertical* political metaphor that previously classified the estates hierarchically as the monarchy and nobility, the church, and the mass public. One historian traces the precise date of the establishment of the left–right divide to 28 August 1789, when the *Estates-General* – in session since May and by August a constituent assembly – began in Versailles to debate whether the king should have veto rights and consequently authority above that of the representatives of the people. Representatives in favour of the royal veto sat to the right of the speaker and those in opposition to the left.[22] Caute also highlights that in the debate over popular sovereignty, views on the structure of the legislature divided across Left/Right lines, with the Right – and Centre – favouring an upper chamber, and the Left opposing any hereditary element and calling for a single-chamber legislature.[23] Significantly for Ignazi, the horizontal 'spatial uni-dimensionality founded upon the Left-Right antinomy clearly identifies, at the moment of its foundation, a basic opposition: equality against privilege'.[24] Crucially, even at its moment of inception, the Left/Right metaphor represented a simplification of the actual state of political conflict. Similarly, we might argue in general that it is a simplification to say that the French Revolution was entirely reducible to a clash between equality and privilege. In the Constituent Assembly of 1789–91, we can in fact distinguish four primary groups which – although shifting positions on different issues – could be labelled the Right (Cazales, Maury), the Centre-Right (*Les Monarchiens*), the Centre-Left (Le Chapelier, Grégoire, Lafayette, Bailly) and the Extreme Left (Robespierre, Pétion de

---

[22] Alain de Benoist, 'The End of the Left-Right Dichotomy: The French Case', *Telos*, 1:10 (1995), pp. 73–89.
[23] David Caute, *The Left in Europe since 1789* (London: Weidenfeld and Nicolson, 1966), p. 26.
[24] Ignazi, *Extreme Right*, p. 8.

Villeneuve).[25] Left/Right was not, even at the point of its origin, a way of thinking about politics that totally avoided simplification. It seems likely that simplifying complex reality is one of the characteristic functions of common sense understandings of any social phenomenon.

It seems possible, though, that the 'birth and sporadic use' of the Left/Right metaphor was a 'false start' because 'although it distinguished opposed political groupings in the legislatures (initially those for and against the king's suspensive veto), the predominant preoccupation during this period was to abolish all political divisions'.[26] Instead, argues Lukes, its 'true birth dates from the restoration of the French monarchy following the defeat of Napoleon, and in particular from the parliamentary session of 1819–20', when the terms Left and Right entered into political practice as distinguishing liberals from ultras and deriving from the memory of 1789.[27] Further, according to Marcel Gauchet, 'The 1819–1820 session of parliament marks one of the great moments in the history of political vocabulary. The whole lexical system was apparently clarified and consecrated at this time. Newspapers, pamphlets, and private correspondence all confirm that the terms *left* and *right* now began to be used not just in isolated instances but in a consistent and regular fashion.'[28] Thus, the entry of Left/Right into the common sense of French politics is likely to have occurred considerably later than the time of the French Revolution, when perhaps it identified a division within the political elite but was not yet widely used by the French people to make sense of politics.

Already, then, at the time of its entry into common sense the main use of Left/Right was to call up a previous political conflict, and to present, in a stylized fashion, the protagonists of one debate in the terms of an older one. The solidification of the Left/Right framework as a common sense understanding of politics became widespread

---

[25] See Caute, *The Left in Europe*, p. 26.

[26] Lukes, 'Epilogue', p. 606.

[27] Ibid., p. 606.

[28] Marcel Gauchet, 'Right and Left', in: Pierre Nora (ed.), *Realms of Memory: Rethinking the French Past, Vol. 1: Conflicts and Divisions*, translated by Arthur Goldhammer (New York: Columbia University Press, 1996), p. 248.

in French politics with the increasing importance of class in the course of the nineteenth century.[29] Critically, for Lukes 'it was with the achievement of universal manhood suffrage in France in 1848 that Left and Right entered mass politics, applying not merely to the topography of the parliamentary chambers but now as categories of political identity, spreading rapidly across the parliamentary systems of the world'.[30]

We can thus trace the origin of Left/Right as a political metaphor to French politics in the mid-nineteenth century, in which the previous political division of the French Revolution was invoked to make sense of the conflict then occurring. The diffusion of Left/Right varied cross-nationally over the course of the nineteenth century, except in Britain where Left/Right terminology continued to be outweighed by the Whig–Tory dichotomy.[31] Indeed, Brittan notes that the terms 'Left' and 'Right' were first used in the British context as late as 1837, and even then did not gain general currency until the 1920s.[32] In short, the most we can conclude in the absence of detailed national studies is that Left/Right only became decisively established in Western Europe with the spread and increasing salience of the class cleavage, and even then not unproblematically. It would be interesting to trace the development of the language of Left/Right in the British context, and particularly its relation to the previously dominant Whig–Tory dichotomy.

Even the brief account given here suggests that the common sense view that 'politics is about Left versus Right' has an important history, initially emerging in France in the nineteenth century to recall the earlier division of the French Revolution. Importantly, common sense, like all ways of thinking about society, is an inherently historical phenomenon – even if it might not immediately reveal its historicity. Starting to make an inventory of this history is an important step in the critical analysis of common sense.

---

[29]See Stefano Bartolini, *The Political Mobilization of the European Left, 1860–1980* (Cambridge: Cambridge University Press, 2000).
[30]Lukes, 'Epilogue', p. 606.
[31]Ignazi, *Extreme Right*, p. 5.
[32]Samuel Brittan, *Left or Right: The Bogus Dilemma* (London: Secker and Warburg, 1968), p. 38.

Analysing common sense:
The formal characteristics of
the Left/Right metaphor

Common sense, we would assert, must be taken seriously and investigated using the methods of close philosophical analysis in addition to attempts to historicize and contextualize it. Specifically, we can as a third step in the critical analysis of common sense investigate the language and the formal structure of the fragment of common sense under analysis, aiming to see how it constrains the understanding of the specific topic to which it refers.

The metaphor of Left/Right, at its most basic level, divides the horizontal dimension of space into at least the two categories of the 'left' side and the 'right' side. It has a number of consequent theoretical attributes. First, it is *symbolic* or 'abstract'. Second, it is *spatial*. Third, the space it refers to is *horizontal*. Fourth, particularly in the language of Left *versus* Right – one possible unpacking of Left/Right – a *conflictual* or at the least oppositional relationship is suggested. Fifth, Left and Right are assumed to be *mutually exclusive* categories. Sixth, Left/Right is flexible – or ambiguous – between positing a *spectrum* or a *binary division*. Finally, we might also ask whether the metaphor of Left/Right purports to apply to *all* aspects of political life since as a consequence of its symbolic nature there are no *formal* barriers to describing any political phenomenon in terms of Left/Right. It may in this sense be an 'exhaustive' description of political life. We address these points in turn below.

First, the metaphor of Left/Right is *abstract*, as it does not refer to specific beliefs or entities in the way that the dualism between, say, 'monarchism' and 'republicanism' does. The symbolic nature of Left/Right has three important consequences. First, we can see how there may be a way in which Left and Right can be thought to be mirror-image opposites. Republicanism is rarely put forward as the opposite or negation of monarchism; it does not simply mean 'no king or queen' but also the belief in the power of the people to govern themselves through a system of popular rule. Second, the terms Left and Right are sufficiently general to be applied to a wide variety of referents, as we observe in political life. Left and Right are ubiquitous, then, partly due to the lack of formal limitations or difficulties in their application to any argument, actor or issue. Third, and most complexly, the symbolic nature of Left and Right means that, for their use in politics, these terms have 'to acquire, to be filled with, concrete meanings'.[33] In other words, the framework of Left/Right is held by some theorists to be formally 'contentless', needing 'outside' political debates to give the division meaning. This contention is considerably complicated by the fact that Left/Right emerged in a specific historical context, and the terms Left and Right were from the very start associated with a set of positions held by French Left and Right in the late eighteenth century. The language of Left/Right emerged to describe a specific political conflict, and when it re-emerged during the Restoration it was on the basis of this intimate link with that conflict. The most that we can say, therefore, on the symbolic or abstract nature of the language of Left/Right is that it is a *formally* abstract metaphor, which the history of the past 200 years shows us has been associated with a historically shifting set of political situations that have given the words content. To put it precisely, the symbolic or abstract nature of the metaphor of Left/Right plausibly is 'filled in' by a relationship to the historically specific political conflict in the political system it is being used to describe.

Second, in addition to being abstract, the metaphor of Left/ Right is also *spatial*, in that it relates to a dimension of physical or hypothetical space. This distinguishes Left/Right from Red/White or Black/White as a common sense description of politics. Interestingly, Black/White might be thought to be a closer relative to Left/Right than Red/White in one sense: black and white are commonsensically thought of as opposites in a way that white and red are not. However, Red/White has historically been an important and evocative symbolic description of politics, most famously in the war between Trotsky's Red Army and the counter-revolutionary Whites in the aftermath of the Revolution. We can also compare Left/Right as a 'political

---

[33]Dieter Fuchs and Hans-Dieter Klingemann, 'The Left-Right Schema', in: M. Kent Jennings and Jan W. van Deth (eds), *Continuities in Political Actions* (Berlin: Walter de Gruyter, 1990), p. 206.

symbolic order', in Dyrberg's terms, to that of similarity/difference as a non-spatial metaphor.[34] Left/Right also, more subtly, presupposes some distance between Left and Right, on whatever dimension is being talked about: the space *between* Left and Right is created by difference between Left and Right in some relevant aspect. Otherwise, Left and Right would occupy the same location within the metaphor, rendering a specifically spatial metaphor redundant or confusing. Here, we can imagine scanning the seated representatives in the French Assembly – or another parliament – from Right to Left: one would see a clear and profound change in political 'positions' as corresponding to the seating positions.

Third, the space described by Left/Right is a *horizontal* plane. Alternative spatial metaphors that could be applied to politics include a metaphor of vertical space (such as of heaven and hell, up and down, or the three ordered estates preceding the French Revolutionary context), one of concentricity, one of proximity or distance, one that divides up space into an included and excluded area, or the overlapping boundaries of Venn diagrams. As Dyrberg notes, other spatial metaphors prominent in contemporary politics include centre/periphery and front/back.[35] Much has been made of the 'principle of parity' in which Left and Right appear to be placed on the same horizontal plane, and so seem to be equals in argumentation and political action.[36] The language of Left/Right, then, allows those using it to make claims about the nature of political conflict – should they choose to – since it contains within it what we might clumsily call 'democratic potential': it formally places two antagonists on a level horizontal plane.

Fourth, the language of Left *versus* Right also suggests a conflict, antagonism or competition between the two camps. Left versus Right suggests that an essential feature of politics is the split of opinion and action into two camps, and the conflict between these

---

[34] Torben Beck Dyrberg, 'The Democratic Ideology of Right-Left and Public Reason in Relation to Rawls's Political Liberalism', *Critical Review of International Social and Political Philosophy*, 8:2 (2005), pp. 161–76.
[35] Torben Beck Dyrberg, 'What Is Beyond Right/Left? The Case of New Labour', *Journal of Political Ideologies*, 14:2 (2009), pp. 133–53.
[36] Lukes, 'Epilogue'.

camps. It is an open question the extent to which a Left versus Right model implicitly leaves space for a ' ... versus Centre' addition.

Fifth, the language of Left/Right is also premised on the idea that Left and Right are *mutually exclusive* categories – simply put, Left/Right is not an appropriate metaphor if both Left and Right refer to the same thing. There is, in addition, an assumption that the mutual exclusivity of Left and Right will be durable over time or, in other words, that the metaphor will make sense tomorrow in the same way as it does today – that is, through the drawing of boundaries of mutual exclusivity.

Sixth, Left/Right can posit either a spectrum or a dichotomous division. In the former case, categories such as Centre, Centre-Right and Far-Right can be introduced as more precise gradations. This flexibility is one of the most useful aspects of Left/Right, since it can present a model with two fundamentally opposed sides, or with more nuanced positions within those sides as depending on the levels of disagreement over the core conflict.

Seventh and finally, it is worth noting that Left/Right may be put forward as an *exhaustive* description of politics; as a fragment of common sense it might be taken to apply to *everything* within politics. The ubiquity of Left/Right within the field of common sense about politics is likely, as noted above, to be related to its flexibility and its ability to incorporate many and varied referents – since the terms Left and Right are formally abstract they must be continually 'filled in' by historical content. In theory, therefore, Left/Right could potentially act as a description of all political events and actions within a given context; it would require, though, an additional claim that Left/Right was relevant to all dimensions of political life. It may be more common that it would be held to be the dominant one. Nevertheless, it is still an important point that there seem to be few political phenomena that are *a priori* not amenable to description in Left/Right terms and that a claim that politics is *equivalent* to Left/Right is at least in theory possible.

In sum, the language of Left/Right provides the formal limits on how Left/Right as a fragment of common sense can describe politics. A Gramscian approach to the analysis of common sense should attempt to specify these limits. Left/Right provides a set of resources and potential tropes for thinking about politics, and it should be emphasized that it is not the case that each dimension of the language of Left/Right must be foregrounded in every instance in which Left/Right is used in thinking about politics.

The conception of the world contained in common sense: The conception of politics underlying Left/Right

Even the brief analysis of the language of the metaphor of Left/ Right in the previous section suggests that fragments of common sense that may appear simple can in fact be highly complex. Importantly, Gramsci held that 'even in the slightest manifestation of any intellectual activity whatever... there is contained a specific conception of the world'.[37] As a fourth step in the critical analysis of common sense, then, it is possible to investigate the 'conception of the world' that lies behind the formal structure of a fragment of common sense. Accordingly, we try to uncover behind Left/Right a more or less complete understanding of politics, and a privileging of certain ways of doing politics, which together form a 'conception of politics'.

Our argument here is that each aspect of the language of Left/ Right puts forward, in the guise of a *description* of politics, an assertion about what politics *should* be about or how politics *should* be done. In other words, the evaluative and the descriptive are very close together, such that a fragment of common sense that purports or appears only to describe a social phenomenon might also be giving a set of prescriptions about what that social phenomenon *should* be like. Table 6.3 illustrates our argument here. The aspects of the conception of politics put forward by Left/Right, when taken together, form something of the notion of the 'conception of the world' Gramsci saw as contained in every intellectual activity.

First, then, we can see that Left/Right as a fragment of common sense about politics does not assume any specific content of political

---

[37] Q11§12; *SPN*, p. 323.

Table 6.3 The conception of politics underlying Left/Right

Aspect of formal structure of Left/Right metaphor	Aspect of conception of politics underlying Left/Right
Abstract metaphor	Politics has no necessary or pre-assumed content (e.g. class conflict)
Spatial metaphor	Political alternatives are different from each other
Horizontal space	Political actors are equal adversaries
Conflictual or oppositional relationship	Politics is centred on conflict
Mutually exclusive categories	Similarity within the Left and the Right over time and across national contexts
Flexible between binary division and spectrum	Binary division: politics as choice between two alternatives; spectrum: politics has one core dimension of conflict
Possibly exhaustive description of politics	Politics does not include practices not fitting with Left/Right model

conflict. Instead, specific positions must be constructed and named as 'Left' or 'Right'. The criterion for the 'legitimate' use of the term 'Left' or 'Right' is then whether the interest or group that wants to assume that label – or is given that label by another political actor – adequately represents the heritage of legacy of the Left or the Right. What 'the Left' and 'the Right' struggle over is, importantly, left open.

Second, the spatial nature of the Left/Right metaphor suggests that the Left and the Right stand some distance from each other – if they are at the same point then the spatial metaphor loses all meaning. One way to illustrate this could be in terms of individual political attitudes towards redistribution of income led by the State.[38]

---

[38] See for instance Geoffrey A. Evans, Anthony F. Heath, and Mansur Lalljee, 'Measuring Left-Right and Libertarian-Authoritarian Values in the British Electorate', *British Journal of Sociology*, 47:1 (1996), pp. 93–112.

In this case it would be possible to establish one's reasonably precise location on this spectrum. The grouping of individuals into Left/Right would then come from the calculation of the two local modal values. As a consequence, Left/Right as a common sense description of politics would tend simultaneously to constrain and to polarize differences, by grouping political actors around two poles. Those in the more central categories would be moved outwards to the Left or Right position and those in more extreme or peripheral categories moved inwards. The usefulness of Left/Right might be questioned, in this context, if all respondents were centrally positioned because then there would be no 'distance' between alternatives. With reference to the positioning of political parties or movements, Left/Right similarly suggests or creates political distance between two alternatives, while marginalizing extreme positions. At the same time, Left/Right seems to describe a politics of distinct alternatives, pushing the positions of Left and Right apart from one another in imaginative or political 'space'. Importantly, if political positions converge in the centre of political space, then Left/Right becomes a less plausible common sense account of politics.

Third, Left/Right as a fragment of the common sense about politics is based on the postulation of a *horizontal* political space in which the Left and the Right appear as equals in a way that the centre and the periphery or the included and the excluded (or the higher and the lower) do not. The horizontal nature of the Left/Right metaphor may plausibly be seen as a claim about the validity of whatever conflict *does* exist: since the participants of the conflict are placed on the same plane, neither is advantaged and so the conflict is seen as 'fair' and as reinforcing the processes of mutual recognition that also provide the preconditions for conflict. In this sense, Left/Right as a fragment of common sense may be related to 'democratic thinking' within the political system through promoting a form of political conflict and debate based on a 'principle of parity' that supposes political adversaries are predisposed to solving conflict through democratic processes.[39] At the same time, as noted above, the 'Far Left' and 'Far Right' groups that may be critical of the democratic

---

[39]Lukes, 'Epilogue'.

political system are also marginalized by the description of politics in terms of Left/Right. Left/Right foregrounds an adversarial relationship as the central feature of the political process, standing as an attempt to *legitimize* conflict by describing it as *legitimate*.

Fourth, Left/Right as a fragment of common sense tends to promote political conflict, through the oppositional relationship between the Left and the Right, as central to the meaning of politics. Importantly, then, consensual political processes are de-emphasized by the commonsensical idea that 'politics is about Left versus Right'. Left/Right, in other words, depends on the presence of political conflict to remain a tenable understanding of politics. Left/Right is likely to be heavily contested as part of the common sense of politics to the extent that societies enter a 'post-political' age in which consensus on the basic structure of society, as a form of welfare-state capitalism, has been achieved.[40]

Fifth, the Left and the Right are posited as mutually exclusive categories in a description of politics in terms of Left/Right (this point is related to the idea that Left and Right cannot occupy the same space within the metaphor). We can extend this idea by saying that there an additional assumption here, namely that the mutual exclusivity of Left and Right will be durable over time. In other words, Left/Right as a part of the common sense of politics is premised on the idea that the Left/Right metaphor will make sense tomorrow in the same way as it does today – that is, through the drawing of boundaries of mutual exclusivity. Left/Right thus tends to emphasize two aspects of the relationship between politics and time. First, stability in the terms of debate is assumed, in order that Left and Right mean *comparable* things over time. It is not necessary for Left and Right to mean exactly the same things. Second and relatedly, the model of Left/Right imposes similarity (at a given point in time) and continuity (over time) on all the movements described as 'Left' or 'Right', imputing a 'family resemblance' between past, present and future Lefts, and past, present and future Rights. The family resemblance, we can note, may also extend beyond national borders. In other words, the model of Left/Right puts forward the claim that

---

[40]See for instance Anthony Giddens, *Beyond Left and Right* (Cambridge: Polity Press, 1994); Ulrich Beck, *World Risk Society* (Cambridge: Polity Press, 1999).

politics should be about the over-time conflict between Left and Right and it accordingly *imposes a long-term structure* of two competing sides, which may tie together otherwise potentially quite disparate groups. In short, the model of Left/Right explicitly links contemporary political debates with those of the past, postulates complex links with other countries' narratives and suggests similarity within the categories of Left and Right. For instance, seeing twentieth-century politics in Britain as comprehensible in terms of Left/Right tends to give prominence to long-term political divisions within British society, rather than those which may be more short-term. In addition, although it may not be an explicit move, British politics is placed in a specifically European context, rather than the liberal/conservative distinction that may instead situate British politics in relation to the American context.

Sixth, Left/Right is flexible between positing a binary division or a spectrum. To the extent that only two political categories are posited, Left/Right also excludes political positions such as 'Centre', 'Centre-Left' and 'Far Right', and marginalizes the 'Far Left' and 'Far Right' by attempting to assimilate them into the categories of Left and Right. In this case, the meaning of Left and Right is seen as core, with the 'Hard' Left or 'Extreme' Right as extensions of that meaning rather than anything qualitatively different or new. Therefore, the process of *constraining* political distance may be an important function of the political narrative of Left/Right, as well as the attempt to *create* it. A spectrum, on the other hand, might be seen as a way to understand a whole set of political positions or ideologies in relation to one another on the basis of a single *dimension*. That dimension is then put forward as central to politics, precisely because it allows us to understand the relative position of a range of political ideologies.[41]

Seventh, Left/Right may be put forward as an 'exhaustive' description of politics, in the sense that it applies to and explains all political conflicts within a given system. In this case, if a political

---

[41] One possible extension of this idea then becomes the 'horseshoe' description of Left/Right: the far Left's and far Right's totalitarianism (or other characteristic) actually distorts and bends the entire horizontal space of Left/Right, such that, for instance, supposed similarities between fascism and communism are emphasized.

practice or phenomenon does not fit into the model advanced, then it is excluded from the 'normal processes of politics'. It this sense we might say that violence represents the breakdown of politics rather than its 'continuation by other means', suggesting both the limits to politics and the delegitimizing of violence to the extent that 'politics' is seen as a preferred human activity.[42] Accordingly, the conception of politics underlying Left/Right tends to exclude from 'politics' those practices grounded in 'illegitimate' conflict or conflict between two undifferentiated adversaries. The former may be seen in a military coup, the latter in intra-party disputes or claims about the increasing similarity of policy programmes in contemporary politics and the falling back to managerial differences rather than 'genuine' political differences. The drawing of the boundaries of politics is an important part of any account of politics, and Left/Right stands as no exception, despite its apparently simple nature as part of the common sense of politics. We can see the process of exclusion at work in Left/Right in two further ways. First, a group which does not accept the validity of its opponents or the rules of the democratic game may be marginalized or, at most, excluded from 'politics' to the extent that the model of Left/Right is argued to necessitate the mutual recognition of the adversaries within a conflictual relationship. Second, to rephrase a point made above, we can see exclusion also as the reverse of the creation of political space. In other words, since Left and Right represent the *limitations* of political space, anything outside of the furthest boundaries of the Right is either drawn into the Right, having its differences elided, or is 'excluded' from the Left/Right model. Thus, a central function of Left/Right as a fragment of common sense about politics, most strongly but not exclusively put forward in claims about its exhaustiveness, is the *drawing of boundaries*. Specifically, in this case, the boundaries concern which practices and what orientations to political adversaries count as properly political and which do not.

In sum, we can categorize the conception of politics underlying Left/Right in the following way. Left/Right is premised on, and tends to reinforce, an understanding of politics based on conflict, and

---

[42] See Hannah Arendt, *On Violence* (London: Allen Lane, 1970).

specifically a conflict in which two equal antagonists present clearly differentiated (or 'distanced') political alternatives, and then engage in a encounter of equals to determine the side that will be victorious. Importantly, Left/Right as a fragment of the common sense of politics does not impute any necessary or pre-assumed content to the conflict. At the same time, the politics of any national context are linked to past conflicts between the Left and the Right (as far back as revolutionary France) and also to conflicts in other national contexts, perhaps particularly those of continental Europe. A Left/ Right understanding of politics is also premised on a conception of politics that excludes consensual practices and marginalizes extreme positions. We can thus see that an analysis of the formal structure of Left/Right shows it to be based on a surprisingly developed and sophisticated conception of politics. Following Gramsci, we take this as support for the proposition that fragments of common sense are likely to contain within them a conception of the world; it is the task of those who would engage in the critical analysis of common sense to reveal these conceptions of the world and try to map something of their complexity.

The critique of common sense: Interpreting Left/Right as a political narrative

The fifth step in the methodology of the critical analysis of common sense that we have been developing in this chapter involves the interpretation and critique of a given fragment of common sense as a story about society. Specifically, the conception of the world underlying the fragment of common sense under investigation, as following from a close analysis of the formal structure of a contextualized and historicized fragment of common sense, should be compared to the conception of the world of the philosophy of praxis. Accordingly, in this section we attempt in a tentative way to compare the understanding of political conflict contained in the Left/ Right metaphor with a conception of class struggle.

The first part of this argument involves extending Gramsci's thought by suggesting that Left/Right might illustrate one of the characteristic ways in which common sense *makes sense* of the social world: through the telling of stories. Here we suggest that Left/Right can be understood as a story about politics or a *political narrative*.

Above all, Left/Right is a stylized way of understanding politics, and one in which contemporary debates of Left against Right are compared to older ones in the attempt to establish over-time continuity and offer an interpretation of contemporary conflict. In the straightforward sense of providing an account of the relationship of historical events, Left/Right stands as a *narrative*. In addition, if we think of 'narrative' in the most general terms as a relayed account of connected events, then it becomes hard to deny that Left/Right is one of the great organizing narratives of modern politics.

Telling stories, including those about politics, is a pervasive and important human activity. It is part of common sense as a way of *making sense* about politics. The term political narrative here means, in the first instance, just the stories we tell about politics. We see the telling and re-telling of political narratives as something in which we all engage, and as a reflection of the complexity and creativity of everyday thinking about politics. A concept of political narrative may allow us to begin to conceptualize the ways in which our everyday thinking about politics is an important moment in the construction of ideologies.

Immediately, though, the question is raised of how we can *assess* the story of Left/Right. Interestingly, the anthropologist Clifford Geertz writes, 'Like Lear, the New Testament, or quantum mechanics, common sense consists in an account of things which claims to strike at their heart. Indeed, it is something of a natural rival to such more sophisticated stories when they are present, and when they are not to phantasmagoric narratives of dream and myth.'[43] We might suggest that Geertz's understanding of common sense captures much of the *authority* of Left/Right: Left/Right presents *an account*

---

[43] Clifford Geertz, 'Common Sense as a Cultural System' in his *Local Knowledge: Further Essays in Interpretive Anthropology* (New York: Basic Books, 1983), p. 84.

of things which claims to strike at their heart, and in popular accounts of politics this manifests itself as the political narrative that 'Politics is about Left versus Right'. It is not so much, therefore, that Left/Right is true or false, but that it is a useful, compelling, accessible, stylish and exciting story. It does not rely on being true but rather on its narrative qualities, which are much more difficult to define and point out. It is thus of interest to assess the characteristics by which we accept or reject stories about politics.

One advantage to seeing Left/Right as a story about politics is that it opens up a variety of new research methods and perspectives in the examination of common sense. In particular, one method of the interpretation of narratives involves our 're-reading' them in the terms of another narrative. A potential model for this 're-reading' process is Fredric Jameson's influential understanding of the interpretation of narrative from *The Political Unconscious* (1981), in which a given narrative is understood – in addition to other elements of an analysis – in its relationship to a master narrative.[44] For Jameson, this master narrative, which defines the terms with which we re-read other narratives, is 'class struggle'. Jameson's model might add an important additional dimension to our historicized understanding of Left/Right as common sense. The second part of our argument here thus involves comparing the conception of politics underlying Left/Right with a notion of class struggle, in order to provide a critique of Left/Right as a fragment of *common sense*.

Explicitly relating the conception of political conflict underlying Left/Right to a conception of political conflict as class struggle provides a whole range of basic insights about its role as a political narrative. Left/Right postulates a division at one level – Left/Right – that is contained within a unity at a higher level: whatever it is that is split *between* Left and Right. Suggested here are conceptions of the nation, or perhaps an overarching consensus in which Left and Right compete. By basing itself on difference, it prompts the question of what allows us to group together those elements divided on the basis of Left and Right. One suggestion might be 'liberal democracy'

---

[44] Fredric Jameson, *The Political Unconscious: Narrative as a Socially Symbolic Act* (London: Routledge, 1981).

or 'bourgeois democracy'. To the extent, then, that Left/Right may be thought of as a division between two halves of liberal democracy, it might be rejected as a distinction without a difference. Moreover, we can see that the idea of Left/Right is fundamentally different to that of class conflict for a number of reasons. For instance, 'Workers Versus Capitalists!' is an entirely different *sort* of narrative, as both its antagonists are historically generated and, even more crucially, the solution of the opposition is only possible *historically* through a movement from present society to a qualitatively different one. The substitution of a social *contradiction between classes* for a surface *opposition between groups* is an important function of the political narrative of a conflict between the Left and the Right. Thus, Left/Right may be the *capitalist common sense of politics par excellence*: it was not only initially generated by a developing capitalism in the context of debates within the bourgeoisie over the nature of its political freedoms, but it also disguises this fact and ideologically masks a deeper, more generative and less resolvable conflict: that between the minority of capitalists and the majority of workers. Therefore, Left/Right as a common sense story about politics offers *a formal and aesthetic resolution of the contradictions between classes in capitalism*. The 'resolution' in this case takes the form of a postulation of formally empty and ahistorical conflict between Left/Right and the obfuscation of the deeper class conflict of between labour and capital. Even if, of course, class actors come entirely to embody the two poles of the conflict, the historicity of the factors generating the conflict in the first place is effaced. Left/Right presents itself as a 'pristine' political division: the notion of contradiction (which cannot be resolved) is reduced to one of *opposition*. 'Labour versus capital' does not suggest the equality of adversaries, nor mutually agreed rules of engagement. The implicit suggestion of the reconcilability of the Left and the Right – they are positional, and have moved in the past and so may move 'toward' each other in the future – is based on a specific view of *conflict*. This is a crucial insight to be gained from seeing Left/Right as a story told about politics, and therefore as open to different types of interpretive analysis.

Importantly, conflict between the Left and the Right is seen as a *political* conflict rather than one based on *economic* or class factors. Accordingly, 'the Left' has denoted a succession of groups that struggled, successively, for political rights, for class interests and for social rights.[45] 'The Right', on the other hand, has referred to a heterogeneous set of responses to the Left and political groups, including the reaction to the French Revolution; the moderate Right of Burke, de Tocqueville and Constant; the response to socialism in the late nineteenth and early twentieth centuries; the extreme Right of nationalist and anti-immigration parties in Europe from the end of the twentieth century; and, most recently, the neo-conservative and neo-liberal New Right.[46] Also, we can note that Left/Right conflict is seen as equal, both as between equals and also balanced. However, the conflict between 'the people' and 'the monopolists', to take a Popular Front slogan, or the conflict between the '1%' and the '99%' are both *deliberately* unbalanced to show that in fact the conflict is precisely between a majority and a minority. Alternatively, 'workers' versus 'capitalists' may suggest that the latter may be more financially powerful than the former, opposing one side of the struggle's power with the other's numerousness. Finally, the conflict between Left and Right is static, since there is nothing internal to either that suggests a third unifying or transcending category: the Centre is exactly *between* Left and Right, and it requires a complex ideological construction to oppose 'forward' to Left/Right.[47] Importantly, the conflict is not going to be 'resolved' or 'transcended' by either the Left or the Right, since both antagonists remain within the terms of Left/Right conflict.

Conclusion

This chapter has aimed to show that Gramsci's thought on *senso comune* can be developed through the detailed examination of a

---

[45] Eric Hobsbawm, 'What's Left of the Left?' in his *The New Century: In Conversation with Antonio Polito* (London: Abacus, 2000), pp. 95–116.
[46] Roger Eatwell, 'The Right as a Variety of "Styles of Thought"', in: Roger Eatwell and Noël O'Sullivan (eds), *The Nature of the Right* (London: Continuum, 1989), pp. 62–76.
[47] See Bastow and Martin, *Third Way Discourse*.

specific 'fragment' of common sense, namely Left/Right as part of the common sense of politics.[48]

We have hoped to show that common sense is composed of immensely complicated thought-products, and that these thought-products warrant serious attention from those interested in developing Gramsci's thought today, and perhaps within the field of political theory more generally. We have suggested that Left/Right as part of the common sense of politics stands in a set of complex relations to Left/Right as a general way of making sense of the world, has a complex and multifaceted history, exhibits an interesting and complicated formal structure, contains within it a conception of the world and acts as a story about politics – or a political narrative – that can ultimately be subjected to critique through a process of interpretation that involves relating it to class struggle. This five-part methodology is proposed as usable by anyone who might wish to investigate common sense.

In theoretical terms, we have suggested that Gramsci's 'philosophy of *senso comune*' might be extended by seeing fragments of common sense as part of the process of telling stories to make sense of our world and our place in it. Common sense might not have to be straightforwardly 'true' to be successful but instead might gain traction by providing a compelling, interesting or useful *story*. The tools of literary theory might then be relevant to the difficult analytical task of examining common sense as it actually exists and linking it to the forms of hegemony that exist in a given society at a given point in time. Finally, Gramsci's philosophy of *senso comune* in

---

[48] Subsequent steps in the investigation of Left/Right as part of the common sense of politics might be as follows: an investigation of the groups in a specific national context that use the label 'the Left' or 'the Right' and how they use this label; an attempt to chart the use of Left/Right in politics textbooks, divided by subject, and how this piece of common sense provides the starting point for more complex explanations of politics, as reaching towards the 'upper level of philosophy' of accounts of politics given by political scientists; an attempt to map the use of Left/Right in concrete examples of popular political commentary, paying close attention to how it functions in different cases and whether there might be a pattern to any differences that the material reveals; and the comparison of Left/Right as part of the common sense of politics with other important stories about contemporary politics, perhaps starting with the notion that 'there is no alternative' to today's liberal capitalism.

general warrants more attention from scholars interested in Gramsci. Extending the philosophy of *senso comune* could involve thinking about what it might mean for common sense to be our 'sixth' or social sense, a critical way we have of 'making sense' of the world. Linked to this idea is Marx's claim in his *Economic and Philosophic Manuscripts of 1844* that our senses are social, and that the forming of the (five) senses is a 'labour of the entire history of the world down to the present'.[49] We might then extend Gramsci's thought by considering that *senso comune* might not be just a product of ways of making sense of the world but could instead be *a mode of perception of the social*, at once foundational and deceptively complex.

---

[49] Marx and Engels, *Collected Works*, vol. 3, p. 302.

7

Thinking through Gramsci in Political Economy: Neo-Liberalism and Hegemony in Britain and France in the 1980s

Introduction

The previous chapter drew on the notion of 'common sense' to show how a Gramscian perspective can illuminate our most essential, everyday conceptions of politics such as Left/Right. The present chapter shifts the focus to the terrain of Political Economy. We will show how some of Gramsci's key categories of historical analysis – such as the historic bloc, hegemony and transformism – may deepen our understanding of one of the most momentous developments of the past decades, namely the diffusion of neo-liberalism across the globe. It testifies to the richness and diversity of Gramsci's thought that it may be equally relevant to the study of areas as (conventionally) distant as Political Theory and Economic History.

In this chapter, we compare the historical experiences of Britain and France in the 1980s, during the earlier and most decisive phase of their respective neo-liberal transitions. In his book entitled *Le grand bond en arrière* ('the great leap backward'), a historical enquiry into the origins of neo-liberalism, editorial director of *Le Monde Diplomatique* Serge Halimi half-seriously asks, 'Were the neo-liberals ... "Gramscian"?'[1] Halimi specifically has in mind processes of ideological mobilization orchestrated by neo-liberal advocates in the United States and in Britain. The 'Gramscian' epithet serves to describe neo-liberalism *qua* hegemonic strategy, a power project that is at once economic, political and cultural. To be sure, Thatcherism in the UK (as Reaganism in the United States) spelt more than mere economic restructuring. It was accompanied by, and relied upon, corresponding dynamics in the spheres of political life (redefining Conservatism) and social mores (a consumerist mindset, a new culture of individualism and so on). As we will see, the notion of Thatcherism as 'Gramscian' resonates with the cultural theorist Stuart Hall's interpretation of British politics in the 1980s, as expounded in an influential series of articles published in *Marxism Today*.

Yet a defining feature of neo-liberalism on a global scale has been its unevenness and variegation across national settings. Hardly any place on the planet has been untouched by the tidal wave of neo-liberalism and by the attendant policies of marketization and privatization. But at the same time, each country can tell its own unique story of how neo-liberal norms and prescriptions have percolated and been carried out within its borders. The ideological crusades of Reaganism and Thatcherism, highly successful on their own terms, and bearers of an 'intellectual and moral reform' of sorts, have not always found equally potent cultural mobilizations echoing them abroad. In many parts of the developing world, neo-liberal reforms were chiefly outside impositions, implemented at the behest of foreign power-holders – such as the International Monetary Fund – irrespective of domestic support, not to speak of home-grown hegemony. In most of Europe, even, neo-liberalism has been more often than not experienced as a passive adaptation

---

[1] Serge Halimi, *Le grand bond en arrière: Comment l'ordre libéral s'est imposé au monde* (Paris: Fayard, 2004), p. 203.

to exogenous trends, a more or less adjustable ensemble of policy steps necessary to keep the nation afloat in a competitive world economy. In such cases, neo-liberal transformation may be justified by the governing class in a strictly instrumental way, as an economic expedient, unencumbered by any discourse about values or morals: if anything, an argument for political and cultural demobilization as opposed to mobilization. To return to Halimi's quip, then, it can be said that many if not most of historical neo-liberalizers were not 'Gramscian', since they were either unable or unwilling to subsume the economic recipes of neo-liberalism within a coherent, political-cum-cultural, hegemonic transformative project.

France's own neo-liberal transition, starting as early as 1982–3, fits this non-hegemonic type of configuration, only with an added, highly paradoxical twist. In the spring of 1981, for the first time in its history, the French people voted into office a Socialist president – François Mitterrand – together with an absolute majority of Socialist deputies in the *Assemblée nationale*, the French lower house of parliament. This was an all the more remarkable turn of events since the Right had held power continuously ever since the foundation of the Fifth Republic under General de Gaulle in 1958. As if this was not enough to dampen the prospects of neo-liberalism in France at the time, the electoral campaigns of 1981 had been fought by the French Socialist Party (*Parti Socialiste*, hereafter PS) on an unusually radical platform of 'rupture with the capitalist system'. During its first twelve months in power, the Socialist government presided over a rapid increase in social expenditure and a wave a nationalizations that put most of the large industrial concerns and virtually all of the financial sector under public ownership.

By 1986, however, all of the expectations built up in 1981 and 1982 had been upended. In four years, the country had witnessed an economic policy reversal of extraordinary magnitude. Macro-economic policy had become firmly monetarist. Industrial policy had been pared down to the point of not only running against previous PS pronouncements, but in fact to the extent of putting to rest decades of interventionist practice dating back to the immediate post-war years. The financial system had been reshaped from top to bottom, away from the 'credit rationing' system put in place in the late 1940s and towards an open market model inspired by U.S.

financial institutions. When Jacques Chirac and the Right swept back to power after the PS's defeat at the 1986 elections for the *Assemblée nationale*, many of the building blocks of neo-liberalism had already been erected by the French Left.

It is our claim that a Gramscian perspective is capable of illuminating not just hegemonic patterns of neo-liberalization – or 'Gramscian' configurations in Halimi's sense – but also the many non-hegemonic trajectories of neo-liberal transformation evidenced across much of the world. By devoting this chapter to a comparison between Thatcherite Britain in the 1980s and Socialist France from 1981 to 1986 – that is, between two markedly different neo-liberal transitions – we seek to illustrate the potency and open-endedness of Gramscian historical analysis. In so doing, we will draw on the notions of hegemony, historic bloc and transformism as 'living' ideas, by specifying and refining them in intimate connection with the concrete historical configurations at hand. In particular, this will entail on our part an original addition to Gramsci's theory of the historic bloc, which appears as key to elucidating the contrast between the British and French social formations in the 1980s. We will delineate two broad types of historic blocs at the generic level, namely coherent (hegemonic) and split (non-hegemonic) historic blocs, and show how this distinction can be brought to bear on our Franco-British comparison.

The following sections will not feature our two case studies on an equal footing; instead we will mostly foreground the French case. This is chiefly because Thatcherism has already been very persuasively analysed through a Gramscian lens by Stuart Hall. Therefore, we will essentially rely on Hall's valuable insights on British politics in the 1980s when characterizing the British case. On the other hand, our Gramscian interpretation of French neo-liberalization between 1981 and 1986 proceeds from our own original research on the period.

We first introduce Hall's seminal analysis of Thatcherism, which will thereafter serve as a reference point against which to appraise French political developments. The following three sections recount these developments, starting with the build-up to the 1981 elections and the Left orientation of the PS at that point, to the vicissitudes of economic policy-making between 1981 and 1986, and then the resulting ideological embarrassment afflicting PS political discourse. The penultimate substantive section elaborates on Gramsci's notion of the historic bloc as a way to grasp the essential determinants of the macro-social contrast between the two cases. The final section draws on the idea of transformism to shed light on the French intellectual elite's fatalistic embrace of neo-liberalism in the context of a split, non-hegemonic historic bloc.

Stuart Hall:
Thatcherism as hegemonic project

With hindsight, what is striking about the 1980s in Britain is the conjunction of major economic, political and cultural change over a relatively short time span. These serial dynamics, affecting virtually all areas of society, were mutually reinforcing, and indeed they tightly relied on each other. The economics of neo-liberal restructuring – disinflation, privatization, financialization – were premised on the durable political supremacy of a transformed Conservative Party as well as on a set of new dispositions and habits within the population at large. Margaret Thatcher led the Tories to discard much of the post-aristocratic paternalism that had given her party an aloof and ineffective image in the preceding decades. Instead, a hard-headed, distinctively uncompassionate individualism was adopted as the new Conservative social philosophy. As council houses and public companies were sold off, the British citizenry itself was being enticed to join in this emergent society in which each household ought to behave as a miniature capitalist unit. Booms in marketing and advertising – and household debt – fuelled a new culture of consumerism. Concurrently, the divisions and the electoral collapse of the Left, the repeated defeats of defensive industrial action and the institutional weakening and decimation of the trade-union movement all seemed to close off alternatives. The economic, political and cultural 'moments' of social life were fast converging, pointing to a new neo-liberal order.

Stuart Hall was one of the first to discern the momentous, structural character of the ongoing transformation of Britain. In four short articles published in *Marxism Today*, he proposed to 'think in a Gramscian way' about the implications of Thatcherism.[2] As early as 1979, in 'The Great Moving Right Show', Hall called upon the Left not to underestimate the originality and potency of the Thatcherite political project, insisting on the way in which it weaved together new economic doctrines – monetarism as opposed to Keynesianism – with processes of populist mobilization. In 1987, in a piece entitled 'Gramsci and Us', Hall went as far as to contend that 'Thatcherism aimed for a reversal in ordinary common sense'.[3]

Thatcherism, for Hall, combined destructive and constructive aspects. As a negative project, it took aim primarily at the Welfare State, both as an institution and as a nexus of popular expectations built into the British psyche since the immediate post-war: 'Thatcherism's project was to transform the State in order to restructure society: to decentre, to displace, the whole post-war formation; to reverse the political culture which had formed the basis of the political settlement – the historic compromise between labour and capital – which had been in place from 1945 onwards.'[4] The dramatic expansion of public welfare provisions under the Attlee government after 1945, including but not limited to the set-up of the National Health Service, transformed the very fabric of State–society relations. For decades, it assumed a 'taken-for-granted' quality, evidenced by the fact that neither of the two governing parties would make a significant policy move against it. This is often referred to as the 'post-war consensus' of British politics, or 'Butskellism' (a portmanteau of Conservative Chancellor of the Exchequer R. A. Butler and Labour politician Hugh Gaitskell). To put it in Gramscian terms, the existence of the welfare State had seeped into the 'common sense' of the 'people-nation' of Britain.

---

[2] Stuart Hall, 'The Great Moving Right Show', *Marxism Today*, January 1979, pp. 14–20; 'Gramsci and Us', *Marxism Today*, June 1987, pp. 16–21; 'Blue Election, Election Blues', *Marxism Today*, July 1987, pp. 30–5; 'Thatcher's Lessons', *Marxism Today*, March 1988, pp. 20–7. The phrase 'to think in a Gramscian way' appears in 'Gramsci and Us', p. 16. *Marxism Today* was a political magazine associated with the Communist Party of Great Britain. It became known for its iconoclastic take on traditional Left-wing orthodoxies, and enjoyed some success with a peak circulation of 15,000 copies in 1989.
[3] Hall, 'Gramsci and Us', p. 17.
[4] Ibid., p. 17.

The Conservative Party under Thatcher aimed to upturn that very common sense. As early as 1975, the year she took on the position of party leader, the struggle against 'statism', 'collectivism' and 'socialism' took prominence in Tory discourse. Welfare provisions were framed as handouts to 'scavengers', nurturing a 'dependency culture' harmful to the British spirit. The economic crises of the 1970s had at times led the Labour governments of Harold Wilson and James Callaghan to increase spending commitments, either in the form of social relief or subsidies to embattled industries. This in turn was portrayed by the Right as 'creeping collectivism'. Thatcher herself famously declared in 1977, 'My job is to stop Britain going red.' The assault on welfarism was pursued consistently under Thatcher's governments in the 1980s. Actual anti-statist reforms fell short of the rhetoric, and the welfare State itself, if weakened, remained in place. Yet at the turn of the 1990s the future of welfare was hardly 'taken for granted' anymore.

More original was Thatcherism's 'positive' project, meaning the infusion in society of specific values resonant with its economic plans, as well as of a 'political imagery' and a 'vision of the future'.[5] Indeed the attack on the State was always couched in value-laden terms. To welfare and dependency were opposed the thematics of individual responsibility, self-reliance, enterprise, competition, choice and so on. To these was typically added a layer of even more traditional notions such as 'nation, family, duty, authority'.[6] Paradoxically, then, the Thatcherite 'revolution' remained discursively tethered to social conservatism. The rallying cry for freedom in the economic realm was matched – indeed was backed – by an authoritarian turn in politics and social norms. Yet Hall insisted that the modernizing, forward-looking aspect of Thatcherism is no mere illusion. The 1980s did witness economic renewal, albeit in definite directions and to the benefit of particular interests. And they did coincide with a modernizing cultural drive – witness the consumerist fever, and the resonance of 'enterprise culture' – albeit in association with a number of regressive ideological tropes. Thus Hall writes of 'the

---

[5] See Hall, 'Blue Election', p. 33; 'Thatcher's Lessons', p. 20.
[6] Hall, 'The Great Moving Right Show', p. 17.

reactionary modernization of Thatcherism': genuine modernization at the service of no-less-genuine reaction.[7]

One of Hall's most perceptive arguments concerns Thatcher's 'populism', that is the way in which Thatcherite discourse not only repeatedly appealed to popular anxieties and aspirations to draw support for its policies, but also, in so doing, sought to redefine the very meaning of 'the people' in British politics. He writes that 'Thatcherism has a perfectly focused conception of who its ideal subjects are', namely a serial collection of individual-minded (or household-minded) consumers and investors, on the lookout for value-for-money not only when purchasing commodities, but also when 'consuming' public services such as education and healthcare.[8] Thus the Thatcherite 'people' is one stripped of its identity as political collective, or as democratic citizenry. Its logical counterpart is a State that may well be overbearing, overtaxing and parasitic, but is never construed as the recipient of a democratic political will. As a result of Thatcherism's constant ideological interpellations, the very meanings of 'people' and 'State' were modified. This was part and parcel of the Thatcherite 'reversal in ordinary common sense'.

Thus Hall sought to understand Thatcherism through the lens of hegemony. The Thatcherite 'reversal of common sense' echoes Gramsci's 'revolution of common sense' (see Chapter 5), with the inescapable, bitter irony that the latter expression was meant to refer to a coming proletarian hegemony, not a neo-liberal one. In 1987, Hall wrote that Thatcherism 'entered the political field … not just for power, but for popular authority, for hegemony'.[9] A year later, he contended that it 'moulds people's conceptions as it restructures their lives as it shifts the disposition of forces to its side'.[10] As will be recalled, the success of a hegemonic project can be measured by its capacity to co-opt some social groups while neutralizing the potential for 'scission' of others. Thatcherism succeeded in altering the subjective, commonsensical referents of much of the British population in a

---

[7] Hall, 'Gramsci and Us', p. 21.
[8] Hall, 'Thatcher's Lessons', p. 27.
[9] Hall, 'Gramsci and Us', p. 17.
[10] Hall, 'Thatcher's Lessons', p. 23.

way conducive to some degree of depoliticization in everyday life. This was well captured by Hall's warning to his Left-leaning readers: 'make no mistake, a tiny bit of all of us is also somewhere inside the Thatcherite project. Of course, we're all one hundred percent committed. But every now and then – Saturday mornings, perhaps, just before the demonstration – we go to Sainsbury's and we're just a tiny bit of a Thatcherite subject'.[11] Blurring the very lines of political divide served to weaken pre-existing forms of organized opposition to neo-liberal politics – such as the British trade-union movement – while thwarting the emergence of new ones. To be sure, no hegemony is ever complete, hegemony being a process rather than a state-of-things. With this caveat in mind, we may retain Hall's characterization of Thatcherism as a hegemonic project.

Socialist politics in France before 1981: A Left turn

The political course France was charting at the start of the 1980s appeared to observers as the exact opposite of the British one. The political Left was on the rise, and in 1981, for the first time since the foundation of the Fifth Republic in 1958, a Left president, François Mitterrand, was voted into office. The following month, at the French legislative elections, the PS obtained an absolute majority in the *Assemblée nationale*, a feat that the party founded in 1905 had never achieved.[12] With the most crucial levers of State power at hand, and a platform proposing no less than to part ways with 'the capitalist system', the PS seemed poised to leave a durable mark on French economy and society. Before we proceed to describe the somewhat dramatic post-1981 turn of events, it is necessary first to put the PS victory in context.

---

[11] Hall, 'Gramsci and Us', p. 19.
[12] Formerly, the PS was known as the *Section Française de l'Internationale Ouvrière* (French Section of the Workers' International), or SFIO. The name change was decided at the Alfortville Congress in 1969.

The origins of the 1981 victory, and of the markedly Left-oriented platform that accompanied it, should be traced ten years prior, to the PS's so-called 'unification' congress held in the town of Epinay in 1971. On that occasion, François Mitterrand joined the PS to be voted its *premier secrétaire* (party leader). Prior to 1971, his long experience in French politics was in several smaller Left-of-centre parties and groupings. A minister at the early age of thirty in 1947, he had thereafter held several governmental positions in the Fourth Republic (1946–58), before becoming one of General de Gaulle's most stubborn critics and opponents under the Fifth. That this deeply pragmatic, 'Florentine' politician – as he was often described – with no historical association with socialism would come to embody the Left orientation of the PS after 1971 is not the smallest paradox of the period.

At the Epinay Congress, PS delegates entrusted the party leadership to Mitterrand in the wake of a string of humiliating defeats, the latest being the 5 per cent of votes obtained by PS candidate Gaston Deferre at the 1969 presidential election. The Gaullist Right was firmly ensconced in government, and the Communists (the *Parti Communiste Français*, hereafter PCF) constituted by far the most potent political force on the Left. The PCF had scored between 19 and 28 per cent at every major election since 1945, up to the 1969 presidential election when its candidate, Jacques Duclos, had obtained 21 per cent.

Mitterrand carried the day at the Epinay Congress against the party's 'old guard' after putting forward a singularly offensive, unabashedly Leftist political line. His victory over the more moderate positions of several PS seniors was premised, in turn, on his alliance with the most Left-leaning of intra-PS groupings, the *Centre d'Etudes, de Recherches et d'Education Socialiste* (CERES). The CERES was an avowedly Marxist, disciplined 'party within the party' led by Jean-Pierre Chevènement, without whose support Mitterrand's bid for leadership would have failed. From the latter's point of view, the PS's new-found radical stance was to enable it to cast off its dusty, politics-as-usual image which had plagued its electoral showings ever since the Fourth Republic. Most importantly, a Left discursive turn held the promise of future gains at the expense of the PCF or, as the French expression has it, of 'poaching' millions of voters on PCF territory.[13]

Mitterrand's final speech at the Epinay Congress provides a taste of the PS's anti-capitalist rhetoric at the time. Indeed the following excerpts are scarcely imaginable in the mouth of any post-war Labour Party leader in Britain:

> The one who does not accept rupture with the established order..., with capitalist society, that one cannot be a member of the Socialist Party!....There is no, there will never be a socialist society without collective property of the great means of production, exchange and research....The true enemy, indeed the only one, because everything transits through it...is monopoly! [This is] an extensive term, that refers to all the powers of money, money that corrupts, money that buys, money that crushes, money that kills, money that ruins, and money that rots the very consciousness of mankind!

In 1971 the PS also decided on an alliance with the PCF. This policy, which led to the proclamation of a 'Left Union' (*Union de la Gauche*) in 1972, had been energetically defended by Mitterrand and by the CERES at the Epinay Congress. In the following years, the PS's electoral results steadily improved at the expense of both the Right and the PCF. In the second round of the 1974 presidential election, Mitterrand lost by a thin margin (49.2 to 50.8 per cent) to Valéry Giscard d'Estaing, who had been Finance Minister under de Gaulle in the 1960s. Feeling – rightly – threatened by the PS's Left assertiveness, the PCF decided to distance itself by scuttling the Left Union in 1977. This was to no avail, as the communist electoral decline went on apace and the Socialists maintained their Left orientation. At the 1978 legislative elections, the Left was once again narrowly defeated. At the PS's 1979 Metz Congress – the last prior to the 1981 presidential race – Mitterrand renewed his alliance with the

---

[13] For further implications of 'competitive pluralism' within the French Left, see George Ross and Jane Jenson, 'Pluralism and the Decline of Left Hegemony: The French Left in Power', *Politics and Society*, 14:2 (1985), pp. 147–83.

CERES, staving off intra-PS dissent and holding on to the Left line. Significantly, Chevènement was tasked with drafting the outline for the 1981 campaign platform.

The PS went to battle in 1981 promising to the French people a 'rupture with the capitalist system' in case of victory. The chief embodiment of this rupture was to be the nationalization of the 'great means of production', namely the large industrial concerns and the financial sector (banking and insurance). As election day approached, however, the thematics of 'rupture' tended to be de-emphasized by Mitterrand and the PS, most likely in view of offering a more reassuring image to voters. Interestingly, the nationalization policy was increasingly presented, not as a systemic overhaul directed against capitalist relations of production, but as a means to economic growth. Given the dreary French economic climate at the time, such an argument was susceptible to echo favourably within the electorate. In 1979 the second oil shock, combined with the steep rise in American interest rates imposed by Federal Reserve President Paul Volcker that year (the 'Volcker shock'), had dimmed European economic prospects. As a result, sluggish growth, declining investments and rising unemployment had tarnished President Giscard d'Estaing's economic record. During the 1981 campaign, the PS pinned most of the crisis on to a lack of industrial investment. This, in turn, was chiefly attributed to French private capital's unwillingness to take investment risk, betraying a deplorable 'Malthusian' mind-set among company owners.[14] Given French private capitalists' excessive timidity, the PS argument went in 1981, the State had a duty to step in, carry out nationalizations, and lead the newly nationalized units on an investment drive that would revive growth and improve competitiveness.

On the eve of the Left's victory, a contradiction was thus lurking in the wings of PS discourse between, on the one hand, the depiction of nationalization as the chief means of breaking away from the capitalist system, and on the other, the much more prosaic, economistic justification of public ownership as growth-inducing.

---

[14] 'Malthusianism' was an – admittedly odd – expression commonly used in France in the post-war decades to describe excessive restraint in economic decision-making.

This – as yet merely potential – difficulty was compounded by the PS's inability to take a coherent stand prior to 1981 on the issue of the pre-existing French *dirigiste* apparatus. It should be stressed that in the immediate post-war period, France had put in place interventionist State institutions that were uniquely pervasive in comparison with other Western capitalist nations. In the French context, this is usually referred to by the terms *dirigisme* (noun) and *dirigiste* (adjective), meaning the organization and the ideology of State dominance in capitalist economic activity (the French verb *diriger* means 'to lead', 'to direct'). This institutional set-up included, among other features, a Planning Commission (putting out five-year plans), a host of public firms nationalized in 1945 and 1946 (energy, transport, retail banking and so on) and perhaps most importantly, a 'credit rationing' system in which most financial flows in the economy came with *ad hoc*, individualized interest rates fixed by Treasury officials or executives in public or semi-public credit institutions. The 'credit rationing' system meant that for decades France did not have an economy-wide interest rate; instead lending activity – and thus monetary creation – was mostly micro-managed by a public technocracy.[15] This whole *dirigiste* apparatus had remained firmly in place during the political turmoil of the Fourth Republic and had, if anything, been strengthened under General de Gaulle and his successors.

Prior to the 1981 elections, Mitterrand and the PS revealingly failed to tell the electorate whether France's *dirigiste* institutions would be strengthened, reformed or dismantled under a Socialist government. If anything, a new, sweeping wave of nationalizations appeared to imply heightened *dirigisme*. The PS, however, took care to refute any such notion. Having been run for decades by a coalition of high-ranking civil servants and politicians of the Right, the *dirigiste* apparatus must have been perceived as foreign if

---

[15] On the 'credit rationing' system, which was rapidly dismantled from 1984 onwards, see Andrew Shonfield, *Modern Capitalism: The Changing Balance of Public and Private Power* (Oxford: Oxford University Press, 1965), Part II, 'The Approach to Planning'; John Zysman, *Government, Markets, and Growth: Financial Systems and the Politics of Industrial Change* (Ithaca: Cornell University Press, 1983), Chapter 3, 'The Interventionist Temptation: The French Case'; Michael Loriaux, *France after Hegemony: International Change and Financial Reform* (Ithaca: Cornell University Press, 1991).

not hostile by the PS establishment at the time. This transpires in the text presenting the PS political project in 1980, describing the 'system embodied by Mr Giscard d'Estaing' as a combination of 'inflation, unemployment, inequality, *dirigisme*, [and] subservience to foreign capitalist interests'.[16] Another reason for the PS's discomfort with *dirigisme* may be explained by the anti-statist, anti-hierarchical mood which permeated much of the French Left (with the notable exception of the PCF) in the wake of the May 1968 protests. In the ideological atmosphere of the 1970s, it was hardly possible to avow any positive construal of State institutions within the PS mainstream. The refusal to embrace *dirigisme*, or to specify a plausible path for its transformation or supersession, was a notable blind spot of the 1981 PS platform that boded ill for future Socialist economic leadership.

Five years of Socialist government: A rocky path to neo-liberalism

On 10 May 1981, Mitterrand was elected President of the Republic in the second round of the election, beating Valéry Giscard d'Estaing with 52 per cent of the votes. When sworn in, on 21 May, he famously declared, 'the democratically expressed political majority of the French people has come to identify itself with its social majority'. This was meant to convey the sense that well before 1981, the sociological make-up of the country was pointing towards a Left victory.[17] France's post-war 'rural exodus' and urbanization, the decline of independent workers (artisans, shopkeepers and so on), the rise of salaried employment generally and of women's employment in particular,

---

[16] http://miroirs.ironie.org/socialisme/www.psinfo.net/documents/conventions/france80/present.html [accessed 10 August 2014]. The inclusion of '*dirigisme*' in this collection of evils strikes a very incongruous note today, at a time when both Left and Right loudly mourn the ineffectiveness of 'industrial policy'.

[17] Tellingly, a book of electoral sociology on the 1978 legislative elections was entitled 'Left-wing France, Right-wing vote'; see Jacques Capdeville, Elisabeth Dupoirier, Gérard Grunberg, Etienne Schweisguth and Colette Ysmal (eds), *France de gauche, vote de droite* (Paris: Presses de la Fondation Nationale des Sciences Politiques, 1981).

secularization and post-May 1968 sexual liberation all appeared to French observers to tilt the balance of political forces away from the Right and towards the Left.[18] A secondary socio-political plot was of course the steady, seemingly irreversible decline of the PCF vote count within the Left, as the manual working class population started dwindling from the 1970s onward.

Once in office, Mitterrand swiftly dissolved the *Assemblée nationale*. The ensuing elections handed it to the PS with an absolute majority of deputies. Mitterrand picked as Prime Minister Pierre Mauroy, the long-time mayor of Lille and a member of the PS old guard. Jacques Delors, a former 'social Catholic' trade-unionist, became Finance Minister, and Chevènement took the Industry portfolio. The government's early economic measures, in 1981 and 1982, were a faithful implementation of the PS's campaign platform. Nationalizations were carried out apace – with generous compensation to owners – so that, by 1982, a third of industrial output and 96 per cent of banking deposits were under public ownership.[19] Spending was also ratcheted up, with significant rises in industrial investment (via State-owned firms) and welfare commitments. The country-wide retirement age was brought down to sixty, a fifth week of yearly paid vacation was granted, and most social transfers and subsidies were revised upward.

Soon enough, however, the government faced an increasingly precarious macro-economic situation. Mitterrand and Mauroy's refusal to contemplate new protectionist measures against foreign goods led the Keynesian-type spending increases of 1981 and 1982 to induce a dramatic growth in imports and a corresponding deterioration of the trade balance. At the same time, France's own industrial production was in no position to experience a significant export expansion as many of the world's advanced economies were stagnant in the wake of the 'Volcker shock'. Repeatedly, the government had to resort to international loans to remain afloat.

---

[18] Interestingly, those were the very years when observers of British politics were coming to terms with the country's structural shift towards the Right. See Hall, 'The Great Moving Right Show'; and also Eric Hobsbawm's influential 'The Forward March of Labour Halted?', *Marxism Today*, September 1978, pp. 279–86.

[19] See Vivien A. Schmidt, *From State to Market? The Transformation of French Business and Government* (Cambridge: Cambridge University Press, 1996), p. 117.

As early as November 1981, Jacques Delors had publicly demanded a 'pause' in the Socialists's economic policies. Although he was sternly rebuffed by Pierre Mauroy at the time, it only took a few more months for the whole government to abandon its original economic plans and to engage on a radically different path. With hindsight, however, economic policy between 1982 and 1986 was hardly about 'pausing' the initial socialistic drive, nor merely about renouncing it. Instead, in four highly significant steps, the government methodically dismantled major components of France's *dirigiste* apparatus, laying in their place the bases of a new, neo-liberal economic order.

The first step occurred in June 1982 when the Socialists enacted a freeze on all wages in order to fight inflation and restore international competitiveness. This was mostly justified at the time as an unpalatable yet unavoidable solution to stave off the threat of an external debt crisis. Delors had actively fought for these measures and his government colleagues had eventually relented.[20] In truth it represented an important break from past practices, since wages in France had been indexed to inflation on the basis of a 'movable scale' (*échelle mobile*) arrangement since the 1950s. As wages were blocked in 1982 while inflation persisted, all salaried people in France underwent declines in purchasing power (it took until late 1985 for inflation to fall under the 5 per cent benchmark).

Besides, in the short term, the wage freeze proved insufficient to avert a looming debt crisis. By March 1983, France's deteriorating competitiveness had fostered an acute sense of emergency in decision-making circles. Mitterrand was under intense pressure from Delors to cut spending drastically, while his Left advisors and Chevènement argued that if France were only to break away from the European Monetary System (EMS) of fixed currency parities, the *franc* would slide enough for exports to rebound and for the government to remain committed to its ambitious 1981 programme of socialist reforms. This alternative facing the government was echoed throughout the country's media, so that the choice to remain in or leave the EMS came to symbolize French socialism at the crossroads. Proponents of the EMS, who were highly sceptical of

---

[20] Philippe Bauchard, *La guerre des deux roses: Du rêve à la réalité, 1981–1985* (Paris: Grasset, 1986).

the prospects of 'socialism in one country', as they put it, were the most vocal. They prevailed, and on 25 March Delors announced a string of austerity measures including new taxes and reductions in public investment. Chevènement left his post as Industry Minister to be replaced by a young Socialist technocrat, Laurent Fabius.

The policy turnarounds of June 1982 and March 1983 durably modified the pattern of macro-economic policy in France. Disinflation became the supreme order of the day, with Delors declaring at the *Assemblée nationale* that 'permanent complicity with inflation' was 'the root of evil'.[21] Moreover, these decisions opened the way for further paradigm shifts in the areas of industrial policy and finance.

Now in charge of the Industry portfolio, Fabius laid ambitious plans for 'public sector restructuring'. These plans' steady implementation between 1983 and 1986 entailed tens of thousands of job suppressions within State-owned firms. Steel works, coal and naval construction were among the hardest hit. Indeed the government's commitment to 'restructuring' was only strengthened when Fabius was appointed by Mitterrand to replace a discredited Mauroy as Prime Minister in July 1984. Since March 1983, a public investment drive was off the table and as a result, mass layoffs were arguably the only plausible strategy left for public companies to survive and prosper in a fast-globalizing world economy.[22] What is striking in retrospect is the lack of widespread defensive industrial action against a State throwing its own employees *en masse* into unemployment. As of the early 1980s, the wave of militancy that had characterized industrial relations in the 1970s was fast receding, as unemployment put a dent in trade-union membership and Socialist policy reversals generated disillusion and cynicism rather than active resistance.

The fourth and last milestone in France's neo-liberal transition between 1982 and 1986 was the complete overhaul of the financial system. It was decided upon in 1984 and overseen by Pierre

---

[21] Quoted in Michel Beaud, *La politique économique de la gauche, vol. 2: Le grand écart* (Paris: Syros, 1985), p. 22.

[22] The French public sector did in fact perform remarkably well from the mid-1980s to the turn of the 1990s. See Steven Greenhouse, 'State Companies Thrive in France', *New York Times*, 9 May 1989.

Bérégovoy, the new finance minister who replaced Jacques Delors when the latter became president of the European Commission. The new restrictive macro-economic policy framework put in place in 1983 was putting great strains on France's 'credit rationing' system. When Delors made disinflation the overriding priority of macro-economic policy, the 'credit rationing' system ground to a halt because policy-makers would no longer countenance financial expansion by State financial institutions lest it fuel inflation. With a stagnant economy and a paralysed system of public credit creation, Bérégovoy and his Finance Ministry officials opted for a top-to-bottom liberalization of the financial system. No longer would loans come with *ad hoc* terms and conditions; instead, lenders would take their cues from an economy-wide, market-driven interest rate. The *Bourse de Paris* (the French stock market) was thoroughly deregulated, breaking the historical monopoly of the *agents de change*, a corporation of State-sanctioned brokers in place since the *Ancien Régime*. Moreover, a new futures exchange modelled on the Chicago Mercantile Exchange was set up. As noted by Philip Cerny: 'The Fabius Government of 1984–6 took a quantum leap forward in financial market deregulation, although the consequences were not visible until 1986, just as the Socialists were voted out.'[23]

After having promised a 'rupture with the capitalist system' prior to 1981 and carrying out a sweeping nationalization programme in 1981 and 1982, Mitterrand and the PS government went in sharp reverse mode thereafter, tearing down whole swathes of France's pre-existing interventionist model and establishing in their place the fundamentals of a neo-liberal system. The Delors-engineered, macro-economic shift of 1982–3 spelt France's swift transition away from decades of Keynesian management towards monetarist orthodoxy. Meanwhile, in the industrial realm, there were mass redundancies aimed at cutting costs and restoring international competitiveness, a business strategy well-known for bearing the hallmark of neo-liberal globalization. And in the area of finance, a decades-old *dirigiste* arrangement granting the State preponderant influence over credit

---

[23] Philip Cerny, 'The Little Big Bang in Paris: Financial Market Deregulation in a Dirigiste System', *European Journal of Political Research*, 17:2 (1989), p. 173.

was discarded in favour of an 'open-market' system modelled on the United States. From 1982 to 1986, the pace and thoroughness of French neo-liberalization were breath-taking, and compared 'favourably', in terms of the neo-liberal thrust, with any four-year period within Margaret Thatcher's eleven-year tenure as British prime minister.

One should also note the outsize role played by external factors in pushing for domestic change in France at the time. This is an essential source of contrast between the British and French experiences of neo-liberalization in the 1980s. The 1982 wage freeze and the 1983 austerity plan were justified by French decision-makers as emergency responses to a deteriorating trade balance and a debt crisis. 'Public sector restructuring', with its mass layoffs of State employees, was also framed as a matter of survival for the State-owned sector in the face of unforgiving external competition. Finally, the complete overhaul of France's financial system occurred at the very time when, in the context of a global shift to disinflation following the 'Volcker shock', finance experienced explosive growth worldwide. Finance Ministry officials were keenly aware that this surging wave of mobile capital would shun any country that did not provide it with a hospitable marketplace. An international race was taking shape for first-mover advantage in finance – the City of London famously underwent its own 'Big Bang' in 1986 – and the fear of being left on the wayside of global financialization spurred France's ministers and technocrats to take radical action.

Parti Socialiste discourse during neo-liberalization: Dissonance and demobilization

As seen in the first section, Thatcherism subsumed the specific policy steps of neo-liberalization within a hegemonic project that aimed for a 'reversal of common sense' in Britain. This hegemonic strategy relied on a set of coherent and resonant ideological messages. As argued by Stuart Hall, Conservative politicians and spokespersons – and none more than Thatcher herself – proved remarkably skilful at gradually disseminating 'social market values' within the citizenry through repeated ideological appeals to the British 'people'.[24] In this respect, the situation in France under the PS government between 1981 and 1986 was almost the exact reverse of Britain's. Having embarked, *nolens volens*, on a path of radical neo-liberal restructuring of the economy, the French Socialists were confronted with an all-too-obvious quandary that they were never able to solve. Renouncing publicly their pre-1981 commitment to socialism and to the 'rupture with the capitalist system' would have had the advantage of bringing their words in line with their actions, even though it would have given rise to the accusation of Left betrayal. On the other hand, a continued adherence to the PS Left line of the 1970s would have ensured surface ideological continuity, but one readily vulnerable to the accusation of hypocrisy. The French Socialists chose neither of these options. Instead, they steered an uneasy and inconsistent course, eliciting a profound ideological embarrassment.

The policy shifts of 1982 and 1983 did induce new inflections in official discourse. In January 1983, Mitterrand declared on television that 'enterprise is a priority that overrides all others. We must produce, produce more, produce better, limit social and financial burdens, invest, know how to sell goods in order to be competitive ... I have always supported freedom of initiative and the enterprising spirit'.[25] A few months later, in an interview with the newspaper *Libération*, he stated that 'social flexibility and technological modernization are the two keys to overcome crisis'.[26] Fabius's accession to the position of prime minister in July 1984 accentuated these neo-liberal soundings in government circles. 'Enterprise', 'freedom', 'competitiveness' and, most of all, 'modernization' became choice words. Fabius's own personal motto as prime minister, from 1984 up to and including the 1986 electoral campaign, was the somewhat vacuous '*moderniser et rassembler*' ('to modernize and to build consensus').

---

[24] Hall, 'The Great Moving Right Show', p. 17.
[25] Quoted in Bauchard, *La guerre des deux roses*, p. 125.
[26] *Libération*, 10 May 1984.

These discursive revisions did not go unnoticed and by 1984, French media and public intellectuals were busy debating the ongoing ideological makeover of the French socialist movement. References to the German Social-Democratic Party's 1959 Bad-Godesberg Convention – when it renounced Marxism – were cropping up in the mainstream press, with many a columnist foreseeing an imminent 'French Bad-Godesberg'. By 1985, Alain Madelin, a Right politician and the most vocal advocate of neo-liberalism within the French political class at the time, was only too happy to announce the death of socialism on French radio: 'Today, everyone is a liberal. Nobody considers the question of socialism anymore. Laurent Fabius has buried it for good.'[27]

But although Madelin might have been right about PS policy practice, socialism had not been buried as far as PS discourse was concerned. In effect, the expected 'French Bad-Godesberg' did not occur, and 'socialism' continued to make regular appearances in governmental utterances alongside the rising tropes of 'enterprise' and 'modernisation'. However, the persistent reference to 'socialism' had now become ambiguous, to put it mildly, as neo-liberalization developed at an increasing pace. Mitterrand himself excelled in the art of ambiguity. In the same interview to *Libération* in which he commended 'social flexibility', he stated, 'I am fighting the theory and practice of "economic liberalism", which is a dupery'. To which he added, 'there is no easy path for one who is aware of his duty to France and, if I may add, to socialism'.[28] The PS, far from renouncing socialistic discourse, actually organized the 1986 legislative campaign around the theme of 'socialist values'.

By continuing to uphold the verbal banner of 'socialism' while carrying out radical neo-liberal restructuring, the Socialists, unsurprisingly, were increasingly perceived by voters as being self-contradictory. The PS's ideological awkwardness is well encapsulated in Finance Minister Pierre Bérégovoy's defence of financial deregulation in a 1985 ministerial publication: 'France has had a long tradition of *dirigisme* and State intervention ... As a socialist,

---

[27] 'Club de la Presse', on Europe 1, quoted in 'M. Madelin: M. Fabius a déposé le bilan', *Le Monde*, 5 November 1985.
[28] *Libération*, 10 May 1984.

my conception of freedom does not accord with this tradition. The State ought to fix a general rule that organizes – and allows – the functioning of markets.'[29] Bérégovoy's attempt to fit 'socialism' in the Procrustean bed of neo-liberal reformism is incongruous, to the say the least.

The electorate became increasingly disaffected with the government as the 1986 elections for the *Assemblée nationale* were approaching. On the Left in particular, the simultaneous sense of betrayal and hypocrisy was acute, and dissenting voices multiplied. The PCF's four token ministers resigned from the Socialist government in the 1984 reshuffle, and the Communists were hoping to take advantage of its discrediting to improve their electoral prospects.[30] From within the PS, Chevènement and the CERES did not hesitate to air their disapproval with ongoing policies, mounting rabid verbal attacks against 'liberalism' and 'social-democracy'. Importantly, however, Left dissent and opposition did not produce any significant remobilization. As noted above, trade-union membership and industrial militancy were on the decline, and both the PCF and labour leaders deemed it too risky to call for a general strike. In a few years' time, the joy and hopes of millions of Mitterrand voters had turned into Left disengagement and dispersion. To put it in Gramscian terms, no credible hegemonic project was discernible, whether embodied by the State – the dissonance of PS discourse precluded that – or emerging from within civil society.

Coherent vs. split historic blocs

The economics of neo-liberalism in Britain and France in the 1980s were quite alike, with regard to actual policy steps and to their sequencing in time. In both cases, for instance, macro-economic stabilization and the implementation of monetarist orthodoxy in the

---

[29] In *L'Agefi*, January 1985, quoted in Pierre Rimbert, '"Nous avons eu le pouvoir, maintenant il nous faut l'argent"', *Le Monde Diplomatique*, April 2009.
[30] This did not happen. In 1986, the PCF obtained 9.8 per cent of the vote. Jean-Marie Le Pen's National Front made its entrance in the *Assemblée nationale* for the first time on this occasion.

early 1980s opened the way for accelerated financial deregulation by the middle of the decade.[31] Yet the political and ideological configuration of forces involved could not have been more different. In Britain, Thatcher's government attempted to mobilize the public on the basis of a coherent, unabashedly Rightist discourse. By appealing to reason and sentiment simultaneously, and by projecting future-oriented 'political imagery' – as Stuart Hall put it – the Conservatives sought not only to explicate and justify neo-liberal reforms, but to make them look attractive and desirable. Another way to put it is that Thatcherism pursued, and achieved, an organic articulation of policy practice and State ideology. As seen in the previous section, this form of organic articulation was precisely what was lacking in France.

We wish to suggest that Gramsci's notion of 'historic bloc' is uniquely capable of illuminating this contrast between the British and French cases; that is, provided that it is developed a bit further than in Gramsci's original formulation. In other words, we seek to adapt and refine the theory of the 'historic bloc' in connection with these concrete existing social formations.

Let us first briefly return to the definition provided by the *Prison Notebooks*: 'Structures and superstructures form an "historical bloc". That is to say the complex, contradictory and discordant *ensemble* of the superstructures is the refection of the *ensemble* of the social relations of production.'[32] As we argued in Chapter 4, the historic bloc emphasizes modes of interaction and interpenetration between the different 'moments' – economic, political, ideological – of social life. Gramsci is building on the Marxian conceptual couplet of base-superstructure but taking it in a less deterministic direction. In his careful study of this concept, Hugues Portelli rightly comes to the conclusion that 'to ask whether one element or another of the historic bloc has primacy is to ask the wrong question'.[33] An accurate understanding of the historic bloc should guard against preconceived

---

[31] A noteworthy contrast is privatization policy. The French Socialist government subjected the State-owned industrial sector to radical restructuring from 1983 to 1986 but did not sell it off. Large-scale privatization did not have to wait for long, however, as it was implemented by the Chirac government after 1986.

[32] Q8§182; *SPN*, p. 366.

[33] Portelli, *Gramsci et le bloc historique*, p. 63. A similar point is made by Peter Thomas in his *The Gramscian Moment*, p. 100.

notions of the ontological or causal priority of any single 'moment' or 'level' of social reality. The historic bloc, moreover, serves to stress that society as a whole or as a totality – *pace* Louis Althusser – is not reducible to any of its parts. Its heuristic promise lies in the study of concrete social articulations that are, as everything else, subject to open-ended historical becoming. Gramsci is innovating from within Marxism and opening up new perspectives for macrosocial analysis.

From this starting point, it is possible to make a step towards the development of a typology of historic blocs. Ultimately, of course, each historic bloc, reflecting the features of a single spatio-temporal configuration, is unique. Yet it should be equally obvious that shared structural attributes may be identified across the whole spectrum of past and present historic blocs. Crucially, some historic blocs sustain hegemonic processes while others do not.

The following passage from the *Prison Notebooks* sheds some light on this issue: 'An appropriate political initiative is always necessary to liberate the economic thrust from the dead weight of traditional policies – i.e. to change the political direction of certain forces which have to be absorbed if a new, homogeneous politico-economic historical bloc, without internal contradictions, is to be successfully formed.'[34] Gramsci appears to be describing in general terms the conditions of emergence of hegemonic historic blocs, only instead of appealing explicitly to the concept of hegemony, he is writing of a 'homogeneous politico-economic historical bloc'. We have already remarked upon the place accorded to homogeneity and homogenization in Gramsci's thought.[35] The above excerpt implies that hegemony is premised on homogeneity within the historic bloc, specifically on the coherence – or organic articulation – of its economic and political 'moments'. It refers, moreover, to the capacity of progressive or *avant-garde* political organization at the superstructural level ('political initiative') to overhaul the economic structure and force its advance along the path of historical development ('liberate the economic thrust from the dead weight of traditional policies').

---

[34] Q13§23; *SPN*, p. 168.
[35] See Chapter 2 on the homogenizing function of intellectuals and Chapter 3 on homogeneity within the political party.

What Gramsci has in mind here, of course, is the political capacity of the proletariat to actuate the transition from a capitalist to a socialist economic structure through revolution. Yet it is striking how this sentence from the *Notebooks* is evocative of the Thatcherite transformation of Britain's post-war economic structures. (Again, the irony of historical reversals has it that neo-liberal reformism has been substituted for proletarian revolutionism.)

As a counterpoint to the hegemonic, coherent historic bloc, we put forward the notion of an incoherent, or split – and by implication non-hegemonic – historic bloc. The split type of historic bloc may be defined by a disjunction or disarticulation between its different 'moments'. By contrast with Gramsci's 'homogeneous politico-economic historic bloc', the split historic bloc manifests a heterogeneity of political and economic dynamics in society.

The idea of a split historic bloc appears especially well-suited to characterizing France's early phase of neo-liberalization under the PS from 1981 to 1986. On the political plane, the Socialist electoral victory of 1981 was the result of specific developments (as described above). The PS's renovation at the 1971 Epinay Congress under Mitterrand's impulse made it a credible contender for power. Its new-found assertive Left orientation enabled it to lure voters away from the PCF, while definite sociological trends were arguably diminishing the electoral prospects of the Communists and of the Right. Yet we have also seen how, after the 1981 victory, the prior political dynamic of Left ascendancy seemingly ran into an economic wall. Between 1982 and 1986, PS policy became orthogonal to the very aspirations that had brought it to power. France was experiencing a sharp, painful incoherence of the political and economic elements of the historic bloc. From then on, PS discourse became a terrain on which the tension of the split historic bloc was played out. As seen in the previous section, official utterances could only, in a somewhat pathetic form, register the country's structural contradiction together with the impossibility of overcoming it by discursive means.

Furthermore, one should stress the extent to which the decisive Socialist policy turnarounds in the period from 1982 to 1986 were responses to external pressures and inducements, from the trade deficit and foreign debt crisis of 1982–3 to the perceived need to overhaul finance in order to attract international mobile capital.

By contrast, the pre-1981 dynamic of socio-political change that conditioned the PS's accession to power was largely a domestic story. It so happened that the French electorate was moving Left in the 1970s, although this can hardly be said of most Western European countries in the period. In Britain, by contrast, the Thatcherite political project was not only synchronized with neo-liberal reformism, it was defined by it. And both could gather strength from the contemporary worldwide ascendancy of monetarism, financialization and generally heightened economic globalization.

As regards our French case study, might one say that base (the economy) trumped superstructure (politics), thereby confirming Marx's original insight about where causal primacy lies? This appears to be the case in this concrete, unique instance, although we would do well to guard against a deterministic interpretation of French developments. Ultimately, France's neo-liberal reforms were not the mechanical effects of economic forces, but resulted from political choices. As bearers of State power, Mitterrand and the members of the government found themselves at the interface of competing political, economic, domestic and external pressures. From June 1982 onward, they decided on a definite political course, which we have characterized as one of neo-liberalization. France's split historic bloc was brought about by this decision.

Neo-liberalism and intellectuals in France: Transformism and fatalism

As a final section of this chapter, it is possible to draw attention to further repercussions of the split historic bloc in the ideological sphere. Previously, extending Gramsci's original understanding, we primarily defined the distinction between hegemonic and split historic blocs as one between politico-economic homogeneity and heterogeneity. However, the structural features of the historic bloc are also played out in the areas of ideology, common sense and cultural life in the widest sense. Of particular interest in this connection is how intellectuals register and grapple with the wider social configurations in which they are enmeshed.

We have already insisted on the central role of intellectuals in Gramsci's thought (see Chapter 2). Some of the *Prison Notebooks*' essential insights concern intellectuals' insertion in the superstructures and their contribution to the politics of hegemony. Indeed, Portelli has argued that Gramsci's very notion of the historic bloc is unintelligible if abstracted from his theory of intellectuals, since intellectuals – described by Gramsci as the 'functionaries' of the superstructures – embody the concrete, living junction between the different 'moments' of the historic bloc.[36] Therefore, whether a historic bloc is coherent (hegemonic) or split (non-hegemonic) should carry definite implications for the way in which intellectuals relate to economic and political developments.

To return to our Franco-British comparison, it can be noticed that the tight articulation of State ideology and policy practice under Thatcherism delineated a hegemonic project in relation to which the intellectual milieu could feel compelled to take sides. Partisans of the Conservative government could act as the neo-liberal State's organic intellectuals. This is Stuart Hall's point when referring to 'leader writers in the *Telegraph*, the *Economist* and the *Spectator*, opinion leaders in the *Mail* and *Express* and many others … constructing for "Thatcherism" a populist common sense'.[37] Many others, of course, actively opposed Thatcherite politics, while still others remained aloof vis-à-vis the ideological expressions crystallizing around emergent neo-liberal hegemony. Whichever way individual intellectuals went, it was possible, in Britain, to pin down ongoing economic restructuring and dislocation on a coherent political project.

This was not the case in France once Mitterrand and the PS had embarked on the path of neo-liberal reform after 1982. In the context of a split historic bloc – that is, of structural politico-economic heterogeneity – no coherent State project could be identified as carrying neo-liberalization forward. Socialist discourse became dissonant and self-contradictory. Although the project of breaking away from capitalism had been *de facto* abandoned, the breakaway from socialism was not acknowledged. Whereas in Britain neo-liberal

---

[36] Portelli, *Gramsci et le bloc historique*. See Q8§182; *SPN*, p. 12.
[37] Hall, 'The Great Moving Right Show', p. 17.

reforms were accompanied by, and embedded in, a definite Right ideology, in France they occurred in ideological murky waters.

The overall configuration of the split historic bloc informed the range of choices open to French intellectuals in the face of neo-liberalization. After 1982, the absence of any mobilizing project for neo-liberal reformism – or indeed for any kind of socio-economic transformation – emanating from the Socialist government left intellectuals in a vacuum of sorts regarding the political meaning or implications of ongoing reforms. Combined with this vacuum was the absence of any credible alternative hegemonic project emerging from within civil society. This would have been, of course, the kind of revolutionary aspiration that had gripped French students and workers in May 1968, and that had persisted throughout the 1970s, dogging the presidencies of Georges Pompidou and Valéry Giscard d'Estaing in the shape of radical student politics and sustained labour militancy. By the early 1980s, however, this wave of contestation had subsided. Meanwhile, in the intellectual milieu itself, the influence of Marxist thinking on academic research and public debate was experiencing a rapid, continuous decline that had started in the mid-1970s. Of course, it could not help Marxism's standing in intellectual life that the PS, a Marxist-sounding party prior to 1981, swiftly abandoned socialist policy once in power. It was tempting – if mistaken – for opponents and cynics to read in the PS's turnaround the bankruptcy of Marxism itself.

In such a political and ideological context, French intellectuals tended to absorb neo-liberalism in a passive and fatalistic way. Because State-imposed economic restructuring could not be associated with any explicit political project, it could be framed as being itself apolitical. For many French columnists and commentators, disinflation, mass industrial redundancies and financial deregulation were hardly political choices at all, but instead unavoidable adaptations to new pressures originating from the world economy. Policy reversals were depicted not as expressions of political will, but rather as realism in the face of necessity.

After the first turnaround of 1982–3, the failure of 'socialism' became a common thread in French public debate. From then onward, in a gradual manner, intellectuals who had supported the Left in 1981 forewent their erstwhile communistic or socialistic convictions. This shift of the French intellectual milieu away from the Left and towards the centre of the political spectrum did not occur in any organized or coherent way. Instead, it was premised on an accumulation of individual revisions and renouncements – what Gramsci would have described as a 'molecular' process of change.[38]

The notion of 'transformism' is well-suited to characterize the experience of the French intellectual Left during the Mitterrand years. As will be recalled, Gramsci used this term to describe how, in post-*Risorgimento* Italy, Left and Right politicians molecularly converged towards the centre in the Italian parliament, thereby disintegrating the party system (see Chapter 3). In 1980s France, 'transformism' can be applied to the process whereby intellectuals shed their Left orientation in a molecular, atomized fashion, within the configuration of the split historic bloc. This in turn led to a broadly felt, fatalistic recognition of the apparent necessity of neo-liberal restructuring. The molecular quality of the change involved is well captured by Didier Eribon: 'the conservative restoration resembled less a historical rupture than a geographical mutation or geological slide: while one type of thinking was replacing another, the two continued to coexist, and one could observe individual transitions from one to the next'.[39]

Thus the 'common sense' of the French intellectual milieu was altered. The new accepted wisdom bore the mark of fatalistic consent to neo-liberalism: it implied a radical disconnect between economic and political realms, a supposed imperviousness of the former to the interventions of the latter. By the mid-1980s, political voluntarism in the economic sphere was construed as hubris if not delusion – witness the failure of 1981–2 policy – while the word 'realism' – often applied in a laudatory way to post-1982 PS decision-making – came to mean precisely the adaptation of policy to objective economic phenomena. As the intellectual

---

[38] Elements of critical history on these socio-cultural shifts can be gleaned in Didier Eribon, *D'une révolution conservatrice et de ses effets sur la gauche française* (Paris: Léo Scheer, 2007) and in François Cusset, *La décennie: Le grand cauchemar des années 1980* (Paris: La Découverte, 2006). See also, in English, Perry Anderson's 'Dégringolade', *London Review of Books*, 26:17 (2004), pp. 3–9, and its sequel 'Union Sucrée', *London Review of Books*, 26:18 (2004), pp. 10–16.

[39] Eribon, *D'une révolution conservatrice*, pp. 86–7.

milieu experienced a sudden amnesia about France's own history of pervasive *dirigisme* and high-speed growth in the post-war decades, this new common sense reified the economy into a self-contained domain with its own *sui generis* laws that politicians were powerless to alter.

Such a mindset is reminiscent of what Gramsci meant by 'economism'. In the *Prison Notebooks*, this term serves to characterize – and criticize – the tendency among Marxists to fetishize economic relations, leading to fatalism, mechanism and abstentionism among would-be revolutionaries (see Chapter 3). In 1980s France, economism captured the thinking of the new intellectual centrists. As the new accepted wisdom, it was invoked to justify one's turn away from Left ideals.

Whereas economic transformation was utilized as a mobilizing cause by Thatcher in Britain – as it was by Ronald Reagan in the United States – it thus became in France an argument for popular demobilization. It is pointless, naturally, to mobilize against unalterable laws, or to resist 'realism'. It is true that Thatcherism is popularly associated with TINA ('there is no alternative'), yet it should be remembered that Thatcher, her associates and her supporters took care to embed neo-liberal reformism in a moralistic, value-heavy discourse. In a sense, then, the more passive and fatalistic French embrace of neo-liberalism in the 1980s expresses the pared-down gist of TINA better than the British one. At the height of Reagan's popularity in early 1985, Alain Minc, one of France's most prominent economic commentators, enjoined his compatriots to draw the right lessons: 'The United States's success is exercising a diffuse pressure that is forcing us to overcome our own rigidities. Let us hail the miracle, accept its mystery, and, most important, let us follow suit.'[40] Such a statement is highly revealing of France's peculiar translation of Anglo-American neo-liberal politics. Reform here is not about embodying a positive political project. Instead, the French are called upon to respond adequately to objective forces, the true necessity of reform lying outside the country's borders and, so it seems, beyond the mind's grasp.

---

[40] In *L'Expansion*, 8 February 1985, quoted in Halimi, *Le grand bond*, p. 403.

Conclusion

This chapter has attempted to put some of Gramsci's concepts to use in elucidating patterns of neo-liberal transition. The so-called Thatcherite 'revolution' in Britain forwarded a hegemonic project, working relentlessly towards the overhaul of economic structures, political life and the very 'common sense' of the public. Comparatively, however, hegemonic politics has not always been the preferred route to neo-liberalism. By offering a detailed account of the French experience, we have sought to illustrate how neo-liberalization could proceed within a markedly fractured socio-political landscape. Under the French Socialist Party, which had vowed no less than to break away from capitalism prior to its accession to power, the French economy underwent high-speed, drastic neo-liberal restructuring between 1982 and 1986. All the while, the government maintained its verbal commitment to 'socialism', eliciting popular reactions of disaffection and cynicism. Ideological lines of divide became fuzzy, and political agency in the process of economic change appeared elusive. Left ideals lost their appeal as intellectuals fatalistically came to terms with neo-liberalization.

A remarkable fact about the Franco-British comparison is that analogous economic policies grew out of two vastly divergent political-cum-cultural configurations. This chapter has argued that Gramsci's notions of hegemony, historic bloc and transformism are possible keys towards a deeper understanding of these contradictory real-world dynamics. Hegemony/non-hegemony encapsulates the root condition of the opposition between the British and French trajectories. Types of historic bloc shed light on the articulation – or lack thereof – between the economic, political and ideological 'moments' of social life. In 1980s Britain, economic transformation, policy action and State ideology cohered under the aegis of the Thatcherite project, while France, on the other hand, experienced radical politico-economic heterogeneity. We related this contrast to a wider distinction between coherent and split historic blocs. Finally, the notion of transformism was used to describe shifts and revisions in French intellectual life in the context of the split historic bloc.

Overall, in this chapter and the previous one we have tried to draw on Gramsci's writings not in the search of settled interpretive schemas, but in a quest for 'living' ideas that may be worked upon and made relevant to the study of past and present developments. Crucially, Gramsci's concepts are at their most potent when they are refined in order to adhere as closely as possible to concrete historical situations.

PART FOUR

Legacy

8

Mapping Gramsci's Legacy

Introduction

In this chapter, we attempt to map Gramsci's influence on contemporary critical thought. This map is necessarily somewhat limited and schematic, not least because Gramsci has had an influence on virtually all subjects within the humanities and also because Gramsci's legacy has been tied up with the fortunes of Italian communism, particularly until the 1980s, and with the availability, strengths and weaknesses of collections of his prison writing.[1]

These difficulties notwithstanding, we can begin to trace the outlines of Gramsci's theoretical and political legacy today.[2] First, Gramsci must be understood in the context of twentieth-century

---

[1] See Fabio Frosini, 'Beyond the Crisis of Marxism: Gramsci's Contested Legacy', in: Jacques Bidet and Stathis Kouvelakis (eds), *Critical Companion to Contemporary Marxism* (Leiden: Brill, 2008), pp. 663–78 for an excellent historical account of Gramsci's legacy, and Eric Hobsbawm, 'Introduction', in: David Forgacs (ed.), *The Gramsci Reader: Selected Writings, 1916–1935* (New York: New York University Press, 2000), pp. 10–13 for a shorter overview.

[2] For a good overview of Gramsci's reception in English see Geoff Eley, 'Reading Gramsci in English: Observations on the Reception of Antonio Gramsci in the English-Speaking World, 1957–82', *European History Quarterly*, 14 (1984), pp. 441–78, and for the British context David Forgacs, 'Gramsci and Marxism in Britain', *New Left Review*, 1:176 (1989), pp. 70–88 is an excellent account, though the state of Gramsci studies has changed since the publication of these articles. For an explicitly global view of the various interpretations of Gramsci, see Michele Filippini, *Gramsci globale: Guida pratica alle interpretazioni di Gramsci nel mondo* (Bologna: Odoya, 2012).

Marxism, as one of the leading figures within the current of 'Western Marxism', even if he does not fit unproblematically into that current. Gramsci's relation to Italian communism and the political uses of Gramsci must also be taken as a key situating context for a map of Gramsci's legacy. Gramsci's influence within contemporary critical thought is most keenly felt in four fields: post-Marxism, Postcolonial Studies, Cultural Studies and International Political Economy.[3] Gramsci's academic legacy, of course, extends beyond these disciplines, but in these four fields his influence has been particularly profound.

Gramsci and Western Marxism

The first step in mapping Gramsci's legacy today is to place him in the trajectory of twentieth-century Marxism. Gramsci is one of the key figures in European Marxism, and in particular in the trend of Marxist thought usually termed 'Western Marxism', which developed in response to the three key political events of the early twentieth century: the First World War, the October Revolution in Russia and the failed German Revolution of 1918–23.[4] We would contend that Gramsci can be admitted only problematically into the general current of Western Marxism, and that his nature as a 'problem case' for inclusion in this intellectual tradition – which is partly caused by his biography, as we explain below – is closely related to the later interpretations of his work and his development into a key thinker within contemporary critical thought.

---

[3] An important recent collection of essays on Gramsci from the *Rethinking Marxism* journal from 1988 to 2011 divides scholarship specifically on Gramsci into four sections: cultural studies, literature and criticism; philological studies; political philosophy (and Gramsci's relationship to Marxism); and the translation and organization of Gramsci's *Prison Notebooks*. See Marcus E. Green (ed.), *Rethinking Gramsci* (London: Routledge, 2011).

[4] The term comes from Maurice Merleau-Ponty, *Les aventures de la dialectique* (Paris: Gallimard, 1955). Göran Therborn, in his *From Marxism to Post-Marxism?* (London: Verso, 2008), p. 84, defines Western Marxism as a 'politically autonomous trend of thought in the advanced capitalist countries after the October Revolution', which does not apply as well to Gramsci, Lukács and Korsch as to later theorists.

The defining account of Western Marxism's genesis and characteristics is given by Perry Anderson, and we largely follow it in the comments that follow.[5] The constituent thinkers of Western Marxism, according to Anderson, can be divided into generations with shared characteristics. The first generation includes Georg Lukács (b. 1885, Budapest), Karl Korsch (b. 1886, Saxony), Gramsci (b. 1891, Sardinia), Walter Benjamin (b. 1892, Berlin), Max Horkheimer (b. 1895, Stuttgart), Galvano Della Volpe (b. 1897, Romagna) and Herbert Marcuse (b. 1898, Berlin). The second generation comprises Henri Lefebvre (b. 1901, Gascony), Theodor Adorno (b. 1903, Frankfurt), Jean-Paul Sartre (b. 1905, Paris), Lucien Goldmann (b. 1913, Bucharest) and Louis Althusser (b. 1918, Algeria). Lucio Colletti (b. 1924, Rome) stands as a single borderline case of a third generation.

If Gramsci stands as part of the first generation of Western Marxism, then we can ask what differentiates his generation from the one that preceded it. Despite its difficulties, an understanding of Marxism that takes into account generational and geographical shifts has the singular benefit of allowing us to begin to relate the overall characteristics of the thought of a set of thinkers to wider political events and deeper changes in capitalism. The generation that preceded Gramsci's included such figures as Lenin (b. 1870, Simbirsk), Luxemburg (b. 1871, Galicia), Hilferding (b. 1877, Vienna) and Trotsky (b. 1879, Kherson), and was formed as European capitalism moved towards the First World War.[6] Lenin's generation, which took its major figures from East of Berlin, was composed of thinkers who also played a key role in the leadership of national parties – unlike the generation that preceded them – and responded

---

[5] Perry Anderson, *Considerations on Western Marxism* (London: New Left Books, 1976). See also Martin Jay, *Marxism and Totality: The Adventures of a Concept from Lukács to Habermas* (Berkeley: University of California Press, 1984); Russell Jacoby, *Dialectic of Defeat: Contours of Western Marxism* (Cambridge: Cambridge University Press, 1981).
[6] The generation of which Lenin was the leading figure can thus be seen as the third generation of Marxism, with Marx (b. 1818, Trier) and Engels (b. 1820, Westphalia) comprising the first generation (in which Marxist theory was developed before the emergence of industrial working-class parties), and the second including Labriola (b. 1843, Campania), Mehring (b. 1846, Pomerania), Kautsky (b. 1854, Bohemia) and Plekhanov (b. 1856, Central Russia), which sought in different ways to systematize historical materialism.

to the transformation of capitalism into an (increasingly) monopolistic and imperialist economic system.[7]

Western Marxism as a departure from the political problems and solutions of Lenin's generation can be characterized, briefly, as follows. Born of the defeat of proletarian revolutions after the First World War as representing the failure of the socialist revolution to spread outside Russia, Western Marxism is marked above all by an increasing divide between (Marxist) theory and (working class) practice. As it develops, its practitioners are increasingly likely to hold a post at a university, be identified as a philosopher and be interested in non-Marxist systems of thought; as a whole Western Marxism exhibits a focus on abstract questions of method, aesthetics and philosophy rather than political economy or questions of political strategy or party organization. Western Marxism, also, represents a geographical concentration of European Marxism from the 1920s in Germany, France and Italy, as the three countries that combined a relatively large Communist Party with a numerous intelligentsia.

Gramsci, Anderson notes, is the greatest and least typical representative of Western Marxism.[8] There are a number of reasons why he seems to stand apart from the other thinkers of Western Marxism. Perhaps most importantly, as noted above, Gramsci stands as part of the transitional first generation of Western Marxism. Along with Lukács and Korsch, identified in all accounts as the 'founding figures' of Western Marxism, Gramsci was a major political leader within his party (see Chapter 1). Importantly, Gramsci – alone in his generation – was a product of the 'periphery' of European capitalism, a 'barbed gift of the backwoods'.[9]

---

[7] See Rudolf Hilferding, *Finance Capital* (Vienna: Verlag der Wiener, 1910), Rosa Luxemburg, *Accumulation of Capital* (Berlin: Buchhandlung Vorwärts, 1913), and V. I. Lenin, *Imperialism: The Highest Stage of Capitalism* (1917), in: V. I. Lenin, *Selected Works* (Moscow: Progress Publishers, 1963), pp. 667–766.

[8] Anderson, *Considerations*, p. 67.

[9] See Tom Nairn, 'Antonu Su Gobbu', in: Anne Showstack Sassoon (ed.), *Approaches to Gramsci* (London: Writers and Readers, 1982), p. 161. For the importance of Gramsci's geographical origins see Michael Ekers, Gillian Hart, Stefan Kipfer and Alex Loftus, '"A Barbed Gift of the Backwoods": Gramsci's Sardinian Beginnings', in: Michael Ekers, Gillian Hart, Stefan Kipfer and Alex Loftus (eds), *Gramsci: Space, Nature, Politics*, Oxford: Wiley-Blackwell, 2013, pp. 3–5; Robert J. C. Young, 'Il Gramsci meridionale', in: Neelam Srivastava and Baidik Bhattacharya (eds), *The Postcolonial Gramsci* (London: Routledge, 2012), pp. 17–33.

Gramsci again stands apart from the main current of Western Marxism due to his exceptional upbringing in poverty (although not as a member of the peasantry or the proletariat). Gramsci is also, along with Benjamin,[10] the only member of his generation or the next to die before the 1960s. More importantly, Gramsci's years in prison served to isolate him from the Stalinization of the USSR and further differentiate his thought from the other representatives of Western Marxism.[11] Nevertheless, Gramsci's life and intellectual legacy most closely fit the general characterization of Western Marxism as an intellectual response to political defeat. Gramsci's *Prison Notebooks* were composed in conditions of very real defeat, political and personal. Gramsci alone among the thinkers of Western Marxism sought to address this defeat fully and to determine the specificity of the Russian Revolution and the nature of bourgeois rule of his time.[12] This is perhaps the ultimate origin of, and key context for assessing the importance of, his concept of hegemony.

Gramsci's intellectual legacy must therefore first and foremost be placed within the context of the development of Western Marxism. Within Western Marxism Gramsci came to be identified as the thinker who, above all others, takes the autonomy of ideology, of culture and of 'superstructures' taken in their most general sense as a *political* problem that must be linked to power and to practical questions of maintaining, resisting or overthrowing a social order.[13] In Keucheyan's assessment, by the beginning of the twenty-first century Gramsci had come to be understood as 'the author in the Marxist tradition who makes it possible to pose the problem of culture more sharply'.[14]

---

[10] Another victim of fascism, Benjamin committed suicide in September 1940 at the French-Spanish border while attempting to flee from the Nazis.

[11] For instance, Anderson also notes that although Gramsci fits the general pattern of verbal complexity within Western Marxism, the difficulties of Gramsci's language are partly explained by his imprisonment. See *Considerations*, pp. 54–5.

[12] Anderson, *Considerations*, p. 80.

[13] Ibid., p. 78.

[14] Razmig Keucheyan, *The Left Hemisphere: Mapping Critical Theory Today* (London: Verso, 2014), p. 31.

Gramsci and Italian communism

Gramsci is acknowledged today as one of the twentieth century's foremost thinkers and his *Prison Notebooks* enjoy worldwide academic recognition. However, during the decades that followed his death and until the 1970s, his influence was chiefly localized in a single country – Italy – and was overwhelmingly political, not academic.

At the time of Gramsci's demise in 1937, the (exiled) head of the PCI was his past comrade-in-arms Palmiro Togliatti, who would keep this position until his death in 1964. During his long tenure as the PCI's leader, Togliatti always took care to claim Gramsci's authority, casting the latter as the party's chief theoretician and a martyr of Italian communism. Togliatti's successors, notably Luigi Longo (1964–72) and Enrico Berlinguer (1972–84) did very much the same. The PCI itself, through its experience of wartime anti-fascist resistance and peacetime electoral politics, went on to become the largest Communist Party in the Western bloc after the Second World War, reaching over two million members in the late 1940s. Gramsci remained the party's prime 'patron saint' until its eventual decline and dissolution forty years later, at the close of the Cold War. This ensured a wide circulation for Gramscian ideas among Italian Left circles during the post-war decades, but simultaneously – when conveniently plucked out of context – Gramscian notions and assertions could fall prey to all manner of misinterpretations and manipulations aimed at justifying the party line of the day. For better or worse, Gramsci's first major historical legacy was the mark he left on the Italian communist movement. Incidentally, such a posthumous aura within a mass party is yet another trait that sets him apart from the other members of his 'Western Marxist' generation.

Togliatti started to make arrangements for the publication of Gramsci's prison writings immediately after the war. The prison letters, published in 1947, won a prestigious literary award – the Viareggio Prize – much to the PCI's delight. Then, between 1948 and 1951, the publisher Einaudi put out five thematic volumes of excerpts from the *Prison Notebooks*. The Einaudi edition remained, for lack of alternatives, the essential reference for students of Gramsci until Valentino Gerratana's chronological, complete edition in 1975. Yet the early edition is now acknowledged to be a deeply problematic treatment of Gramscian thought. To regroup Gramsci's scattered, exploratory notations into thematic rubrics – such as 'Historical materialism and Croce's philosophy' or 'Literature and national life' – conveyed a false impression of completeness, while the original notebooks were inaccessible to the general public. The very open-endedness of Gramsci's writings was masked; instead the Einaudi volumes tended to turn him into a petrified 'classic' of Italian political thought. Moreover, the compilers of these volumes expunged passages that were perceived as compromising to the PCI in the post-war context. References to Bordiga and Trotsky, as well as scathing remarks on Italian parliamentarianism, were censored.

It is difficult to doubt the sincerity of Togliatti's admiration for Gramsci, or the fact that he drew practical inspiration from him. Yet it remains that Togliatti and the PCI leadership chose to use Gramsci's figure and ideas in specific ways that were consonant with the policies they were pursing and with the image they wished to project in post-war Italian society. On the one hand, the PCI sought to depict Gramsci as a summit in the nation's intellectual history, an embodiment of Italian high culture, a mind that had inherited the genius of Giambattista Vico's historicist philosophy and carried it forward into the twentieth century. That the PCI would not only countenance but actively promote such a rigid, traditionalist reading of Gramsci can be explained by its thirst for cultural prestige at the time. Togliatti was eager to establish the communist movement at the heart of Italian civil society, and the intellectual brilliance of Gramsci's writings seemed to allow his party to have a claim on the high ground of national culture.

On the other hand, in the early post-war years, Togliatti attempted to present Gramsci's life and prison martyrdom as that of an impeccable Stalinist hero. Gramsci's writings on party discipline were appealed to when loyalty to the PCI leadership had to be enforced within the ranks, while passages of the *Prison Notebooks* that could be interpreted as damning for the Soviet Union were comfortably out of sight.[15]

As a result of this peculiar post-war PCI embrace, Gramsci became a quasi-mythological figure for the party rank and file. His pictures and busts abounded in PCI local sections across the country, fuelling a form of hero folklore that eschewed critical engagement with his actual writings.[16] By contrast, for those on the Italian Left that became alienated from the PCI leadership – such as the *operaismo* group in the 1960s and 1970s – Gramsci could appear, understandably, as a stale icon legitimating the status quo.[17]

A second phase in Gramsci's political legacy in Italy came with the PCI's so-called 'Eurocommunist' turn. The term 'Eurocommunism' was used frequently in the 1970s and 1980s to describe the tendency of certain communist parties in Western Europe – specifically in Italy, Spain and France – to distance themselves from orthodox Marxism-Leninism and the Soviet Union. The PCI went the farthest in that direction, and is therefore considered the chief exemplar of 'Eurocommunism'.[18] In so doing, it typically appealed to Gramsci's thought, finding new ways to interpret and inflect his ideas in order to justify its new political course.

Following the Soviet invasion of Czechoslovakia in 1968, the PCI became increasingly vocal in criticizing the Soviet Union's authoritarian model, arguing instead for a 'democratic road to socialism' suited to Italy's own political conditions and parliamentary tradition. Such a position resonated with the wider call, across both Western and

---

[15] See Costanzo Preve, 'De la mort du gramscisme au retour à Gramsci: La crise actuelle de perspective politique du marxisme gramscien en Italie', in: André Tosel (ed.), *Modernité de Gramsci: Actes du colloque franco-italien de Besançon, 23–25 novembre 1989* (Paris: Les Belles Lettres, 1992), pp. 293–313.

[16] Anderson, *Considerations*, pp. 40–1.

[17] For Perry Anderson's take on the trajectory of the post-war Italian Left, see his 'An Invertebrate Left', *London Review of Books*, 31:5 (2009), pp. 12–18.

[18] The PCF dabbled in 'Eurocommunism' for a few years in the mid-1970s, at the time of the 'Left Union' (see Chapter 7), but quickly reversed its course and returned to the Soviet fold, going so far as to support Russia's invasion of Afghanistan in 1979. The Communist Party of Spain (CPE) under Santiago Carrillo opted for a 'Eurocommunist' politics of accommodation with the Spanish monarchy following the death of Franco in 1976, but was swiftly marginalized by the social-democratic Socialist Workers' Party (PSOE) in Spanish political life thereafter.

Eastern blocs, in favour of more Soviet respect for national differences in ways of attaining and practising socialism. Under Enrico Berlinguer, the PCI took great care to avoid any association with revolutionary violence or any kind of subversion, adopting as unsympathetic a position to Left terrorism as Italy's governing Christian Democrats.[19] In order to cast itself as a potential partner in government, it ceased to put into question Italy's membership in NATO, Berlinguer famously telling a journalist in 1976, 'I feel safer on this side'. In the mid-1970s, in what was known as the 'historic compromise', the PCI even offered its support to Giulio Andreotti's Christian Democratic government (although Andreotti did not return the favour by appointing PCI ministers).

It was common for party authorities at the time to justify their new accommodating orientation in Gramscian terms. The publication of Gramsci's pre-prison writings, together with the 1975 Gerratana edition of the *Prison Notebooks*, had given more visibility to his own rejection of political and intellectual dogmatism, which in turn could be used as an argument against the rigid Soviet system under Leonid Brezhnev. Most crucially, the proponents of the 'Eurocommunist' turn drew on Gramsci's writings to imply that 'ideological hegemony' and the 'war of position' were viable alternatives – as opposed to being complementary – to the coercive seizure of power by revolutionary forces. Togliatti had already succeeded during his tenure in turning the PCI into a potent ideological force in Italy, whose positions were well echoed throughout the country's cultural and intellectual spheres. In turn, it was tempting for PCI leaders in the 1970s to argue that time was on the side of socialism, and that their party's ideological pre-eminence would eventually translate into the peaceful assumption of State power by legal means. They construed the Italian State not as a coercive apparatus of class rule, but as an arena that could be progressively influenced and then taken over by parliamentary means, bringing about a new society-wide consensus and a new hegemony under the auspices of the PCI.

It is no surprise that Left critics of 'Eurocommunism' keenly denounced the instrumentalization of Gramsci's thought in the service of a politics of accommodation of which Gramsci himself

---

[19] Anderson, 'An Invertebrate Left'.

would have been very unlikely to approve.[20] In effect, by turning a blind eye to the coercive aspect of hegemony, by renouncing the war of movement and by overlooking the class foundations of the State, the 'Eurocommunists' were deforming Gramsci's intent and arguably leaving Marxism behind altogether. Ernest Mandel, one of the most scathing critics of 'Eurocommunism', argued that it amounted to substituting reformism for revolution, and that it embodied a 'Right' move drawing the West European communist movement closer to social democracy.[21]

By the late 1980s, however, little was left of the 'Eurocommunist' impulse. Far from time being on the side of Italian communism, the PCI's electoral fortunes steadily declined from the late 1970s onward and the party ingloriously dissolved into two rival organizations in 1991. In 1989, reflecting on the fact that Gramsci had ceased to be the 'patron saint' of a mass movement in his home country, Costanzo Preve could find solace in the fact that, as a result, his thought had been freed from circumstantial manipulation for party-political ends.[22]

Gramsci and post-Marxism

Gramsci has emerged as a key figure in debates over 'post-Marxism', or whether the Marxist model of society and politics is 'outdated' and thus needs to be replaced.[23] A key political context of the rise of post-Marxism has been the 'challenge' of New Social Movements – those struggles for women's rights, gay rights, ecology, peace and a range of other causes in the last decades of the twentieth century.

---

[20] Peter Gibbon, 'Gramsci, Eurocommunism and the Comintern', *Economy and Society*, 12:3 (1983), pp. 328–66.

[21] Ernest Mandel, *From Stalinism to Eurocommunism: The Bitter Fruits of 'Socialism in One Country'* (London: New Left Books, 1978).

[22] Preve, 'De la mort de Gramsci'.

[23] Therborn defines post-Marxism as denoting authors with 'an explicitly Marxist background, whose recent work has gone beyond Marxist problematics and who do not publicly claim a continuing Marxist commitment', while he uses the term 'neo-Marxism' to refer to a group of theorists who retain an explicit commitment to Marxism (while departing from its classical forms). See Therborn, *From Marxism to Post-Marxism?*, p. 165.

Post-Marxists typically contend that the Marxist focus on the working class as the 'universal' class that can liberate everyone must be replaced by a theorization of the ways in which diverse groups in opposition to capitalism can be united. Gramsci's thought is used at a key point by post-Marxist writers, as his concept of hegemony is said to establish the principle – contended to be central to any adequate recognition of the political possibilities of a world of fragmented struggles – that politics involves a process of 'articulation' in which interests are made and then represented, rather than pre-given by their economic position. A core theme in post-Marxism is the question of the relation between class and politics.

While there is disagreement as to the intellectual heritage of post-Marxism,[24] its contemporary instantiation represents an intellectual current within its own right (rather than existing as a part of Marxism).[25] The starting point of this 'contemporary post-Marxism' can be dated to the publication of, and subsequent heated discussion over, Ernesto Laclau and Chantal Mouffe's *Hegemony and Socialist Strategy: Towards a Radical Democratic Politics* (1985).[26] Laclau and Mouffe's aim is to deconstruct Marxism and sketch how to replace it with a post-Marxism whose aim would be a 'radical democracy' in which the irreducible

---

[24] Richard Howson, 'From Ethico-Political Hegemony to Post-Marxism', *Rethinking Marxism*, 19:2 (2007), pp. 234–44 sees Luxemburg's spontaneism, Kautsky's social democracy and the contradictory class positions in Wright's analytical Marxism as moments of post-Marxism within Marxist intellectual development. Eric Hobsbawm on the other hand sees Croce as the first post-Marxist, in which case Gramsci is clearly positioned as against the post-Marxism of his time, and by implication ours (cited in Adam David Morton, 'A Double Reading of Gramsci: Beyond the Logic of Contingency', *Critical Review of International Social and Political Philosophy*, 8:4 (2005), p. 440).

[25] Stuart Sim, *Post-Marxism: An Intellectual History* (London: Routledge, 2000).

[26] Ernesto Laclau and Chantal Mouffe, *Hegemony and Socialist Strategy: Towards a Radical Democratic Politics* (London: Verso, 1985). For reasons of space, a full discussion of Laclau and Mouffe is not possible here: see Sim, *Post-Marxism*, chapter 3 for an overview of the contemporaneous responses to Laclau and Mouffe in *New Left Review*. While Howson, 'From Ethico-Political Hegemony to Post-Marxism', sees in Laclau and Mouffe's work a continuation of Gramsci's project of analysing power, Chris Harman's 'Gramsci, the Prison Notebooks and Philosophy', *International Socialism*, 114 (2007), pp. 105–23 sees hegemony counterposed in their account to notions of class struggle and revolution. For critical assessments of Laclau and Mouffe's reading of Gramsci see Morton, 'Beyond the Logic of Contingency' and Peter Ives, 'Language, Agency, and Hegemony: A Gramscian Response to Post-Marxism', *Critical Review of International Social and Political Philosophy*, 8:4 (2005), pp. 455–68.

plurality of different struggles would receive proper recognition. The initial stress of *Hegemony and Socialist Strategy* is on Gramsci's break with a solely class-based conception of ideology in favour of a positive or 'material' perspective that rejects the deterministic base-superstructure model. Laclau and Mouffe talk of the Gramscian 'watershed', understood as a move from seeing politics as governed by the principle of representation – in which political actors and centrally the party represent a class core – to understanding as central to politics a notion of articulation, which sees the unity between social agents not as the expression of a common essence but as achieved through political work and struggle.[27] They criticize Gramsci as 'essentialist' with regard to the economy, since, as we have seen, Gramsci understands hegemony as stemming ultimately from a social group's position within the relations of production (see Chapter 5). As Laclau and Mouffe write, the 'inner essentialist core' of Gramsci's thought remains the predicate that the economy 'constitutes an insurmountable limit to society's potential for hegemonic recomposition' (while also existing as 'a homogeneous space unified by necessary laws').[28]

Instead, they propose a divisive break with Gramsci's concept of hegemony in two ways: they argue that there cannot be a single hegemonic pole within a political formation (such as a class actor), and they emphasize that all individual and group interests are *entirely* constructed through the process of articulation. The rejection of the idea of a leading group within a bloc raises a number of serious issues with regard to the interpretation of Gramsci's work.[29] Centrally, Gramsci's theorization of hegemony is clearly designed to provide an understanding of dominant groups' hegemonic strategies – and the notion of (class) leadership is clearly central to the conceptual origins of hegemony. As Laclau and Mouffe point out, for Gramsci 'there must always be a *single* unifying principle in every hegemonic formation, and this can only be a fundamental class'.[30] Rejecting this, hegemony is seen by Laclau and Mouffe as a 'federation' of

[27] Laclau and Mouffe, *Hegemony and Socialist Strategy*, p. 65.

[28] Ibid., p. 69.

[29] See Steve Jones, *Antonio Gramsci: Routledge Critical Thinkers* (London: Routledge, 2006).

[30] Laclau and Mouffe, *Hegemony and Socialist Strategy*, p. 69.

groups, or in terms of an ideal situation of politics, rather than – as in Gramsci's hands – a tool of analysis and a strategy. As Laclau and Mouffe put it, 'the expansion and determination of the social logic implicit in the concept of "hegemony" – in a direction that goes far beyond Gramsci – will provide us with an *anchorage* from which contemporary social struggles are *thinkable* in their specificity'.[31] The corresponding political project is to set up a 'chain of equivalences' that can then link varied anti-capitalist struggles. It is thus Laclau and Mouffe's engagement with Gramsci's concept of hegemony that forms the basis of their attempt to move beyond Marxism.[32]

Gramsci would likely have criticized Laclau and Mouffe's idealist notion of the free association of progressive forces and their dismissal of economic issues as 'voluntaristic'. Hegemony, instead, refers in Gramsci to a sort of leadership carried out at the material level, in the State and civil society (see Chapter 5). The question remains today of the weight to be attached to class as opposed to other salient divisions such as gender, ethnicity and age, and how these can be incorporated into a socialist political project. It is unsurprising that Gramsci's work provides the foundation of one of the most searching challenges to 'class primacy' in contemporary critical thought since he, like Laclau and Mouffe, is sensitive to the plurality and fluidity of the social as well as to how political categories are constructed rather than pre-given. However, it is important to note that Gramsci's Marxism was not, for him, a relativism – in his view the ultimate task of the theoretician is to relate the concreteness of the social in all its variety to positions of ascendancy in production, and thus ultimately to class.

Gramsci and Postcolonial Studies

Postcolonial Studies may be characterized, briefly, as the academic field that emerged out of developments in literary studies in the late

---

[31] Ibid., p. 3.

[32] Laclau and Mouffe state that their 'principal conclusion is that behind the concept of "hegemony" lies hidden something more than a type of political relation *complementary* to the basic categories of Marxist theory. In fact, it introduces a *logic of the social* which is incompatible with those categories'. Ibid., p. 3.

1970s, tending to exhibit the following characteristics in its relation to Marxism: the repudiation not only of Marxism but all struggle-based models of politics; the aversion to dialectics and hostility to totality; and the rejection of all forms of nationalism and consequent celebration of hybridity, liminality and migrancy.[33] It is in this context of Postcolonial Studies' 'constitutive anti-Marxism', as Lazarus and Varma put it, that Gramsci's legacy must be outlined.[34] Gramsci's influence in Postcolonial Studies runs along two primary axes: the work of Edward Said, particularly his extremely influential *Orientalism* (1978), and the work of the Subaltern Studies group of historians that emerged in the 1980s.[35]

The 1978 publication of Said's *Orientalism* is one of the key moments in the development of Postcolonial Theory, with Young going as far as to suggest that Postcolonial Studies has actually defined itself, at least initially, as an academic discipline through critiques of Said's work.[36] Said's project in *Orientalism* begins with the assumption that the Orient, as much as the idea of 'the West', 'is not merely *there*' but rather 'is an idea that has a history and a tradition of thought, imagery, and vocabulary that have given it reality and presence'.[37] Said attempts to investigate the construction by Europe of an 'image outside of history' of the Orient, one that was unchanging and acted as a naturalization (and therefore reduction) of the culture of the Orient. Crucially, the European idea of the Orient served as its ideal Other: by representing the Orient as uncivilized, uncultured and repressed, Europeans were then able to represent themselves as a civilizing, cultured and scientific force (turning this science, from Napoleon onwards, into the expert gaze of the Orientalist and the anthropologist). One interesting aspect of Said's

---

[33] Neil Lazarus and Rashmi Varma, 'Marxism and Postcolonial Studies', in: Jacques Bidet and Stathis Kouvelakis (eds), *Critical Companion to Contemporary Marxism* (Leiden: Brill, 2008), pp. 309–32.

[34] Ibid., p. 309.

[35] For a more detailed account see Timothy Brennan, 'Antonio Gramsci and Postcolonial Theory: "Southernism"', *Diaspora*, 10:2 (2001), pp. 143–87; Neelam Srivastava and Baidik Bhattacharya, 'Introduction', in: Neelam Srivastava and Baidik Bhattacharya (eds), *The Postcolonial Gramsci* (London: Routledge, 2012), pp. 1–15.

[36] Robert J. C. Young, *Postcolonialism: An Historical Introduction* (Oxford: Blackwell, 2001) p. 384.

[37] Edward Said, *Orientalism* (Harmondsworth: Penguin, 1978), pp. 4, 5.

argument is that he considers that Orientalism's power depends less on its claims to truth than on aspects of its internal consistency, the considerable material investment made in networks that create and disseminate Orientalist ideas and its ultimate foundation in asymmetric power relations that allowed the Europeans to categorize their Oriental 'Others'.

Gramsci is central to this intellectual enterprise – second only perhaps to Foucault in Said's theoretical framework – and it is possible to discern two related ways in which Said uses Gramsci's thought.[38] First, the concept of hegemony is used by Said to explain the operation and power of Orientalist notions. Citing a distinction between civil and political society drawn from Gramsci, Said continues by asserting the role of culture in maintaining power: 'Culture … is to be found operating within civil society, where the influence of ideas, of institutions, and of other persons works not through domination but by what Gramsci calls consent.'[39] It is the pre-eminence of some cultural forms over others and the fact that some ideas are more influential than others that Said understands by hegemony, and it is this hegemony that 'gives Orientalism the durability and the strength' that characterize it.[40] Crucially, then, Said understands Orientalism in terms of its causes in and consequences for European culture: 'the major component in European culture is precisely what made that culture hegemonic both in and outside Europe: the idea of European identity as a superior one in comparison with all the non-European peoples and cultures'.[41] We can see clearly that Gramsci is used by Said to begin to think through the relationship between culture and power in the context of imperialism. Said is careful to make clear that he does not consider the highlighting of the necessary relation between 'politics in the form of imperialism' and 'the production of literature, scholarship, social theory, and history writing' to be the same as asserting that 'culture is therefore a demeaned thing'.[42] Instead, he argues that 'we can better understand the persistence

---

[38] See Alastair Davidson, 'The Uses and Abuses of Gramsci', *Thesis Eleven*, 95 (2008), pp. 68–94 for a fuller account.

[39] Said, *Orientalism*, p. 7.

[40] Ibid., p. 7.

[41] Ibid., p. 7.

[42] Ibid., p. 14.

and durability of saturating hegemonic systems like culture when we realize that their internal constraints upon writers and thinkers were *productive*, not unilaterally inhibiting'.[43] *Orientalism*, despite problems that later scholars might have had with it, stands as a pathbreaking account within Postcolonial Studies that investigates the ways in which ideologies – in this case the constellation of ideas Said terms 'Orientalism' – cannot be understood only as constraining knowledge, but in fact helping to *create* a certain body of (partial and politically non-neutral) knowledge.

Said also draws on Gramsci to understand what he terms the 'personal dimension' of Orientalism. Said cites one of Gramsci's most famous passages from the *Prison Notebooks*: 'The starting point of critical elaboration is the consciousness of what one really is, and is "knowing thyself" as a product of the historical process to date, which has deposited in you an infinity of traces, without leaving an inventory.'[44] He then points out that the translation in Hoare and Nowell-Smith's *Selections from the Prison Notebooks* strangely leaves out Gramsci's further thought: 'Such an inventory must therefore be made at the outset.'[45] Said notes that his awareness of being, himself, an 'Oriental' as a child growing up in the British colonies of Palestine and Egypt persisted through his Western education in those colonies and in the United States, and remarks that he felt it important to be conscious of trying to produce a Gramscian inventory of his personal relation to Orientalism. He concludes, 'my study of Orientalism has been an attempt to inventory the traces upon me, the Oriental subject, of the culture whose domination has been so powerful a factor in the life of all Orientals'.[46]

If Said draws on Gramsci's concept of hegemony (see Chapter 5) to think about the relation between culture and power and gestures towards what we might call Gramsci's philosophical anthropology (see Chapter 4) to begin to understand his own personal relation

---

[43] Ibid., p. 14.

[44] Q11§12; *SPN*, p. 324.

[45] Q11§12; see *GR*, p. 326. Cited in full in Said, *Orientalism*, p. 25. But cf. Antonio Gramsci, *The Modern Prince and Other Essays*, edited by Louis Marks (London: Lawrence and Wishart, 1957), p. 59.

[46] Said, *Orientalism*, p. 25.

to Orientalism and his formation as an 'Oriental' subject, then the use of Gramsci by the thinkers around the Subaltern Studies group demonstrates an additional dimension of Gramsci's legacy in contemporary critical thought. Subaltern Studies is a radical current in recent Indian historiography that emerged in the 1980s around the figure of Ranajit Guha and the *Subaltern Studies* journal, with the objective of developing a history 'from below' against both British colonial and Indian 'bourgeois-nationalist' historiography since the country's independence. Guha situates the political project of Subaltern Studies as against both these 'varieties of elitism' that 'share the prejudice that the making of the Indian nation and the development of the consciousness – nationalism – which informed this process were exclusively or predominantly elite achievements' that are then credited either to British colonial rulers, administrators and culture or to Indian elite personalities and ideas.[47] Instead, Subaltern Studies has sought to give a voice to issues of caste, age, gender and class as aspects of subaltern history.

In the preface to their first collection of essays, Guha links the project of Subaltern Studies to Gramsci's six point plan in a note titled 'History of the Subaltern Classes: Methodological Criteria'. Gramsci's note runs as follows:

> The subaltern classes, by definition, are not unified and cannot unite until they are able to become a 'State': their history, therefore, is intertwined with that of civil society, and thereby with the history of States and groups of States. Hence it is necessary to study: 1. the objective formation of the subaltern social groups, by the developments and transformations occurring in the sphere of economic production; their quantitative diffusion and their origins in pre-existing social groups, whose mentality, ideology and aims they conserve for a time; 2. their active or passive affiliation to the dominant political formations, their attempts to influence the programmes of these formations in order to press claims of their own, and the consequences of these attempts in determining

---

[47] Ranajit Guha, 'On Some Aspects of the Historiography of Colonial India', in: Ranajit Guha (ed.), *Subaltern Studies I: Writings on South Asian History and Society* (Oxford: Oxford University Press, 1982), p. 1.

processes of decomposition, renovation or neo-formation; 3. the birth of new parties of the dominant groups, intended to conserve the assent of the subaltern groups and to maintain control over them; 4. the formations which the subaltern groups themselves produce, in order to press claims of a limited and partial character; 5. those new formations which assert the autonomy of the subaltern groups, but within the old framework; 6. those formations which assert the integral autonomy, ... etc.[48]

From this starting point, the problematic of the investigation of the history of subaltern groups in South Asia in the Gramscian sense has proved to be enormously generative, even taking into account the growing influence of Foucault on many thinkers within Subaltern Studies.[49] Gramsci thus provides not only the term 'subaltern' but also a set of open methodological guidelines for the practice of investigating subaltern history. The contemporary popularity of subaltern analysis has another important root in the work of Gayatri Chakravorty Spivak and in particular her famous article 'Can the Subaltern Speak?'.[50] Of particular importance in Spivak's complex and influential critique of the methodology and focus of Subaltern Studies is the notion that the subaltern *cannot* speak, in the sense that they must always be represented by British, nationalist and colonialist records. The influence of Gramsci on Spivak is considerable but her development of the notion of the subaltern includes a focus on questions of gender and individual agency within subaltern groups, and her use of the term 'subaltern' in the singular, which would have

---

[48] Q25§5; *SPN*, p. 52. See Ranajit Guha, 'Preface', in: Ranajit Guha (ed.), *Subaltern Studies I: Writings on South Asian History and Society* (Oxford: Oxford University Press, 1982), pp. vii–viii. As Green explains, Gramsci uses the term subaltern in a way that develops through his prison notebooks, from the literal sense of an inferior position or rank in a military context to a figurative use in non-military senses to denote a position of subordination or lower status. See Marcus E. Green, 'Gramsci Cannot Speak: Presentations and Interpretations of Gramsci's Concept of the Subaltern', *Rethinking Marxism*, 14:3 (2002), pp. 1–24.

[49] For an excellent starting point, see Ranajit Guha and Gayatri Chakravorty Spivak (eds), *Selected Subaltern Studies* (New York: Oxford University Press), 1988.

[50] Gayatri Chakravorty Spivak, 'Can the Subaltern Speak?', in: Cary Nelson and Lawrence Grossberg (eds), *Marxism and the Interpretation of Culture* (Urbana: University of Illinois Press, 1998), pp. 271–313.

been less familiar to Gramsci.[51] Green notes that although the notion of 'subalternity' for Spivak and Guha in many ways follows aspects of Gramsci, they rely heavily for their understanding of subaltern social groups on the limited notes included in the *Selections from the Prison Notebooks*.[52]

Overall, Gramsci remains influential in Postcolonial Studies and his thought has represented a key resource in theorizing conceptual issues of agency, representation, the role of the intellectual and the possibilities for the formation of counter-hegemonies in the post-colonial context. We can also note that a major influence of Gramsci's thought in Postcolonial Studies today stems from his sensitivity to the problem of the proletariat – peasantry alliance and his analysis of this in terms of the geographical North–South division within Italy as expressed most fully in his 1926 *Alcuni temi* essay, which seems strikingly to anticipate global North–South divisions as developed subsequently in dependency theory.[53]

Gramsci and Cultural Studies

Gramsci is also a key figure in Anglophone Cultural Studies, particularly in British Cultural Studies of the 1970s, and above all in the work of Stuart Hall.[54] Cultural Studies emerged in Britain in earnest in the late 1950s and early 1960s, with Richard Hoggart's *The Uses of Literacy* (1957), Raymond Williams's *Culture and Society* (1958) and *The Long Revolution* (1961), and E. P. Thompson's *The Making of the English Working Class* (1963) as founding texts. By the 1970s the initially dominant paradigm of the 'culturalism' influenced by Hoggart, Williams and Thompson and the political climate of the New Left had been joined as one of the two major streams of thought in Cultural Studies in Britain by the 'structuralism' of those influenced by the intellectual followers of Saussure (Lévi-

---

[51] See Young, 'Il Gramsci meridionale'.
[52] Green, 'Gramsci Cannot Speak'.
[53] See Young, *Postcolonialism*, p. 353.
[54] For an excellent overview, see David Morley and Kuan-Hsing Chen (eds), *Stuart Hall: Critical Dialogues in Cultural Studies* (London: Routledge, 1996).

Strauss, Barthes, Lacan and Althusser).[55] In analysing culture, the structuralists were concerned with the deep rules (or structures) of phenomena, rather than specific local forms; accordingly, they were suspicious of human agency, treating culture as a structure that rigidly determines people's thoughts and practices. As culturalism took its inspiration from analyses of British culture, and in particular working class culture, it tended to look to privilege what it saw as the creative practices, and previously suppressed voices, of subordinate social groups. These two schools – structuralism focusing on texts, culturalism on history, sociology, sport and youth subcultures – however both essentially accepted that bourgeois ideology had been imposed *from without* on subordinate classes, albeit with varying degrees of success.[56]

In this context, the 'turn to Gramsci' represented a decisive advance from the impasse that had been developing between culturalism and structuralism: it enabled cultural theorists to think about popular culture as a terrain of struggle rather than *either* the authentic expression of popular values *or* the servant of dominant interests. Those influenced by Gramsci also began to investigate the interaction of class with other dimensions of subordination such as ethnicity.[57] The use of Gramsci's thought was situated, in the context of discussions in Cultural Studies about Marxism, as a movement beyond an Althusserian account of ideology that did not seem to leave sufficient room for the heterogeneity of actually existing cultural forms.

A central institution in the development of what we might term 'Gramscian Cultural Studies', which peaked in the late 1970s, was the Birmingham Centre for Contemporary Cultural Studies (BCCCS), initially founded in 1964 as a postgraduate research centre under the directorship of Hoggart and led by Stuart Hall from 1968 to 1979. The thinkers around the BCCCS and the Open University produced

---

[55] Stuart Hall, 'Cultural Studies: Two Paradigms', *Media, Culture, and Society*, 2:1 (1980), pp. 57–72.

[56] Tony Bennett, 'Introduction: The Turn to Gramsci', in: Tony Bennett, Colin Mercer and Janet Woollacott (eds), *Popular Culture and Social Relations* (Milton Keynes: Open University Press, 1986), pp. xi–xix.

[57] See for instance Stuart Hall, 'Gramsci's Relevance for the Study of Race and Ethnicity', *Journal of Communication Inquiry* 10:2 (1986), pp. 5–27.

a range of analyses of popular culture and its political importance. Some of the key works in Gramscian Cultural Studies might include the edited collections *Policing the Crisis* (1978) and *Resistance Through Rituals* (1975), on the role of the mass media, crime control agencies and political interests in creating the phenomenon of 'mugging' and the political significance of youth mass culture, respectively; Dick Hebdige's examination of music-centred white working class subcultures in his *Subculture: The Meaning of Style* (1979); and Paul Willis's complex investigation into questions of class, gender, class, resistance and conformity in the school in his *Learning to Labour* (1977).

Similarly to post-Marxism, two of the key concepts in Gramscian Cultural Studies were hegemony and articulation. Among the many uses of the notion of hegemony within Cultural Studies, it was used productively to link practices of representation to structures of domination, sharing with Said the recognition that stereotyping and the representation of others are likely to be most prevalent where there are inequalities of power. Here, the relationship of hegemony to a notion of normalcy can be foregrounded, with what is 'normal' as contrasted to 'oppositional' or even 'deviant' subcultures:

> The establishment of normalcy (i.e. what is accepted as 'normal') through social- and stereo-types is one aspect of the habit of ruling groups ... to attempt to fashion the whole of society according to their own world view, value system, sensibility and ideology. So right is the world view for ruling groups that they make it appear (as it *does* appear to them) as 'natural' and 'inevitable' – and for everyone – and, in so far as they succeed, they establish their hegemony.[58]

Replacing an Althusserian conception of ideology as essentially uniform and ahistorical with a Gramscian stress on the provisional

---

[58] Richard Dyer, 'Stereotyping', in: Richard Dyer (ed.), *Gays and Film* (London: British Film Institute, 1977), cited in Stuart Hall, 'The Spectacle of the "Other"', in: Stuart Hall (ed.), *Representation: Cultural Representations and Signifying Practices* (London: Sage, 1997), p. 259.

and constructed nature of hegemony was also seen to represent a political step forward to the extent that 'ideological struggle' as a monolithic battle between ideology and science could be replaced with a plurality of hegemonic struggles between inherently flexible ideologies.[59]

Articulation is another concept within Gramscian Cultural Studies that allowed for the 'thinking through' of the relationship of culture and politics. Articulation describes the processes by which social forces are connected and disconnected from one another, being joined together in a hierarchical and politicized relationship. Thus the *Policing the Crisis* collection mentioned above can be understood as creating a framework that explained how Thatcherism was able to 'disarticulate' the interests of large sectors of the working class from the Labour Party and 'rearticulate' them not only to the Conservative Party but 'through the production of fantasies, dreams and exemplary stories as well as through legislative and administrative changes, to the cultural values of yuppies in the south'.[60] The importance of a notion of articulation provides one important point of contact – and, of course, possible disagreement – between post-Marxism and Cultural Studies.[61]

Gramsci's influence, through Hall, also extends into Media Studies. One of Hall's most influential articles, pathbreaking within the field of Television Studies, is 'Encoding and Decoding in the Media Discourse' (1973).[62] Hall's basic theoretical model of how ideological messages move within society has four moments: production, circulation, distribution/consumption and reproduction. Each stage, Hall asserts, is 'relatively autonomous' from the others, but each is limited by the previous one; at each stage, crucially, messages

---

[59] Colin Sparks, 'Stuart Hall, Cultural Studies and Marxism', in: David Morley and Kuan-Hsing Chen (eds), *Stuart Hall: Critical Dialogues in Cultural Studies* (London: Routledge, 1996), pp. 71–101.

[60] Meghan Morris, 'A Question of Cultural Studies', in: Angela McRobbie (ed.), *Back to Reality? Social Experience and Cultural Studies* (Manchester: Manchester University Press, 1997), p. 46.

[61] See Paul Bowman, *Post-Marxism versus Cultural Studies: Theory, Politics, and Intervention* (Edinburgh: Edinburgh University Press, 2007).

[62] See Stuart Hall, 'Encoding and Decoding in the Television Discourse', CCCS stencilled paper no. 7 (Birmingham: Centre for Contemporary Cultural Studies, 1973).

are imprinted by institutional power relations and the character and content of dominant social relations. Hall sees a TV sign as a visual and aural representation that possesses only some properties of the thing represented, and its message is thus polysemic. Hall concludes that there is 'no necessary correspondence' between the 'encodings' of media producers and the 'decodings' of audiences. Interpretation is thus seen as a social practice, neither fully free or fully forced, in which the audience can take the meaning from the broadcast 'full and straight' (by following a dominant-hegemonic interpretative code), reject the message (following an oppositional code) or mix adaptive and oppositional elements and follow a 'negotiated' code. The last reading, importantly, allows space for conflict with dominant codes.

Despite the productivity and enduring influence of Gramscian perspectives, they were challenged by a variety of postmodernist approaches to the study of culture through the 1980s and Gramscian Cultural Studies was, in the slightly cynical judgement of one commentator, exhausted as a political force by the 1990s.[63] At any rate, during the high-point of Gramsci's influence on Cultural Studies we can note the affinity between Gramscian analyses of culture and those of politics. Hall's use of Gramsci in the analysis of Thatcherism is covered in more detail in Chapter 7, but here we can briefly note that for Hall both cultural and political forces must be analysed as constructed rather than pre-given. For Hall, the elements of any culture, just as those of any politics, 'do not "emerge"; they have to be constructed. Political and ideological work is required to disarticulate old formations, and to rework their elements into new ones'.[64]

---

[63] See David Harris, *From Class Struggle to the Politics of Pleasure: The Effects of Gramscianism on Cultural Studies* (London: Routledge, 1992). Bennett argues that 'the Gramscian problematic' was 'warrened out' by the various attempts made to 'establish some form of accommodation between, on the one hand, the Gramscian theory and project of hegemony, and, on the other, aspects of postmodernism and discourse theory'. See Tony Bennett, 'Putting Policy into Cultural Studies', in: Lawrence Grossberg, Cary Nelson and Paula A. Treichler (eds), *Cultural Studies*, (London: Routledge, 1992), p. 29.
[64] Hall, 'The Great Moving Right Show', p. 15.

Gramsci and International Political Economy

Another academic field where Gramscian thought has had a notable influence is International Relations (IR), and specifically the sub-discipline of International Political Economy (IPE). This might be somewhat unexpected insofar as only a small proportion of Gramsci's writings explicitly address inter-State relations. The emergence of 'neo-Gramscian IPE' – also known as the 'Italian School' – as one of the most prominent critical approaches within IR originates in Robert Cox's innovative work on 'world orders' in the 1980s. Cox introduced Gramscian notions to an academic audience which until then had often had minimal contact with Marxist perspectives, let alone a Gramscian one. Since then, the neo-Gramscian approach has bloomed in a number of directions within IR and IPE, more or less in keeping with Cox's original arguments. Existing differences across the array of departments and researchers engaged in this brand of scholarship mean that there is no 'school' to speak of; instead, as Stephen Gill put it twenty years ago, 'there are clusters of scholars working in ways that address some of the questions raised and posed in Gramscian terms'.[65]

Neo-Gramscian IPE was originally inspired by two articles published by Robert Cox in the IR journal *Millennium* in the early 1980s.[66] In these ground-breaking pieces, Cox took aim at the positivist, 'problem-solving' paradigm that dominated – and in fact still dominates – the discipline of IR, and proposed an alternative historicist research agenda premised upon the study of 'world orders' and their transformation and supersession through time.

At the epistemological level, Cox embraces Gramsci's rejection of economism and mechanism, arguing that objective international

---

[65] Stephen Gill, 'Gramsci and Global Politics: Towards a Post-Hegemonic Research Agenda', in: Stephen Gill (ed.), *Gramsci, Historical Materialism and International Relations* (Cambridge: Cambridge University Press, 1993), p. 2.

[66] See Robert Cox, 'Social Forces, States and World Orders: Beyond International Relations Theory', *Millennium: Journal of International Studies*, 10:2 (1981), pp. 126–55; 'Gramsci, Hegemony, and International Relations: An Essay in Method', *Millennium: Journal of International Studies*, 12:2 (1983), pp. 162–75.

structures have to be related to the collective images and human practices that reproduce or alter them on a daily basis. Methodologically, he argues that a historicist approach to IR should be applied simultaneously to three levels, namely '(1) the organisation of production, more particularly with regard to the *social forces* engendered by the production process; (2) *forms of State* as derived from the study of State/society complexes; and (3) *world orders*, i.e. the particular configurations of forces which successively define the problematic of war and peace for the ensemble of States'.[67] Cox stresses that these three spheres entertain ongoing reciprocal, dialectical relations, very much like the different 'moments' of social life according to Gramsci's own understanding of the Marxian *Basis–Überbau* metaphor. Specifically, 'social forces' – including social classes – are rooted in the production process and emanate from the basic structure, while 'forms of State' should be referred to Gramsci's notion of the *stato integrale* – integral State – as an overarching superstructure encompassing both political and civil society ('State–society complexes'). Cox's purported innovation is to integrate within this Marxian-Gramscian schema the international sphere ('world orders'), as a level of human practice and power in dynamic interaction with national historic blocs.

On this basis, Cox attempts to break new ground by internationalizing the Gramscian conception of hegemony. Highlighting passages from the *Prison Notebooks* in which Gramsci mentions the repercussions of the French Revolution on Italian social and political life – such as the Action Party's 'Jacobin monkeying around' (see Chapter 3) – Cox argues that a powerful State that has undergone socio-economic revolution, and has succeeded in building a domestic hegemonic order, 'unleashes energies which expand beyond the State's boundaries'.[68] He continues, 'A world hegemony is thus in its beginnings an outward expansion of the internal (national) hegemony established by a dominant social class. The economic and social institutions, the culture, the technology associated with this national hegemony become patterns for emulation abroad.'[69]

---

[67] Cox, 'Social Forces', pp. 137–8, emphasis in original.
[68] Cox, 'Gramsci, Hegemony and International Relations', p. 171.
[69] Ibid., p. 171.

Cox considers such a form of development to be the hallmark not only of the French Revolution, but also, crucially, of the expansionary politics of the United States and the Soviet Union into the twentieth century. In this connection, one of the primary focuses of his writings is the way in which post-1945 *Pax Americana* – that is, US hegemony as exercised vis-à-vis other countries of the Western bloc – has evolved during the decades that followed the Second World War. The immediate post-war period, he argues, was defined by an American-led world order premised on the rise of national welfare states in the West. Thereafter, several systemic shifts and strains forced alterations in the post-war settlement, and by the 1970s a new type of world order began to emerge, centred on heightened economic globalization and the political coming-of-age of neo-liberalism. In this new era, the internationalization of economic and political elites in the form of a 'transnational managerial class' echoes the internationalization of the production process and the ascendancy of finance. Cox's focus on the articulation of economic, political and sociological processes, both within and across nation states, is captured in the following assertion:

> Hegemony at the international level is thus not merely an order among States. It is an order within a world economy with a dominant mode of production which penetrates into all countries and links into other subordinate modes of production. It is also a complex of international social relationships which connect the social classes of the different countries. World hegemony can be described as a social structure, an economic structure, and a political structure; and it cannot be simply one of these things but must be all three.[70]

Some of the scholars having taken up the challenge of this ambitious research agenda came together in 1993 to put out a collective volume that may be considered a milestone in the development of neo-Gramscian IPE.[71] In it, contributors such as Robert Cox, Mark Rupert

---

[70] Ibid., pp. 171–2.
[71] Gill (ed.), *Gramsci, Historical Materialism and International Relations.*

and Kees van der Pijl, together with editor Stephen Gill, attempt to take stock of the phase of global turbulence and recomposition following the end of the Cold War. In his introductory essay, Gill argues that capitalist social forces are integrating the world into a 'global civil society' of economic and cultural inter-connectedness while these transnational currents are subjecting domestic political structures to disintegrative strains.[72] Hence a diagnosis of 'patterned disorder', in which global US 'hegemony' is increasingly morphing into mere domination, or 'supremacy'.[73]

As neo-Gramscian IPE rose to prominence within critical IR studies in the 1990s and 2000s, it spawned a number of criticisms.[74] Among these, one in particular, by Randall Germain and Michael Kenny, has proven influential and has arguably aided in the further development of the neo-Gramscian approach.[75] Germain and Kenny take aim at the tendency among the neo-Gramscians merely to 'apply' notions plucked from the *Prison Notebooks* to the current world order, failing to engage critically with Gramsci's writings and disregarding the historical context in which his thought is rooted. This weakness is compounded, they argue, among the 'second generation' of neo-Gramscians 'whose claim to a Gramscian mantle extends no further than an initial reading of Cox, Gill *et al*'.[76] Substantively, they claim that properly historicizing Gramsci leads to the conclusion that his concepts of hegemony and civil society are distorted beyond the point of usefulness if abstracted away from individual States and 'people-nations' and projected onto the international plane.

---

[72] Gill, 'Gramsci and Global Politics', p. 16.

[73] Ibid., p. 7.

[74] For an instance of a critique from a more 'orthodox' Marxist standpoint, see Peter Burnham, 'Neo-Gramscian Hegemony and the International Order', *Capital & Class*, 15:3 (1991), pp. 73–92. Among criticisms arising from Gramscian scholars not working in the field of IR/IPE, one can mention Anne Showstack Sassoon's argument that neo-Gramscians fail to pay sufficient attention to the ways in which consent to global hegemony is experienced concretely by subaltern groups; see her 'Globalisation, Hegemony and Passive Revolution', *New Political Economy*, 6:1 (2001), pp. 5–17.

[75] Randall D. Germain and Michael Kenny, 'Engaging Gramsci: International Relations Theory and the New Gramscians', *Review of International Studies*, 24:1 (1998), pp. 3–21.

[76] Ibid., p. 20.

Germain and Kenny's critique of neo-Gramscian scholarship was predictably met with a number of rebukes.[77] Irrespective of the validity of its restrictive interpretation of Gramscian concepts, however, it had the welcome effect of prodding 'second-generation' neo-Gramscians towards more rigorous engagements with Gramsci's writings. Among these, one may highlight in particular the work of Adam Morton. In his *Unravelling Gramsci*, Morton daringly intertwines close readings of Gramsci's *Prison Notebooks* and pre-prison writings with accounts of neo-liberal hegemony, passive revolution and uneven development in the present period.[78] Against Germain and Kenny's 'austere historicism', Morton claims to adopt an intellectual practice that is closer in spirit to Gramsci's own 'absolute historicism'.[79] Inspired by the way in which Gramsci embraced the 'living' element in Marxism, yet wrote about the 'revolution against *Capital*', Morton purports to 'unravel' Gramsci, absorbing some of his crucial notions while also considering 'what might be historically limited in a theoretical and practical translation of Gramsci's writings to alternative social and political circumstances'.[80]

Conclusion

Thus, Gramsci's legacy, we have argued, is best understood in the context of his place in the first generation of Western Marxism, with Gramsci emerging as the thinker in that tradition most suited to the analysis of cultural problems as political problems. It is also necessary to ground Gramsci's legacy in relation to the Italian communist movement of the post-war decades. Within recent critical thought, Gramsci has been central to post-Marxism,

---

[77] Craig N. Murphy, 'Understanding IR: Understanding Gramsci', *Review of International Studies*, 24:3 (1998), pp. 417–25; Mark Rupert, 'Re-engaging Gramsci: A Response to Germain and Kenny', *Review of International Studies*, 24:3 (1998), pp. 427–34; Adam D. Morton, 'Historicizing Gramsci: Situating Ideas in and beyond Their Context', *Review of International Political Economy*, 10:1 (2003), pp. 118–46.

[78] Adam D. Morton, *Unravelling Gramsci: Hegemony and Passive Revolution in the Global Political Economy* (London: Pluto Press, 2007).

[79] Ibid., p. 17.

[80] Ibid., p. 2.

International Political Economy, Postcolonial Theory and Cultural Studies. Gramsci's thought has been productively used as a starting point in thinking about the ways in which relations of domination and subordination, political subjects, and representations and understandings of ourselves and others are constructed – and especially how they relate to categories of class.

But, of course, this is a map of only some aspects of Gramsci's legacy. Gramsci has also been a key resource in some theories of radical pedagogy and adult education, and has also been influential within anthropology, particularly as filtered through Raymond Williams's reading of hegemony.[81] Gramsci has also been subject to a growing range of interpretations from Right-wing commentators, with some of the more perspicacious contributions noting that Gramsci combines, for the Left, a mix of theoretical influence and personal moral capital.[82] Indeed, only Rosa Luxemburg and Walter Benjamin come close to Gramsci as the foremost martyrs of the Marxist tradition.

Gramsci's future is not easy to assess. The scholarly conditions of Gramsci's current reception and usage seem to suggest that Anglophone studies of Gramsci will continue to be a growth industry, and Frosini talks of a 'world-wide Gramsci renaissance', noting the range and quality of recent work on and using his thought.[83] Joseph Buttigieg's important project of the production of a critical English edition of Gramsci's notebooks continues, with the publication of the third volume in 2007 meaning that the first eight notebooks are now available. While this is of course likely to raise the expectations of textual familiarity among Anglophone scholars (and to a lesser extent students) of Gramsci, even a critical edition of the *Prison Notebooks* cannot remove their essentially open and unfinished character, which have continued to have a determining influence on Gramsci's legacy. Perhaps the most exciting recent engagement

---

[81] Peter Mayo (ed.) *Gramsci and Educational Thought* (Oxford: Wiley-Nicolson, 2010); Crehan, *Gramsci, Culture, and Anthropology*.

[82] See Roger Scruton, 'Thinkers of the Left: Antonio Gramsci', *The Salisbury Review*, 3:2 (1984), pp. 18–22. See Marcus E. Green, 'Gramsci on the World Wide Web: Intellectuals and Bizarre Interpretations of Gramsci', *International Gramsci Society Newsletter*, 10 (2000), pp. 3–5 for an interesting assessment of some other readings of Gramsci.

[83] Frosini, 'Gramsci's Contested Legacy', p. 674.

with Gramsci's thought is Peter Thomas's *The Gramscian Moment* (2009). Thomas argues that Gramsci's philosophy can be understood as an attempt to read from Marx's *Theses on Feuerbach* a conception of Marxist philosophy as absolute historicism, absolute immanence and absolute humanism that can serve as the basis for a radical research programme.[84]

However, it is also the case that the politics of a period determine the resources that critical thinkers need, and the politics of the current period cannot be characterized with certainty. As Keucheyan argues, although it is a trait of contemporary critical theories to argue over issues of periodization, there is a consensus that the years from 1989 to 1993 marked the *end* of a period.[85] Consequently today we seem to be in a transitional period, possibly that of 'Capitalist Realism' in which it seems easier to imagine the destruction of the whole world than it does the historical progression beyond capitalism.[86] Or perhaps the Eurozone crisis of 2008 will be seen by future historians as marking the beginning of a period of increased political participation and contestation. The contours of the present period are not easy to discern, but we would suggest that Gramsci's concepts and method, and in particular his extension and renewal of Marxism, are useful tools for thinking through capitalism today. Gramsci is also one of the foremost theorists of defeat in the history of critical thought, and this would recommend him to a contemporary Left that must start from the conditions of its very real defeat (at least in Europe) while attempting to retain a *Gramscian pessimism* rather than a useless *defeatism*.

---

[84] Other important Gramscian research projects today might include Peter Ives's exploration of the linguistic roots of Gramsci's concept of hegemony and Adam Morton's application of Gramsci to international relations. See Peter Ives, *Language and Hegemony in Gramsci* (London: Pluto, 2004); Morton, *Unravelling Gramsci*.

[85] There is, though, less agreement about whether the period from around 1989 to 1993 marks the end of the short political cycle of the New Left started in 1956, the 'short twentieth century' begun in 1914, or the long political cycle of modernity as initiated by the French Revolution in 1789. See Keucheyan, *The Left Hemisphere*.

[86] See Fisher, *Capitalist Realism*.

Guide to Further Reading

Gramsci in English

The best starting point for an engagement with Gramsci is undoubtedly his *Prison Notebooks*. Readers should start with *Selections from Prison Notebooks*, edited and translated by Quintin Hoare and Geoffrey Nowell-Smith (London: Lawrence and Wishart, 1971) (*SPN*). Despite problems that later scholars have found with selection, presentation and translation, *SPN* is likely to remain the starting point for readers of Gramsci, at least until the arrival of the complete critical edition of Gramsci's *Prison Notebooks* in English. It can usefully be supplemented by *Further Selections from the Prison Notebooks*, edited and translated by Derek Boothman (London: Lawrence and Wishart, 1995).

The critical English edition of Gramsci's *Prison Notebooks* is currently being prepared by Joseph Buttigieg and Columbia University Press; with the most recent volume published in 2007 it now includes notebooks 1–8, and an excellent introductory essay by Buttigieg at the start of the first volume.[1] A very good single-volume reader is *The Gramsci Reader: Selected Writings, 1916–1935*, edited by David Forgacs, which includes both prison and pre-prison writings.

Gramsci's pre-prison writings are available either in *Pre-Prison Writings*, edited by Richard Bellamy and translated by Virginia Cox

---

[1] The first editions of Gramsci's *Quaderni del Carcere* were published by Einaudi (Turin) in six volumes between 1948 and 1951. These have now been superseded by the critical edition published under the auspices of the *Istituto Antonio Gramsci* in Rome: *Quaderni del Carcere*, edited by Valentino Gerratana (Turin: Einaudi, 1975). The critical edition consists of three volumes of the notebooks, and one of critical apparatuses.

(Cambridge: Cambridge University Press, 1994) or in the two-volume *Selections from Political Writings (1910–1920)*, edited by Quintin Hoare and translated by John Mathews (London: Lawrence and Wishart, 1977) and *Selections from Political Writings (1921–1926)*, translated and edited by Quintin Hoare (London: Lawrence and Wishart, 1978).

Selections from Cultural Writings, edited by David Forgacs and Geoffrey Nowell-Smith and translated by William Boelhower (London: Lawrence and Wishart, 1985) is an extremely engaging collection that includes both prison and pre-prison writings, and may be particularly useful to readers interested in cultural questions.

Gramsci's prison letters, some of which are quite moving and which are an excellent companion to his other writings, are available in selection in either *Letters from Prison by Antonio Gramsci*, edited and translated by Lynne Lawner (London: Quartet, 1979) or *Gramsci's Prison Letters*, edited and translated by Hamish Hamilton (London: Zwan, 1988). The complete edition is the two-volume *Letters from Prison*, edited by Frank Rosengarten and translated by Raymond Rosenthal (New York: Columbia University Press, 1994). For Gramsci's pre-prison letters, see *A Great and Terrible World: The Pre-Prison Letters of Antonio Gramsci, 1908–1926*, edited and translated by Derek Boothman (London: Lawrence and Wishart, 2014).

Gramsci's life

The best account of Gramsci's life is Giuseppe Fiori's *Antonio Gramsci: Life of a Revolutionary* (London: New Left Books, 1970). Fiori manages to paint a vivid picture of Gramsci as a person and a revolutionary. We would also recommend the documentary 'Everything That Concerns People', available on YouTube at: https://www.youtube.com/watch?v=51DhvS9abyI.

Secondary sources

There are several good introductions to Gramsci's thought, and we would particularly recommend Roger Simon's *Gramsci's Political Thought* (London: Lawrence and Wishart, 1991) for those interested in Gramsci's thought on politics, while Steve Jones's *Antonio Gramsci:*

Routledge Critical Thinkers (London: Routledge, 2006) has more of a slant towards cultural theory.

There are several useful collections of essays on Gramsci's thought. Readers should probably start with Anne Showstack Sassoon (ed.), *Approaches to Gramsci* (London: Writers and Readers, 1982) as Chantal Mouffe (ed.), *Gramsci and Marxist Theory* (London: Routledge, 1979), though excellent, is not an easy read. Marcus E. Green (ed.), *Rethinking Gramsci* (London: Routledge, 2011) and Joseph Francese (ed.), *Perspectives on Gramsci: Politics, Culture, and Social Theory* (London: Routledge, 2009) represent more closely the current state of Gramsci scholarship. James Martin's (ed.) *Antonio Gramsci: Critical Assessments of Leading Political Philosophers* (London: Routledge, 2002) is an indispensable four-volume collection that contains many of the articles we use here, although it is probably not a first step for the new reader of Gramsci.

In Chapter 8 we began to map Gramsci's legacy on contemporary critical thought, and any of the works referred to there would be suitable further reading. Within post-Marxism, *Hegemony and Socialist Strategy* (Ernesto Laclau and Chantal Mouffe; London: Verso, 1985) is a necessary starting point, but is a difficult read. *The Postcolonial Gramsci*, edited by Neelam Srivastava and Baidik Bhattacharya (London: Routledge, 2012) is an interesting collection, but the uses of Gramsci there are sometimes problematic and it should be read in conjunction with Timothy Brennan's critical review 'Joining the Party', *Postcolonial Studies*, 16:1 (2013), pp. 68–78. A good starting point within cultural studies is Tony Bennett, Colin Mercer and Janet Woollacott's *Popular Culture and Social Relations* (Milton Keynes: Open University Press, 1986).

Two of the most important overall interpretations of Gramsci in English are Perry Anderson, 'The Antinomies of Antonio Gramsci', *New Left Review*, 1:100 (1976), pp. 5–78 and Peter Thomas, *The Gramscian Moment: Philosophy, Hegemony, and Marxism* (Leiden: Brill, 2009).

Other resources

http://www.marxists.org/archive/gramsci/index.htm
Some of Gramsci's writings in English.

http://www.internationalgramscisociety.org
Website of the International Gramsci Society, with a useful website
and mailing list.

http://www.internationalgramscisociety.org/resources/concordance
_table/index.html
Concordance tables linking the *Prison Notebooks* to anthologies
published in English. Very useful for readers of *SPN*.

http://bobjessop.org/2014/04/21/lectures-on-gramsci/
An interesting set of lectures on Gramsci.

http://www.victoryiscertain.com/gramsci/
A useful, if slightly dated, set of links.

A suggestion on reading Gramsci

We wanted to conclude our guide to further reading by suggesting
a very rough plan for a potential Gramsci reading group (although
the outline here could of course also be followed by an individual
reader). We would recommend centring a reading group around *SPN*
as the single volume for the readers of the group. The concordance
tables mentioned above might be useful here. Although we outline a
ten-session reading group plan, readers should of course feel free to
change it in any way they choose.

First, we would recommend reading the introductory essay in *SPN*
(pp. xvii–xcvi) and possibly Stuart Hall's short and powerful 'Gramsci
and Us' (*Marxism Today*, June 1987, pp. 16–21; available online at:
http://www.amielandmelburn.org.uk/archive_index.htm). The second
session could then be on the intellectual and education (*SPN*, pp.
3–43), before two sessions each on the modern Prince (*SPN*, pp. 123–
205) and the State and civil society (*SPN*, pp. 206–76). The seventh
session could then be centred on Gramsci's approach to philosophy
(*SPN*, pp. 321–77) or on his interpretation of Marxism (*SPN*, pp. 378–
419 and pp. 462–5), depending on interests, before an eighth session
on Americanism and Fordism (*SPN*, pp. 277–318), and a ninth session

on Gramsci's 1926 *Alcuni temi* essay (*SPWI*, pp. 441–62). The tenth session could then widen the discussion by examining some chapters of a study that uses, criticizes or develops some aspect of Gramsci's thought; particularly relevant here might be James C. Scott's *Weapons of the Weak: Everyday Forms of Peasant Resistance* (New Haven: Yale University Press, 1985), Paul Willis's *Learning to Labour: How Working Class Kids Get Working Class Jobs* (Farnham: Ashgate, 1977), David D. Laitin's *Hegemony and Culture: Politics and Change among the Yoruba* (Chicago: University of Chicago Press, 1986) or Michael Burawoy's *Manufacturing Consent: Changes in the Labour Process Under Monopoly Capitalism* (Chicago: University of Chicago Press, 1979). Alternatively, the group could choose to engage with Perry Anderson's difficult but important 'Antinomies' essay or another more difficult secondary source. The final session of the reading group could then be followed by a screening of a documentary about Gramsci's life, 'Everything that Concerns People' (https://www. youtube.com/watch?v=51DhvS9abyI).

Bibliography

Althusser, L., 'Idéologie et appareils idéologiques d'État', *La Pensée*, 151 (1970), pp. 3–38.

Althusser, L. and É. Balibar, *Reading Capital*, translated by Ben Brewster, London: New Left Books, 1970.

Anderson, P., 'Origins of the Present Crisis', *New Left Review*, 1:23 (1964), pp. 26–53.

Anderson, P., 'Components of the National Culture', *New Left Review*, 1:50 (1968), pp. 3–57.

Anderson, P., 'The Antinomies of Antonio Gramsci', *New Left Review*, 1:100 (1976), pp. 5–78.

Anderson, P., *Considerations on Western Marxism*, London: New Left Books, 1976.

Anderson, P., 'Dégringolade', *London Review of Books*, 26:17 (2004), pp. 3–9.

Anderson, P., 'Union Sucrée', *London Review of Books*, 26:18 (2004), pp. 10–16.

Anderson, P., 'An Invertebrate Left', *London Review of Books*, 31:5 (2009), pp. 12–18.

Arendt, H., *On Violence*, London: Allen Lane, 1970.

Balibar, É., 'Gramsci, Marx et le rapport social', in: A. Tosel (ed.), *Modernité de Gramsci: Actes du colloque franco-italien de Besançon, 23–25 novembre 1989*, Paris: Les Belles Lettres, 1992.

Barrère, C., 'Gramsci et la Troisième Internationale face à l'évolution du capitalisme', in: A. Tosel (ed.), *Modernité de Gramsci: Actes du colloque franco-italien de Besançon, 23–25 novembre 1989*, Paris: Les Belles Lettres, 1992.

Barthes, R., *Mythologies*, Paris: Seuil, 1957.

Bartolini, S., *The Political Mobilization of the European Left, 1860–1980*, Cambridge: Cambridge University Press, 2000.

Bastow, S. and J. Martin, *Third Way Discourse: European Ideologies in the Twentieth Century*, Edinburgh: Edinburgh University Press, 2003.

Bauchard, P., *La guerre des deux roses: Du rêve à la réalité, 1981–1985*, Paris: Grasset, 1986.

Beaud, M., *La politique économique de la gauche, vol. 2: Le grand écart*, Paris: Syros, 1985.

Beck, U., *World Risk Society*, Cambridge: Polity Press, 1999.

Bennett, T., 'Introduction: The Turn to Gramsci', in: T. Bennett, C. Mercer and J. Woollacott (eds), *Popular Culture and Social Relations*, Milton Keynes: Open University Press, 1986.

Bennett, T., 'Putting Policy into Cultural Studies', in: L. Grossberg, C. Nelson and P. Treichler (eds), *Cultural Studies*, London: Routledge, 1992.

Benoit, K. and M. Laver, *Party Policy in Modern Democracies*, London: Routledge, 2009.

Bobbio, N., 'Gramsci e la concezione della società civile', in: P. Rossi (ed.), *Gramsci e la cultura contemporanea. Atti del convegno internazionale di studi gramsciani*, Rome: Riuniti, 1969.

Bobbio, N., *Left and Right: The Significance of a Political Distinction*, Cambridge: Polity Press, 1996.

Boothman, D., 'The Sources for Gramsci's Concept of Hegemony', *Rethinking Marxism*, 20:2 (2008), pp. 201–15.

Bourdieu, P., 'Reproduction culturelle et reproduction sociale', *Information sur les Sciences Sociales*, 10:2 (1971), pp. 45–99.

Bourdieu, P., *Counterfire: Against the Tyranny of the Market*, translated by C. Turner, London: Verso, 2002.

Bowman, P., *Post-Marxism versus Cultural Studies: Theory, Politics, and Intervention*, Edinburgh: Edinburgh University Press, 2007.

Brennan, T., 'Antonio Gramsci and Postcolonial Theory: "Southernism"', *Diaspora*, 10:2 (2001), pp. 143–87.

Brittan, S., *Left or Right: The Bogus Dilemma*, London: Secker and Warburg, 1968.

Buci-Glucksmann, C., *Gramsci and the State*, translated by David Fernbach, London: Lawrence and Wishart, 1980.

Buissière, E., 'Gramsci et le problème du chef charismatique', in: A. Tosel (ed.), *Modernité de Gramsci: Actes du colloque franco-italien de Besançon, 23–25 novembre 1989*, Paris: Les Belles Lettres, 1992.

Burnham, P., 'Neo-Gramscian Hegemony and the International Order', *Capital & Class*, 15:3 (1991), pp. 73–92.

Capdeville, J. et al. (eds), *France de gauche, vote de droite*, Paris: Presses de la Fondation Nationale des Sciences Politiques, 1981.

Caracciolo, A. (ed.), *La Formazione dell'Italia industriale: discussioni et ricerche*, Bari: Laterza, 1963.

Caute, D., *The Left in Europe since 1789*, London: Weidenfeld and Nicolson, 1966.

Cerny, P., 'The Little Big Bang in Paris: Financial Market Deregulation in a Dirigiste System', *European Journal of Political Research*, 17:2 (1989), pp. 169–92.

Cox, R., 'Social Forces, States and World Orders: Beyond International Relations Theory', *Millennium: Journal of International Studies*, 10:2 (1981), pp. 126–55.

Cox, R., 'Gramsci, Hegemony, and International Relations: An Essay in Method', *Millennium: Journal of International Studies*, 12:2 (1983), pp. 162–75.

Crehan, K., *Gramsci, Culture and Anthropology*, London: Pluto, 2002.

Crehan, K., 'Gramsci's Concept of Common Sense: A Useful Concept for Anthropologists?', *Journal of Modern Italian Studies*, 16:2 (2011), pp. 273–87.

Crow, D., *Left to Right: The Cultural Shift from Words to Pictures*, London: Thames and Hudson, 2006.

Cusset, F., *La décennie: Le grand cauchemar des années 1980*, Paris: La Découverte, 2006.

Dalton, R., 'Social Modernization and the End of Ideology Debate: Patterns of Ideological Polarization', *Japanese Journal of Political Science*, 7:1 (2006), pp. 1–22.

Davidson, A., *Antonio Gramsci: Towards an Intellectual Biography*, London: Merlin Press, 1977.

Davidson, A., 'The Uses and Abuses of Gramsci', *Thesis Eleven*, 95 (2008), pp. 68–94.

de Benoist, A., 'The End of the Left-Right Dichotomy: The French Case', *Telos*, 1:10 (1995), pp. 73–89.

Dirlik, A., 'The Predicament of Marxist Revolutionary Consciousness: Mao Zedong, Antonio Gramsci, and the Reformulation of Marxist Revolutionary Theory', *Modern China*, 9:2 (1983), pp. 182–211.

Durand, P., 'Culture populaire, culture de masse ou culture de mass-médias? Autour de cinq thèses moins une d'Antonio Gramsci', *Quaderni*, 57 (2005), pp. 73–83.

Dyrberg, T. B., 'The Democratic Ideology of Right-Left and Public Reason in Relation to Rawls's Political Liberalism', *Critical Review of International Social and Political Philosophy*, 8:2 (2005), pp. 161–76.

Dyrberg, T. B., 'What Is beyond Right/Left? The Case of New Labour', *Journal of Political Ideologies*, 14:2 (2009), pp. 133–53.

Eatwell, R., 'The Right as a Variety of "Styles of Thought"', in: R. Eatwell and N. O'Sullivan (eds), *The Nature of the Right*, London: Continuum, 1989.

Ekers, M., G. Hart, S. Kipfer and A. Loftus, '"A Barbed Gift of the Backwoods": Gramsci's Sardinian Beginnings', in: M. Ekers et al. (eds), *Gramsci: Space, Nature, Politics*, Oxford: Wiley-Blackwell, 2013.

Eley, G., 'Reading Gramsci in English: Observations on the Reception of Antonio Gramsci in the English-Speaking World, 1957-82', *European History Quarterly*, 14 (1984), pp. 441–78.

Entwistle, H., *Antonio Gramsci: Conservative Schooling for Radical Politics*, London: Routledge, 1979.

Eribon, D., *D'une révolution conservatrice et de ses effets sur la gauche française*, Paris: Léo Scheer, 2007.

Evans, G. A., A. F. Heath and M. Lalljee, 'Measuring Left-Right and Libertarian-Authoritarian Values in the British Electorate', *British Journal of Sociology*, 47:1 (1996), pp. 93–112.

Feher, F., '1989 and the Deconstruction of Political Monism', *Thesis Eleven*, 1:42 (1995), pp. 87–112.

Femia, J. V., *Gramsci's Political Thought: Hegemony, Consciousness and the Revolutionary Process*, Oxford: Oxford University Press, 1981.

Filippini, M., *Gramsci globale: Guida pratica alle interpretazioni di Gramsci nel mondo*, Bologna: Odoya, 2012.

Fiori, G., *Antonio Gramsci: Life of a Revolutionary*, translated by T. Nairn, London: New Left Books, 1970.

Fisher, M., *Capitalist Realism*, London: Zero books, 2009.

Forgacs, D., 'Gramsci and Marxism in Britain', *New Left Review*, 1:176 (1989), pp. 70–88.

Frosini, F., *Gramsci e la filosofia: saggio sui 'Quaderni del carcere'*, Rome: Carocci, 2003.

Frosini, F., 'Beyond the Crisis of Marxism: Gramsci's Contested Legacy', in: J. Bidet and S. Kouvelakis (eds), *Critical Companion to Contemporary Marxism*, Leiden: Brill, 2008.

Fuchs, D. and H.-D. Klingemann, 'The Left-Right Schema', in: M. K. Jennings and J. W. van Deth (eds), *Continuities in Political Actions*, Berlin: Walter de Gruyter, 1990.

Gauchet, M., 'Right and Left', in: P. Nora (ed.), *Realms of Memory: Rethinking the French Past, Vol. 1: Conflicts and Divisions*, translated by A. Goldhammer, New York: Columbia University Press, 1996.

Geertz, C., 'Common Sense as a Cultural System', in: *Local Knowledge: Further Essays in Interpretive Anthropology*, New York: Basic Books, 1983.

Germain, R. D. and M. Kenny, 'Engaging Gramsci: International Relations theory and the new Gramscians', *Review of International Studies*, 24:1 (1998), pp. 3–21.

Gibbon, P., 'Gramsci, Eurocommunism and the Comintern', *Economy and Society*, 12:3 (1983), pp. 328–66.

Giddens, A., *Beyond Left and Right*, Cambridge: Polity Press, 1994.

Gill, S., 'Gramsci and Global Politics: Towards a Post-Hegemonic Research Agenda', in: S. Gill (ed.), *Gramsci, Historical Materialism and International Relations*, Cambridge: Cambridge University Press, 1993.

Gill, S. (ed.), *Gramsci, Historical Materialism and International Relations*, Cambridge: Cambridge University Press, 1993.

Gramsci, A., *The Modern Prince and Other Essays*, edited by Louis Marks, London: Lawrence and Wishart, 1957.

Gramsci, A., *Selections from Prison Notebooks* (SPN), edited and translated by Q. Hoare and G. Nowell-Smith, London: Lawrence and Wishart, 1971.

Gramsci, A., *Selections from Political Writings (1910–1920)* (SPWI),
    edited by Q. Hoare and translated by J. Mathews, London: Lawrence
    and Wishart, 1977.
Gramsci, A., *Selections from Political Writings (1921–1926)* (SPWII),
    translated and edited by Q. Hoare, London: Lawrence and Wishart,
    1978.
Gramsci, A., *Letters from Prison by Antonio Gramsci* (LP), edited and
    translated by L. Lawner, London: Quartet, 1979.
Gramsci, A., *Selections from Cultural Writings* (SCW), edited by
    D. Forgacs and G. Nowell-Smith and translated by W. Boelhower,
    London: Lawrence and Wishart, 1985.
Gramsci, A., *Further Selections from the Prison Notebooks* (FSPN),
    edited and translated by D. Boothman, London: Lawrence and
    Wishart, 1995.
Gramsci, A., *The Gramsci Reader: Selected Writings, 1916–1935* (GR),
    edited by D. Forgacs, New York: New York University Press, 2000.
Gramsci, A., *Prison Notebooks*, Volume 3, translated and edited by
    J. Buttigieg, New York: Columbia University Press, 2007.
Green, M. E., 'Gramsci on the World Wide Web: Intellectuals and
    Bizarre Interpretations of Gramsci', *International Gramsci Society
    Newsletter*, 10 (2000), pp. 3–5.
Green, M. E., 'Gramsci Cannot Speak: Presentations and Interpretations
    of Gramsci's Concept of the Subaltern', *Rethinking Marxism*, 14:3
    (2002), pp. 1–24.
Green, M. E. (ed.), *Rethinking Gramsci*, London: Routledge, 2011.
Greenhouse, S., 'State Companies Thrive in France', *New York Times*,
    9 May 1989.
Guha, R., 'On Some Aspects of the Historiography of Colonial India', in:
    R. Guha (ed.), *Subaltern Studies I: Writings on South Asian History
    and Society*, Oxford: Oxford University Press, 1982.
Guha, R., 'Preface', in: R. Guha (ed.), *Subaltern Studies I: Writings on
    South Asian History and Society*, Oxford: Oxford University Press,
    1982.
Guha, R. and G. C. Spivak (eds), *Selected Subaltern Studies*, New York:
    Oxford University Press, 1988.
Halimi, S., *Le grand bond en arrière: Comment l'ordre libéral s'est
    imposé au monde*, Paris: Fayard, 2004.
Hall, J., *The Sinister Side: How Left-Right Symbolism Shaped Western
    Art*, Oxford: Oxford University Press, 2008.
Hall, S., 'Encoding and Decoding in the Television Discourse', CCCS
    stencilled paper no. 7 (Birmingham: Centre for Contemporary
    Cultural Studies, 1973).
Hall, S., 'The Great Moving Right Show', *Marxism Today*, January 1979,
    pp. 14–20.

Hall, S., 'Cultural Studies: Two Paradigms', *Media, Culture, and Society*, 2:1 (1980), pp. 57–72.

Hall, S., 'Gramsci's Relevance for the Study of Race and Ethnicity', *Journal of Communication Inquiry*, 10:2 (1986), pp. 5–27.

Hall, S., 'Gramsci and Us', *Marxism Today*, June 1987, pp. 16–21.

Hall, S., 'Blue Election, Election Blues', *Marxism Today*, July 1987, pp. 30–5.

Hall, S., 'Thatcher's Lessons', *Marxism Today*, March 1988, pp. 20–7.

Hall, S., 'The Spectacle of the "Other"', in: S. Hall (ed.), *Representation: Cultural Representations and Signifying Practices*, London: Sage, 1997.

Harman, C., 'Gramsci, the Prison Notebooks and Philosophy', *International Socialism*, 114 (2007), pp. 105–23.

Harris, D., *From Class Struggle to the Politics of Pleasure: The Effects of Gramscianism on Cultural Studies*, London: Routledge, 1992.

Hobsbawm, E., 'The Forward March of Labour Halted?', *Marxism Today*, September 1978, pp. 279–86.

Hobsbawm, E., 'Introduction', in: A. Gramsci (ed.) *The Gramsci Reader: Selected Writings, 1916–1935*, edited by D. Forgacs, New York: New York University Press, 2000.

Hobsbawm, E., *The New Century: In Conversation with Antonio Polito*, London: Abacus, 2000.

Howson, R., 'From Ethico-Political Hegemony to Post-Marxism', *Rethinking Marxism*, 19:2 (2007), pp. 234–44.

Ignazi, P., *Extreme Right Parties in Western Europe*, Oxford: Oxford University Press, 2003.

Ives, P., *Language and Hegemony in Gramsci*, London: Pluto, 2004.

Ives, P., 'Language, Agency, and Hegemony: A Gramscian Response to Post-Marxism', *Critical Review of International Social and Political Philosophy*, 8:4 (2005), pp. 455–68.

Jacoby, R., *Dialectic of Defeat: Contours of Western Marxism*, Cambridge: Cambridge University Press, 1981.

Jameson, F., *The Political Unconscious: Narrative as a Socially Symbolic Act*, London: Routledge, 1981.

Jay, M., *Marxism and Totality: The Adventures of a Concept from Lukács to Habermas*, Berkeley: University of California Press, 1984.

Jessop, B., 'Gramsci as a Spatial Theorist', *Critical Review of International Social and Political Philosophy*, 8:4 (2005), pp. 421–37.

Jones, S., *Antonio Gramsci: Routledge Critical Thinkers*, London: Routledge, 2006.

Karabel, J., 'Revolutionary Contradictions: Antonio Gramsci and the Problem of Intellectuals', *Politics and Society*, 6 (1976), pp. 123–72.

Keucheyan, R., *The Left Hemisphere: Mapping Critical Theory Today*, London: Verso, 2014.

Krätke, M., 'Antonio Gramsci's Contribution to a Critical Economics', *Historical Materialism*, 19:3 (2011), pp. 63–105.

Laclau, E., *Politics and Ideology in Marxist Theory: Capitalism, Fascism, Populism*, London: New Left Books, 1977.

Laclau, E. and C. Mouffe, *Hegemony and Socialist Strategy: Towards a Radical Democratic Politics*, London: Verso, 1985.

Landy, M., *Film, Politics, and Gramsci*, Minneapolis: University of Minnesota Press, 1994.

Laponce, J., *Left and Right: The Topography of Political Perceptions*, Toronto: University of Toronto Press, 1981.

Laroche, P., 'Gramsci et le *Risorgimento*', *Italies*, 6 (2002), pp. 313–23.

Lazarus, N. and R. Varma, 'Marxism and Postcolonial Studies', in: J. Bidet and S. Kouvelakis (eds), *Critical Companion to Contemporary Marxism*, Leiden: Brill, 2008.

Lenin, V. I., *Selected Works*, Moscow: Progress Publishers, 1963, pp. 667–766.

Levy, C., *Gramsci and the Anarchists*, London: Bloomsbury, 1999.

Liguori, G., *Sentieri gramsciani*, Rome: Carocci, 2006.

Liguori, G., 'Common Sense in Gramsci', in: J. Francese (ed.), *Perspectives on Gramsci: Politics, Culture and Social Theory*, London: Routledge, 2009.

Loriaux, M., *France after Hegemony: International Change and Financial Reform*, Ithaca: Cornell University Press, 1991.

Losurdo, D., 'Gramsci, Gentile, Marx et les philosophies de la praxis', in: A. Tosel (ed.), *Modernité de Gramsci: Actes du colloque franco-italien de Besançon, 23–25 novembre 1989*, Paris: Les Belles Lettres, 1992.

Losurdo, D., *Antonio Gramsci dal liberalismo al 'Comunismo critico'*, Rome: Gamberetti, 1997.

Lukes, S., 'Epilogue: The Grand Dichotomy of the Twentieth Century', in: T. Ball and R. Bellamy (eds), *The Cambridge History of Twentieth-Century Political Thought*, Cambridge: Cambridge University Press, 2003.

Macciocchi, M.-A., *Pour Gramsci*, Paris: Seuil, 1974.

Macherey, P., '*Verum et factum*: les enjeux d'une philosophie de la *praxis* et le débat Althusser-Gramsci', in: S. Kouvelakis and V. Charbonier (eds), *Sartre, Lukács, Althusser: des marxistes en philosophie*, Paris: Presses Universitaires de France, 2005.

Mair, P., 'Left-Right Orientations', in: R. Dalton and H.-D. Klingemann (eds), *The Oxford Handbook of Political Behaviour*, Oxford: Oxford University Press, 2007.

Mandel, E., *From Stalinism to Eurocommunism: The Bitter Fruits of 'Socialism in One Country'*, London: New Left Books, 1978.

Marx, K. and F. Engels, *Marx Engels Collected Works*, 50 volumes, London: Lawrence and Wishart, 1975–2004.

Mayo, P. (ed.), *Gramsci and Educational Thought*, Oxford: Wiley-Nicolson, 2010.

McManus, C., *Left Hand, Right Hand*, London: Weidenfeld and Nicolson, 2002.

Merleau-Ponty, M., *Les aventures de la dialectique*, Paris: Gallimard, 1955.

Monasta, A., 'Antonio Gramsci', *Perspectives: revue trimestrielle d'éducation comparée*, 23:3 (1993), pp. 613–29.

Morley, D. and K.-H. Chen (eds), *Stuart Hall: Critical Dialogues in Cultural Studies*, London: Routledge, 1996.

Morris, M., 'A Question of Cultural Studies', in: A. McRobbie (ed.), *Back to Reality? Social Experience and Cultural Studies*, Manchester: Manchester University Press, 1997.

Morton, A. D., 'Historicizing Gramsci: Situating Ideas in and beyond Their Context', *Review of International Political Economy*, 10:1 (2003), pp. 118–46.

Morton, A. D., 'A Double Reading of Gramsci: Beyond the Logic of Contingency', *Critical Review of International Social and Political Philosophy*, 8:4 (2005), pp. 439–53.

Morton, A. D., *Unravelling Gramsci: Hegemony and Passive Revolution in the Global Political Economy*, London: Pluto, 2007.

Murphy, C. N., 'Understanding IR: Understanding Gramsci', *Review of International Studies*, 24:3 (1998), pp. 417–25.

Nairn, T., 'The British Political Elite', *New Left Review* 1:23 (1964), pp. 19–25.

Nairn, T., 'Antonu Su Gobbu', in: A. S. Sassoon (ed.), *Approaches to Gramsci*, London: Writers and Readers, 1982.

Needham, R. (ed.), *Right and Left: Essays in Dual Symbolic Classification*, Chicago: University of Chicago Press, 1973.

Needham, R., 'Right and Left in Nyoro Symbolic Classification', in: R. Needham (ed.), *Right and Left: Essays in Dual Symbolic Classification*, Chicago: University of Chicago Press, 1973.

Noël, A. and J.-P. Thérien, *Left and Right in Global Politics*, Cambridge: Cambridge University Press, 2008.

Nun, J., 'Elements for a Theory of Democracy: Gramsci and Common Sense', *Boundary 2*, 14:3 (1986), pp. 197–229.

Paris, R., 'Gramsci en France', *Revue française de science politique*, 29 (1979): pp. 5–18.

Piotte, J.-M., *La Pensée politique de Gramsci*, Montréal: Parti-Pris, 1970.

Portelli, H., *Gramsci et le bloc historique*, Paris: Presses Universitaires de France, 1972.

Preve, C., 'De la mort du gramscisme au retour à Gramsci: La crise actuelle de perspective politique du marxisme gramscien en Italie', in: A. Tosel (ed.), *Modernité de Gramsci: Actes du colloque franco-italien de Besançon, 23–25 novembre 1989*, Paris: Les Belles Lettres, 1992.

Richeri, G., 'Réflexion sur Gramsci et le journalisme', *Quaderni*, 57 (2006), pp. 85–91.

Rimbert, P., 'Nous avons eu le pouvoir, maintenant il nous faut l'argent', *Le Monde Diplomatique*, April 2009.

Roberts, D. D., 'Reconsidering Gramsci's Interpretation of Fascism', *Modern of Modern Italian Studies*, 16:2 (2011), pp. 239–55.

Robinson, A., 'Towards an Intellectual Reformation: The Critique of Common Sense and the Forgotten Revolutionary Project of Gramscian Theory', *Critical Review of International Social and Political Philosophy*, 8:4 (2005), pp. 469–81.

Romeo, R., *Risorgimento e capitalismo*, Bari: Laterza, 1959.

Rosengarten, F., 'The Gramsci-Trotsky Question, 1922–1932', *Social Text*, 11 (1984–5), pp. 65–95.

Ross, G. and J. Jenson, 'Pluralism and the Decline of Left Hegemony: The French Left in Power', *Politics and Society*, 14:2 (1985), pp. 147–83.

Rupert, M., 'Re-engaging Gramsci: A Response to Germain and Kenny', *Review of International Studies*, 24:3 (1998), pp. 427–34.

Said, E., *Orientalism*, Harmondsworth: Penguin, 1978.

Santucci, A., 'La perspective du communisme dans *L'Ordine Nuovo*', in: A. Tosel (ed.), *Modernité de Gramsci: Actes du colloque franco-italien de Besançon, 23–25 novembre 1989*, Paris: Les Belles Lettres, 1992.

Sassoon, A. S., 'Globalisation, Hegemony and Passive Revolution', *New Political Economy*, 6:1 (2001), pp. 5–17.

Schmidt, V. A., *From State to Market? The Transformation of French Business and Government*, Cambridge: Cambridge University Press, 1996.

Schwarzmantel, J., *The Age of Ideology: Political Ideologies from the American Revolution to Postmodern Times*, Basingstoke: Macmillan, 1998.

Scruton, R., 'Thinkers of the Left: Antonio Gramsci', *The Salisbury Review*, 3:2 (1984), pp. 18–22.

Shonfield, A., *Modern Capitalism: The Changing Balance of Public and Private Power*, Oxford: Oxford University Press, 1965.

Sim, S., *Post-Marxism: An Intellectual History*, London: Routledge, 2000.

Simon, R., *Gramsci's Political Thought: An Introduction*, London: Lawrence and Wishart, 1991.

Sparks, C., 'Stuart Hall, Cultural Studies and Marxism', in: D. Morley and K.-H. Chen (eds), *Stuart Hall: Critical Dialogues in Cultural Studies*, London: Routledge, 1996.

Spivak, G. C., 'Can the Subaltern Speak?', in: C. Nelson and L. Grossberg (eds), *Marxism and the Interpretation of Culture*, Urbana, IL: University of Illinois Press, 1998.

Srivastava, N. and B. Bhattacharya, 'Introduction', in: N. Srivastava and B. Bhattacharya (eds), *The Postcolonial Gramsci*, London: Routledge, 2012.

Texier, J., 'Gramsci, théoricien des superstructures', *La Pensée*, 139 (1968), pp. 35–60.

Texier, J., 'Gramsci face à l'américanisme + Examen du *Cahier 22 des Quaderni del carcere*', in: A. Tosel (ed.), *Modernité de Gramsci: Actes du colloque franco-italien de Besançon, 23–25 novembre 1989*, Paris: Les Belles Lettres, 1992.

Therborn, G., *From Marxism to Post-Marxism?*, London: Verso, 2008.

Thomas, P., 'Modernity as "Passive Revolution": Gramsci and the Fundamental Concepts of Historical Materialism', *Review of the Canadian Historical Association*, 17:2 (2006), pp. 61–78.

Thomas, P., *The Gramscian Moment: Philosophy, Hegemony, and Marxism*, Leiden: Brill, 2009.

Tosel, A., *Marx en italiques*, Paris: Trans Europ Repress, 1991.

Tosel, A., 'Modernité de Gramsci?', in: A. Tosel (ed.), *Modernité de Gramsci: Actes du colloque franco-italien de Besançon, 23–25 novembre 1989*, Paris: Les Belles Lettres, 1992.

Tosel, A., *Le Marxisme du XXe siècle*, Paris: Syllepse, 2009.

Watkins, E., 'Gramscian Politics and Capitalist Common Sense', *Rethinking Marxism*, 11:3 (1999), pp. 83–90.

Young, R. J. C., *Postcolonialism: An Historical Introduction*, Oxford: Blackwell, 2001.

Young, R. J. C., 'Il Gramsci meridionale', in: N. Srivastava and B. Bhattacharya (eds), *The Postcolonial Gramsci*, London: Routledge, 2012.

Zysman, J., *Government, Markets, and Growth: Financial Systems and the Politics of Industrial Change*, Ithaca, NY: Cornell University Press, 1983.

Index